Low-Income Housing
in
The Developing World

A WILEY SERIES ON
PUBLIC ADMINISTRATION IN DEVELOPING COUNTRIES

FINANCING REGIONAL GOVERNMENT

International Practices and their Relevance to the Third World
By K. J. Davey: University of Birmingham

LOCAL GOVERNMENT IN THE THIRD WORLD

The Experience of Tropical Africa
Edited by P. Mawhood: University of Birmingham

MANAGEMENT OF PASTORAL DEVELOPMENT
IN THE THIRD WORLD

By Stephen Sandford: Overseas Development Institute

AN INTRODUCTION TO DEVELOPMENT PLANNING
IN THE THIRD WORLD

By Diana Conyers: University of Nottingham
and
Peter Hills: University of Hong Kong

LOW-INCOME HOUSING IN THE DEVELOPING WORLD

The Role of Sites and Services and Settlement Upgrading
By Geoffrey K. Payne

Low-Income Housing in The Developing World

The Role of Sites and Services and Settlement Upgrading

Geoffrey K. Payne
Joint Centre for Urban Design, Oxford Polytechnic

JOHN WILEY & SONS

Chichester · New York · Brisbane · Toronto · Singapore

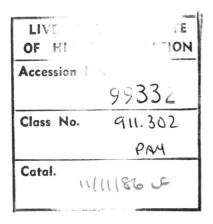
Library of Congress Cataloging in Publication Data:

Payne, Geoffrey K.
  Low-income housing in the developing world.

  (Public administration in developing countries)
  Bibliography: p.
  Includes index.
  1. Housing policy—Developing countries. 2. Public
housing—Developing countries.   3. Housing—Developing
countries.   I. Title   II. Series.
HD7287.5.P36   1984   363.5'8   83-14488

ISBN 0 471 90212 8

British Library Cataloguing in Publication Data:

Payne, Geoffrey K.
  Low-income housing in the developing world. — (A
  Wiley series on public administration in developing countries)
  1. Underdeveloped areas — Housing
  I. Title
  363.5'09172'4   HD7391

ISBN 0 471 90212 8

Phototypeset by Dobbie Typesetting Service, Plymouth, Devon
Printed by Pitman Press Ltd., Bath, Avon

List of Contributors

Francis J. C. Amos
Institute of Local Government Studies, University of Birmingham, UK

Francis Amos is Senior Fellow of the Institute of Local Government Studies at the University of Birmingham, from where he has been an adviser to the governments of India, Kenya, Pakistan, Turkey, Venezuela and Zimbabwe on various aspects of development management and planning. Previously he has been Chief Executive of the City of Birmingham, City Planning Officer of Liverpool City Council and Chief Technical Adviser to the Government of Ethiopia. He has also worked in the UK for the Ministry of Housing and Local Government, the London County Council and Harlow Development Corporation. He is an architect, sociologist and planner and was President of the Royal Town Planning Institute in 1971–72.

Michael Bamberger
Urban Projects Department, The World Bank, 1818 H Street NW, Washington DC 20433, USA

Michael Bamberger was resident adviser to Fundasal's Evaluation Unit from 1975 to 1978, at which time he joined the World Bank to coordinate a four-country evaluation of urban shelter programmes jointly sponsored by the IDRC and the World Bank.

T. S. Chana
Housing Research and Development Unit, University of Nairobi, Nairobi

T. S. Chana worked as Project Architect Planner on the Dandora Sites and Services Scheme, one of Nairobi's earliest and largest. He has for some years been director of the Housing Research and Development Unit at Nairobi University and was recently appointed UN Chief Technical Adviser on Housing to the government of Zimbabwe.

Forbes Davidson
Hogarth House, Paradise Road, Richmond, Surrey, UK

Forbes Davidson was a member of the Master Plan Study team and Clifford Culpin and Partners' team leader in Ismailia on the project design and for the following technical assistance programme, giving a close involvement over an 8-year period. He has also carried out consultancy related to low-income housing and managing urban growth elsewhere in Egypt, Indonesia, Libya, Gambia, and the UK.

Alberto Harth Deneke
Urban Projects Department, The World Bank, 1818 H Street NW, Washington DC 20433, USA

Alberto Harth Deneke was formerly the General Manager of FUNDASAL from 1971 to 1977. He received his PhD in Urban Studies at MIT in 1978 and the following year became Minister of Planning in El Salvador. He joined the World Bank in 1980.

Harrington Jere
Human Settlements of Zambia (HUZA), PO Box 50141, Lusaka, Zambia

Harrington Jere has been involved in community development for most of his working life. He has extensive practical experience in both sites and services and upgrading projects, particularly in Lusaka, and participated in the UK Vancouver Habitat Conference in both official and NGO roles. He is currently Executive Director of the NGO Human Settlements of Zambia.

John Kirke
Gilmore, Hankey, Kirke Partnership, Moor Park Road, London SW6

John Kirke is a partner in the consultancy practice of Gilmore, Hankey, Kirke. He has worked on sites and services and upgrading projects in a number of countries and served on several World Bank missions.

Joram Mghweno
Ministry of Lands, Housing and Urban Development, Housing Development Division, PO Box 9344, Dar es Salaam, Tanzania

Joram Mghweno is Director of Housing Development in the Ministry of Lands, Housing and Urban Development. Before this appointment he was Project Manager for the National Sites and Services and Squatter Upgrading Project for 5 years.

John Parry
JPM Parry Associates Limited, Overend Road, Cradley Heath, Warley, W. Midlands B64 7DD

John Parry is a specialist in building materials production and application. He is Managing Director of JPM Parry Associates Limited, a private building research and development workshop, which has been responsible for the development of several new materials and construction techniques. Fieldwork has been undertaken by the workshop's teams in 25 countries in all parts of Africa, Latin America, and the Caribbean, and several states in the Far East.

Geoffrey K. Payne
Joint Centre for Urban Design, Oxford Polytechnic, Headington, Oxford UK

Geoffrey Payne is an architect and planning consultant specializing in low-income housing and settlement planning. He has undertaken consultancy, training, and research work in a number of countries and teaches at the Joint Centre for Urban Design, Oxford Polytechnic, UK. He published a book, *Urban Housing in the Third World*, in 1977 and is joint Editor of the *Urban Projects Manual*, published in 1983 by Liverpool University Press.

Kirtee Shah
Ahmedabad Study Action Group, Dalal Building, near Hotel Capri, Relief Road, Ahmedabad 380001, India

Kirtee Shah has been involved in community action for several years and has travelled widely to exchange ideas and experiences with other like-minded groups and individuals. He is currently Director of the Ahmedabad Study Action Group.

Johan Silas
47 Jalan Doho, 47, Surabaya, Indonesia

Johan Silas is an Indonesian architect who has carried out extensive research on urban housing, particularly in East Java. He is an adviser to the Municipal Government of Surabaya and a regular contributor to conferences and training programmes.

Bulent Tokman
Building Research Institute, Bilir Sokak No. 17, Kavaklidere, Ankara, Turkey

Bulent Tokman is an architect–planner specializing in housing. He studied architecture in METU, Turkey, and did postgraduate work in The Royal Danish Academy of Fine Arts, and in MIT, USA. He has practised in Europe and Turkey, and currently works for The Building Research Institute of Turkey as a research architect on housing and planning issues.

Roger Tym
Roger Tym and Partners, 26 Craven Street, London WC2

Roger Tym is senior partner of Roger Tym and Partners, a consultancy firm of urban land and development economists based in London and Hong Kong. He has worked in most parts of Asia as well as North and West Africa and the Middle East.

David S. Walton
Halcrow Fox Associates, 3 Shortlands, Hammersmith, London, W6

David Walton is the Director responsible for the planning, development, social and environmental activities of Halcrow Fox Associates, with whom he has worked for 10 years. He has many years of experience in upgrading and minimal-cost new development schemes in most parts of the developing world and has served as a member of various World Bank missions.

Peter Ward
Dept. of Geography, University College London, 26 Bedford Way, London WC1

Peter Ward is lecturer in the Department of Geography, University College London. He worked as adviser on low-cost housing with the Mexican Government between 1978 and 1979 on secondment from the UK Overseas Development Administration. He is editor of *Self-help Housing: a Critique*, and co-author (with Alan Gilbert) of a recently completed study, *Public Intervention, Housing and Land Use in Latin American Cities*.

David Williams
Urban Projects Department, The World Bank, 1818 H Street NW, Washington DC 20433, USA

David Williams is a staff member of the Urban Projects Department of the World Bank, with major responsibilities in the Philippines and Indonesia. He previously worked on the Jakarta Kampung Improvement Programme and was Chief Urban Planner for the Pahang Tenggara Development Authority in Malaysia (1974–76). He is the author of a number of articles in the fields of architecture, sociology, and planning. His most recent publication is *Urban Planning Practice in Developing Countries* (co-editor, 1982).

Roger Zetter
Dept. of Town Planning, Oxford Polytechnic, Headington, Oxford

Roger Zetter has taught, researched, and made working visits to a number of African countries. His main interests are in housing and urban land development and planning processes. He is currently senior lecturer in Urban Development and Planning at Oxford Polytechnic and is carrying out doctoral research on Housing Policy and Economic and Social Change in Cyprus at the Institute of Development Studies, University of Sussex.

Contents

ix

Foreword

This volume is the first comprehensive review of experience in the 'sites-and-services' and 'shelter upgrading' fields published for a general readership. Edited and introduced by Geoffrey Payne, it contains contributions from eighteen professionals and others of wide and varied practical and academic experience of these fields.

Divided into two main parts, the volume describes some of the critical issues involved, examines the past, present and potential role of the principal actors in the housing and urban development sectors, and presents major examples of projects and programmes taken from all the main geographical regions of the developing world, illustrating the evolution of this approach to the provision of shelter.

There can be few more important issues than that of 'housing' to the poor and deprived millions living in developing countries. To them it means more than 'shelter', for it provides the secure base from which they can pursue their activities, and ensure their own survival.

Where their governments are concerned, they must recognize that 'housing', which so often in the past has been considered purely 'social' in character and 'non-economic' in development terms, is one of the principal means through which national development policies and programmes may be achieved. However, this requires that this sector form part of national 'human settlement' or 'urbanization' policies and programmes, based on the distribution of population and related economic and social activities throughout the national territory.

The true nature and scale of the housing problems facing the developing world are rarely fully understood. In his report to the Fifth Session United Nations Commission on Human Settlements (UNCHS), Nairobi, May 1982, Dr Arcot Ramachandran, Executive Director UN Centre for Human Settlements (HABITAT), focused attention on the challenge of urbanization in the developing world. He spoke of the immense task of providing shelter, services and infrastructure for the 1000 million additional people who will inhabit Third World cities by the year 2000, an increase of more than 1 million people every week, as well as for rapidly increasing rural populations.

Similarly at the Sixth Session UNCHS Helsinki, May 1983, Dr Mostafa Tolba, Executive Director UN Environmental Programme (UNEP), reminded delegates that in most major Third World human settlements there are in fact two 'cities'; one for the elite where western standards prevail, and one for the poor with their self-built cities of slums and shanty towns. Spatially, economically, socially and politically, the chasm between the two 'cities' has never been deeper or wider.

The magnitude of such urban growth, the increasing realization that it cannot be prevented, the limited official resources available for housing, allied to the persuasion and financial support of the World Bank, have led many governments to accept 'sites-and-services' and 'settlement upgrading' projects.

Unfortunately, the hope that the lessons of such projects, carried out at the local level, will automatically be learned by governments, incorporated into national policies, and applied through wide-scale programmes available to all of the poor, has proved as forlorn as the former contention that the benefits of large-scale, capital-intensive, projects and increases in GNP would filter down to the level of the urban and rural poor.

Projects of a demonstration character at the local level must support appropriate measures, taken at national policy-making levels, to inform governments and encourage in them changes in understanding and attitude toward human settlement and housing issues. Projects are invaluable but, taken on their own, they deal with a small part only of housing need. Even where the right kind of approach or solution is adopted, projects are usually too few and programmes too small to make any significant impact.

It is essential, though far more difficult, for governments to deal appropriately and effectively with the overall problem of housing. If they are either unable or unwilling to attempt this, the poor and deprived majority of Third World communities will be forced to continue to apply their own unplanned illegal solutions in their efforts to survive.

Whatever governments may wish to believe, it is inevitable that the greater part of future urban growth in developing countries, with few exceptions, will have the characteristics of informal squatter-type settlement, most work being carried out by the people themselves. However, it is possible for this growth to take one of two forms.

Without positive government intervention, taken in support of the people's own efforts, such growth will continue to be unplanned, uncontrolled, illegal, unhealthy, difficult and costly to upgrade, and unbalanced, thus adding to already massive existing urban problems particularly within major settlements.

Alternatively, if such growth forms part of official human settlement and development policies and programmes, prepared in advance of need, it can be planned, controlled, legal, healthy, easy to upgrade with the passage of time, and balanced, forming a recognized and accepted part of communities.

This book is a valuable contribution to the growing debate, knowledge and understanding of a subject of vital concern to the poor majority of Third World populations, pointing the way to the kind of policies and solutions which should be adopted, and implemented on a large scale. It is hoped that it will receive wide distribution and use, and it is strongly commended to the attention of all those concerned in any way with planning and development issues in countries of the Third World.

GEORGE FRANKLIN

Introduction

Geoffrey Payne

Of all the practical ideas for reducing urban housing problems in the developing world, two have emerged during the last 20 years as the most widely adopted: sites and services and settlement upgrading. Although they take a number of different forms and may be carried out separately or in conjunction, these complementary approaches are currently being employed in over 30 countries, from Peru to Pakistan and Papua New Guinea. The considerable experience which has been gained since the early 1960s, and the rate at which new examples are being implemented, now make it desirable and possible to assess their contribution and future potential. This book is therefore addressed primarily to all those considering such approaches or seeking ways of improving their contribution to the housing of rapidly expanding—and predominantly poor—urban populations. It illustrates some of the more significant examples which have been implemented in different parts of the developing world and examines not only their achievements and limitations locally, but some of the more general issues which they raise. It also examines a number of aspects which have to be considered in *any* location. As such, the book attempts to provide a balance between an analysis of the theory and the practice of sites and services and settlement upgrading; it also offers a number of recommendations for future action.

Before describing the individual chapters it may be useful to place both sites and services and settlement upgrading in their historical context. What were the problems to which they were seen as a solution? Who were they intended to benefit and why? What made them so popular with different types of government?

The first factor to consider is the *extent* of housing demand. This is so vast that it is difficult to quantify. It is clear, however, that the problem will be with us for some time and is likely to get worse. A World Bank study has projected that the number of cities with populations over a million will increase from 90 in 1975 to about 300 by the year 2000[1], whilst many smaller cities will also grow rapidly; in fact many medium-sized cities are already growing faster in percentage terms than the metropolitan centres and there are, of course, more of them. The intense pressure which this puts upon urban land and housing resources is intensified still further when the *nature* of demand is taken into account. Since the 1950s the proportion of low-income households to total urban populations has risen steadily, so that the vast majority of people currently have little in the way of capital or incomes with which to obtain a prebuilt and officially approved

1

dwelling. With the private construction industry generally unwilling to accept the high risks and low profits of building for the urban poor, greater responsibility has been placed upon government agencies concerned with housing and urban development.

When rural–urban migration first triggered urban growth in the 1950s the almost universal response was to construct public housing estates on cheap peripheral land. Whilst dwellings in these projects conformed to high standards of construction and services provision, they were far too expensive for the households intended and required such heavy subsidies that they were unable to meet more than a nominal proportion of total housing demand.

The inevitable outcome of this mismatch in demand and supply was the growth of squatter settlements and increased densities in existing low-income areas. By 1970 these accommodated 46% of the population in Mexico City, 60% in Ankara, 33% in Calcutta and as much as 90% in Addis Ababa[2]. Furthermore, such areas were growing at a much faster rate than the formally planned parts of cities. Yet slum clearance and squatter relocation programmes only squandered scarce resources on replacing existing dwellings and the poor simply moved to other parts of the cities.

It was one thing to expose the limitations of this earlier conventional wisdom, however, and another to find a more realistic alternative. Changes therefore began to occur on the basis of individually tailored, or *ad hoc* procedures rather than co-ordinated programmes. Individual low-income settlements which had obtained political support or public attention were provided with basic services and a measure of security, even when official policies may have required their removal. Elsewhere, the prototypes of sites and services were carried out as temporary measures, pending the construction of conventional housing units, or to justify the relocation of squatters from valuable inner-city locations. Occasionally, however, more positive attitudes emerged. During the mid-1960s the governments of Zambia, Columbia, and Kenya, and a number of individual metropolitan administrations in other countries, realized that a more appropriate course of action was to spread limited resources more widely — if thinly — and provide serviced plots in which mutual self-help could be used to construct individual dwellings.

The conceptual foundation which enabled these individual examples to coalesce into an alternative housing strategy, however, was provided by a small number of committed professionals who questioned the negative official view of slum and squatter settlements. Observers such as Abrams, Turner, and Mangin[3] demonstrated convincingly that people were the best judge of what housing they needed, and that in most cases they were perfectly capable of obtaining it. The role of government was to support such initiative by providing inexpensive land, security of tenure, and basic services. So the concept of sites and services was born.

The approach itself was not, however, new. Serviced land sub-divisions, on which occupants organized the construction of their dwellings with some form of assistance and keeping some control, can be found throughout history and have even been adopted in industrialized countries such as Britain as recently as the 1920s[4]. Their attraction for less developed countries was that they reduced unit housing costs, thereby stimulating the supply of planned housing without an equal increase in housing budgets. In this sense they were adopted as much from a desire for 'good housekeeping' as from a desire for a social redistribution of housing resources. They also enabled governments to control the important elements of development such as location, layout, cost and use, which they had lost with the growth of squatter settlements. These aspects appealed to both capitalist and socialist governments faced with enormous demands for housing and urban services and a wide range of countries began to adopt them.

The need to upgrade the large and increasing numbers of slum and squatter settlements was also being recognized. Peru, India, Indonesia, and Turkey were among the countries which adopted upgrading in the 1950s, or even earlier, but others soon followed. In some cases upgrading involved little more than installing basic services, such as communal water taps and toilets, some paved roads, drainage, and street lighting. In others, individual services were provided together with schools, health clinics, and workshops, as well as loans for house improvements or extensions. The nature of the works varied according to the type and location of the settlement and the political pressure residents were able to exert, as well as their ability to pay.

A UN Seminar held in 1970 identified the objectives of settlement upgrading as incorporating the initiative, organizational ability, and capacity for work of the marginal population in the urban community and achieving the greatest social benefit with the limited resources available[5]. A number of other objectives may also have applied, including:

(a) reducing health risks resulting from inadequate provision of clean water and sewerage;
(b) winning political support for entrenched and increasingly active slum or squatter communities;
(c) extending control over officially unplanned areas;
(d) assisting households too poor even to afford a dwelling in a sites and services project, most of whom represent the lowest 10% of a city's population.

The last objective illustrates the complementary nature of sites and services and settlement upgrading policies. They retained the existing housing stock and stimulated the supply of new housing within existing financial limits, whilst enabling both the lower and lowest income groups to participate. In many countries the two approaches were carried out in conjunction. This had the additional benefit of permitting households displaced from an upgrading area to be offered a plot nearby with a minimum of delay, and permitted the installation of facilities such as schools, health clinics, and commercial centres, for which no space was available in an existing settlement. Combining the approaches also enabled local building firms to participate in the development of new areas, whilst studies of existing settlements provided valuable information on the types of layout and infrastructure provision most appropriate for the new ones.

Both sites and services and settlement upgrading were not only attractive to governments. For low-income households they often provided the only legal alternative to squatting or other informal development and enabled them, at least in theory, to determine how *much* they spent on housing, what *form* such expenditure took, and *when* it was spent. For professional observers or consultants and international agencies, the approaches provided the only realistic way of beginning to equate limited government resources with the extent and nature of housing demand.

This apparent combination of interests resulted during the 1970s in more and more schemes being adopted. It is impossible to estimate the total number of plots provided or upgraded so far, but it is clear that a large proportion of projects have been financed through international agencies. The World Bank made its first loan for sites and services (to Senegal) in 1972, and in 1974 extended its operations to upgrading with loans for projects in Calcutta, Manila, and Dar es Salaam. As Williams shows in Chapter 10, the World Bank alone has committed about US $1200 million in loans, plus US $360 million in IDA credits. Similarly, USAID invested about US $100 million a year during the 1970s on slum upgrading, sites and services, core housing and low-cost units specifically intended for low-income groups[6]. This investment, though considerable, has been far outweighed by the influence which the agencies had in senior political and official circles. Of course, a Bank mission with a full portfolio is more likely to persuade governments of the merits of a particular policy than the most articulate academic, though it is also possible that the Bank's reputation as a conservative financial institution gave sympathetic governments the confidence to initiate policy changes with a reasonable hope of achieving success.

ASSESSING THE RECORD

What, then, is the degree of success achieved by sites and services and squatter upgrading in assisting the mass of poorer households throughout the developing world to obtain adequate housing? To what extent do they represent a token response or a radical change in governmental attitudes to housing? What impact have they had upon the economic circumstances of the poor and the constraints of land and housing markets? These are some of the critical issues discussed throughout the book.

Given the varied lengths of experience in each country and the range of approaches adopted, it may be useful to briefly review the experience gained so far and the way other writers have assessed it. In doing this, it has to be remembered that some countries have given priority to upgrading existing settlements, whilst others have focused upon sites and services in an effort to reduce the need for future unauthorized development. A large number of countries have focused—at least initially—upon a 'project' approach in which a specific social group, or 'target population', is provided with a package of 'affordable' housing components in a specific location, whilst some have opted for more indirect approaches such as legalizing squatter settlements. Nonetheless, there has probably been more variety in the approaches adopted towards upgrading existing settlements than in the development of sites and services, where the project approach is overwhelmingly the most common. Examples of some of these approaches are to be found in Part One of the book.

Analysis of experience so far, and of the literature, suggests that a useful distinction can be made in analysis between three broad aspects, namely political/economic, administrative/institutional, and design/technical. These may be loosely related in terms of action to policy, programme, and project levels.

In assessing the political and economic aspects, attention has generally focused upon the experience of what can be broadly termed capitalist countries. This is perhaps inevitable in that more countries in the developing world are capitalist than socialist, and information on the former is generally easier to obtain. Analysis of the political/economic aspects of housing has therefore focused upon the regressive impact of land and property markets and the ways in which the class interests of the ruling elites have been able to co-opt the progressive characteristics of what Turner[7] calls 'bottom-up', or locally determined solutions. There is ample evidence that such problems have seriously restricted the potential contribution of both sites and services and settlement upgrading to improve standards of living for more than a minority. Most countries have been willing to undertake individual projects on a trial basis, and for this the opportunity to acquire soft interest loans from international agencies such as the World Bank has been an obvious attraction. Few, however, have used these initiatives to radically change the way in which housing resources such as land, capital, materials, and labour, are allocated. In fact, Hardoy and Satterthwaite[8] have argued that of the 17 countries to adopt sites and services which they surveyed only Sudan and Tanzania have made them a central part of their urban housing policies. As a result, only a handful of cities can claim that sites and services have enabled the supply of new units to keep pace with demand. Under such conditions, competition increases between *all* income groups and the affluent are always able to outbid the poor. As Crooke has noted, market forces in the developing world are not self-regulating, but thrive under conditions of scarcity, with the result that projects permit such forces to penetrate areas which had previously been cushioned from them[9]. This incorporation into the land and property markets of a city benefits the upper- and middle-income groups in particular, and some of those at the upper end of the low-income groups, but isolates the poorest groups still further from suitable housing and employment opportunities.

The pressure to reduce costs has invariably resulted in new developments being located on sites already in public ownership or on private land which is cheap to acquire. These are invariably on the urban periphery or in areas which are low-lying, steeply sloping, or otherwise difficult to develop. In such cases the additional costs of house construction, site development, and transportation to places of employment are simply transferred to the new low-income residents, and the constraints imposed by market forces remain. Many therefore either fall into permanent default on repayment or sell out to middle-income households who can afford to meet the extra hidden costs, whilst measures to acquire adequate amounts of suitably located land are commonly ineffective or ignored as a result of political opposition.

Reduced subsidies per unit have undoubtedly made it easier to replicate projects, though this is rarely enough to offset the impact of market forces. It is also socially regressive, unless the more affluent groups also pay the full economic cost for all housing and environmental services which they receive, yet in some countries the middle-income groups receive more subsidies than the poor! The very notion of formalizing a housing process which had previously been the exclusive preserve of informal sector groups can be seen as consolidating land and housing markets and therefore intensifying the forces which generated unauthorized settlement in the first place. In countries where land markets already exist, such as most parts of Asia, sites and services have therefore tended to reinforce their regressive characteristics. In many African, Middle Eastern, and Pacific countries, where land traditionally belonged to customary groups, sites and services have *introduced* active markets with potentially disastrous long-term consequences. Peattie's conclusion that the primary need is to change the way land and property markets operate for the urban poor[10], would, therefore appear to be well founded.

It would be naïve, however, to assume that socialist countries are free of such constraints. The regressive characteristics of market forces are commonly replaced by inflexible, complex, and ultimately expensive bureaucratic procedures which can be just as restrictive in their effect. There is also no reason to assume that bureaucratic elites and senior party members are less capable of self-interest than the elites of capitalist countries. Co-optation can therefore exist within *any* political or economic system, though it appears that the greatest progress has been in those countries which, irrespective of their ideological character, have given preferential consideration to the poor. Otherwise the only opportunities for progress seem to occur when the vital interests of a state are threatened—or when the ruling elites consider them to be.

Apart from variations in the degree of support which sites and services or settlement upgrading have received from the state, opposition has frequently been encountered from a number of other groups who benefited—or hoped to—from previous policies. Local politicians, for example, have always been able to use subsidized, high-quality housing projects to dispense favours to their supporters, so that any proposals which met a higher proportion of demand would correspondingly reduce their powers of patronage; administrators are often able to extract large commissions or bribes for approving the allocation of a unit to households not officially eligible, or wishing to jump the long waiting lists; architects and planners are able to indulge their creative energies producing monuments to posterity, whilst tender procedures benefit larger contractors at the expense of small local firms. Even more intransigent has been the way in which prestige housing estates have affected public expectations, for people encouraged in the belief that government should—and could—provide high-quality housing for all can hardly be blamed for demanding it, especially when sites and services appear to offer less and cost relatively more.

Few countries have national or urban housing policies which contain clear and effective measures to deal with the major constraints on increased housing supply as outlined above. All too often, official statements are couched in terms of the numbers of units to be provided or upgraded within a given period; yet these are targets rather than policies and, in any case, even the targets are rarely achieved in full. There is obviously considerable scope for improving the relevance of low-income housing policy to these constraints. Whilst this would inevitably focus attention upon the more overtly political dimensions of housing and urban development, it would be unwise to assume that this can relieve professionals of their responsibilities or, indeed, that such constraints cannot change. Several cases exist in which local political pressures have resulted in the upgrading of existing low-income settlements irrespective of their legal status or conformity to official master plans, and such pressures are likely to increase in the future. Those of us professionally involved in housing should therefore always be prepared to respond quickly and effectively to new opportunities within the political/economic environment. The book illustrates many ways in which this can be done.

In assessing the impact of administrative and institutional aspects on low-income housing supply, a similar number of considerations commonly apply. Inter-agency rivalry is one of these, and applies particularly when a new agency is introduced onto the scene. Existing agencies naturally resist any reduction in their budgets or technical capability and often impose vetoes or delays which impair the new agency's effectiveness. Conflicts may also arise between various levels of government, perhaps because they are controlled by different political parties. It is therefore not unusual for even a small project to take 5 years from inception to completion, during which time demand has escalated further. Feedback from individual projects into large-scale programmes and housing policies takes even longer.

Standardization and administrative inflexibility have also limited the contribution of sites and services and settlement upgrading. Insensitive management can restrict the range of options available to households so that they find it difficult to meet their needs at a cost they can afford. At the same time, excessive institutional control over what residents may do with their own plot can inhibit the potential for providing vitally needed workshops and shops or additional rental accommodation. Once proposals are completed, arrangements for their handover to the relevant local authorities are not always satisfactory, especially if the implementation agency is unrelated to that responsible for long-term maintenance. Projects may therefore be regarded mainly as conventional public works rather than the initial stage of a continuous consolidation process. Lack of co-ordination between agencies may also result in disputes between them, as a result of which services cease to operate, residents withhold repayments, and the project or programme loses all momentum.

Participation can also be a major source of administrative problems. The very mention of sites and services and settlement upgrading implies an active role for the residents concerned and most programmes contain explicit references to its importance. The views of households are sought through social surveys and public meetings, or they are encouraged to contribute their labour in digging trenches or building houses, but active participation rarely extends to the composition or distribution of project components. Some observers[11] argue that the forms of participation which are permitted extend exploitation from the work-place into the home by undervaluing the labour contribution, though the lack of demand for labour in the urban economies and the limited funds available for housing provide little alternative. Such arguments may therefore be regarded as somewhat purist given the realities, but there can be little doubt that it is usually people who participate and project agencies which decide. There are, of course, considerable practical difficulties in generating a genuine participatory decision-making system, especially when people are not accustomed to being consulted. In upgrading programmes expectations can be raised very quickly that participation will solve all problems overnight, so that when a setback occurs, a mood of despondency and recrimination can descend onto a community. In sites and services programmes, many decisions necessarily have to be made before settlers appear on the scene, so that there is a danger of using participation to justify decisions already taken.

It is also by no means certain that the institutional capability generated by carrying out sites and services or upgrading programmes provides an appropriate basis for changing the major constraints to improved housing supply, since the types of expertise involved are of a fundamentally different nature. Yet few countries have the necessary institutional framework or legislation to address the main constraints, and some do not even have sufficient staff resources to expand their existing projects. It could also be argued that the more successful a programme or project is seen to be, the more it is likely to be perpetuated unchanged, thereby diverting attention from the primary responsibilities of housing and planning agencies to regulate urban growth and assist the poor.

One further institutional and administrative aspect relates to the tendency for agencies involved in either sites and services or settlement upgrading to be drawn into the routine administration of settlements long after their developmental function has effectively ceased. This restricts the institutional resources available for other areas and *increases* the dependence of residents upon the housing agency, both of which are contrary to the objectives of sites and services and upgrading approaches.

Finally, design and technical aspects are the ones with which professionals engaged in housing have the most contact, since they apply particularly at the level of the individual project. Most attention has understandably concentrated on the issue of standards. Whilst the desire not to create 'planned slums' is understandable, it can easily lead to the imposition of standards which neither residents nor governments can afford, and which are in some aspects actually higher than are required on conventional housing projects. Thus plot sizes, building separation rules, and road reservations may all be considerably more than necessary. By the time labour contributions, building loans, technical assistance, and the administrative costs associated with self-help are added to the site and on-plot development costs, total net savings may be far lower than envisaged.

The frequent exclusion of all land, financing, and administrative costs from project accounting may be considered to represent positive discrimination in favour of the poor and therefore a socially progressive approach. In practice, however, it is often an excuse to maintain unrealistically high standards, irrespective of their appropriateness. Even realistic initial standards have a habit of rising over time, forcing costs up with them. Naturally, the more that is provided, the more this inflationary pressure is likely to exclude poorer households. Higher standards also make it more likely that large-scale contractors will be required to carry out works which otherwise could be undertaken by small, locally based contractors. By failing to distinguish between standards appropriate for initial and subsequent consolidated development, many early projects failed to stimulate the 'progressive development' which lay at the basis of sites and services and settlement upgrading concepts.

Another major technical consideration which has received considerable attention is the degree of efficiency with which land is used[12]. Since land usually represents a substantial proportion of total project costs and is universally scarce in the locations where it is most needed, it is obviously vital to put each square metre to the best possible use. Over-provision of land for circulation and public open space is therefore difficult to justify, since somebody, somewhere, has to pay to develop and maintain it.

Many considerations relating to implementation have also been discussed in the literature; the difficulty in ensuring that beneficiaries are restricted to those eligible; the high cost of maintenance and problems in recovering costs; excessive restrictions on the provision of rental accommodation; and the tendency for tenants and others to be forced out of a project in favour of higher-income households. Of all the considerations which have restricted the contribution of projects, however, probably the most crucial is time. Even small projects can take so long to prepare and carry out that they become totally engulfed by rapidly expanding unauthorized settlements. In sum, they provide too little, too late, and at too high a cost.

RECENT EXPERIENCE

The above discussion has outlined some of the issues against which the present generation of low-income housing initiatives will need to be judged. In doing so, it also sets the scene for the chapters which follow. Since many of the points mentioned suggest that there are serious limitations on previously completed approaches it may be useful first to ask to what extent these issues are being recognized and tackled in current approaches?

What trends in government prescriptions and actions can be identified? What positive recommendations can be made for the future?

It is to these crucial questions that the main body of the book is addressed. If it has a single message, it is that whilst the lessons of previous experience are rapidly being absorbed, there is an even greater need to develop more comprehensive, flexible, and locally specific responses appropriate to the extent and nature of total housing demand. Many of the examples discussed on the following pages are evidence of a move in this direction. Most provide a range of options on plot size and services networks, priced to generate cross-subsidies from commercial or residential development to benefit poorer households. A range of income groups is often encouraged, not only to generate cross-subsidies, but to create socially mixed communities with enhanced opportunities for local employment. A range of land-uses is frequently permitted, including shops and workshops on house plots, and regulations restricting the provision of rooms for rent are increasingly being relaxed. This enables residents to supplement their incomes and accelerates consolidation, whilst also providing cheap-rental housing to help the poorest households. At the same time land sub-divisions are making more intensive use of available space by increasing the proportion of private, revenue-generating land up to 60-65% of total site areas, though as Rapoport argues[13] insufficient attention is sometimes given to sociocultural aspects which influence the ways in which land is *used*.

The recognition that sites and services have to compete with informally sponsored sub-divisions has forced agencies to revise previously unrealistic standards. This usually involves the design of more cost-effective layouts and lower initial levels of utilities provision, designed in such a way that subsequent upgrading can be achieved with the minimum of cost and disruption. It may also involve designing for higher initial densities. The increasing success of some recent projects has also enabled project agencies to attract a higher calibre of staff and retain them by offering a secure and expanding career structure. The new generation of planners, architects, engineers, and community development staff are also more aware of the need for participation by residents *and* more willing to accept the practical implications for design and implementation and all it involves.

The advantages of combining sites and services with upgrading operations are also becoming more widely accepted, and upgrading itself is being implemented more effectively in both management and social terms. This can be seen in the cases of Jakarta and Surabaya in Indonesia (see Chapter 4) and Ankara in Turkey (see Chapter 5), where upgrading has benefited a substantial proportion of the urban populations. Whilst a major constraint continues to be the ability—or willingness—of governments to upgrade settlements on land held under private or customary tenure, it appears that, in cases where this is not a problem, the costs of upgrading can be significantly less than those of direct provision through sites and services. Under certain conditions, the upgrading of existing settlements may therefore provide an attractive alternative to sites and services. It also provides considerably more scope for effective participation, since residents will have been involved in initial development and will have a vested interest in subsequent consolidation. The experience of Lusaka (see Chapter 3) and El Salvador (Chapter 2) shows that where this human resource can be harnessed, the benefits of upgrading to both residents and local authorities can be considerable.

Unfortunately, the benefits of this learning process have yet to make a sufficient impact upon housing policies, and the time lag between gaining experience from projects and modifying policy *at all* is often too long given the pace at which many cities are growing. At the same time, therefore, that individual projects are becoming more successful, and some are being expanded into large-scale programmes, it is becoming more important to address the political/economic and institutional/administrative constraints. Co-ordinated action is, in fact needed on all three levels and in general a project should be judged by the extent to which it provides a basis for more comprehensive and effective policies to intervene in housing and land markets. In some cases such intervention has taken the form of studies to prepare revised building regulations; in others major institutional reforms and in others a relaxation of restrictions upon informal development. It may also take the form of direct acquisition of areas for land banks, though this tends to be more successful in smaller cities than metropolitan centres with established land markets.

These trends are generally to be welcomed, though many are never officially endorsed or fully implemented. The pace of economic, social, and institutional reform remains slow compared to the rate at which demand is growing, and a continued deterioration in urban living conditions is inevitable unless the position can be reversed. The possibility of achieving this in any given country depends, of course, upon the degree of political will which can be mobilized. This in turn depends upon the importance attached to housing in national development strategies, the political and administrative framework within which housing resources are allocated, and the skills of those actually involved in the provision of housing services. Obviously, governments which favour free enterprise are less likely to embrace policies which require extensive intervention in land and housing markets than those of centrally planned economies, though neither can be guaranteed to find the right balance of control and flexibility. Whilst it is therefore true that many of the constraints to real progress are outside professional control, there is still considerable scope for those of us directly involved in housing to improve the quality of our understanding, advice, and action. This book will have served its purpose if it enables experience gained in different parts of the developing world to reach a wider audience and accelerate the speed with which relevant approaches are put into practice.

ORGANIZATION OF THE BOOK

The selection and organization of material for a book such as this poses a number of obvious problems. So many examples now exist that any solution would inevitably exclude many important ones. At the same time, case studies are not the ideal vehicle for assessing those aspects such as land, finance, and administration, which critically affect *all* housing projects, programmes, and policies.

The book is therefore organized into two distinct but related parts. Part One consists of eight case studies of sites and services and/or settlement upgrading. Each has been selected for its significance in illustrating a particular approach, though an attempt has also been made to cover as wide a range of countries and city types as space permits. Each example is, of course, different from the others. They all, however, contain a general outline of the context in which they were developed, the stated or implicit objectives adopted, the specific proposals and means of implementation used, and an assessment of the consequences both locally and in wider terms. In this way they combine diagnosis with prognosis and will hopefully enable readers to make comparisons with other examples or other cities with which they are more familiar. The chapters are arranged in approximate chronological order so that the evolution of the approach to both sites and services and upgrading can be shown more clearly.

Part Two contains a series of chapters on the roles of major actors and various factors influencing both sites and services and settlement upgrading. These are mostly written by practitioners with considerable experience in their subject area. Their chapters therefore draw upon the case studies in Part One, and on other examples with which they are familiar, to evaluate recent experience and make recommendations for future action.

In the first case study chapter, T. S. Chana assesses one of the earliest and largest sites and services projects carried out in Africa. Chana describes how the Dandora project in Nairobi was designed and implemented, and the role of 'building groups' in assisting self-help initiatives. He also discusses several of the problems typically found in early projects, but shows how the experience gained has benefited later developments.

In Chapter 2, Alberto Harth Deneke and Michael Bamberger describe El Salvador's experience with sites and services. They describe how FUNDASAL, a non-profit organization independent of government, was able to obtain international assistance to develop projects affordable by households in the lowest 17th percentile, based upon community participation and incremental development. Despite the severe political crisis in the country and problems in keeping pace with demand, the authors show how the programme has flourished and why it still has one of the best cost recovery records in the world.

Chapter 3 takes the theme of participation further and shows how it provided the basis for a large-scale programme of sites and services and squatter upgrading in Lusaka, Zambia. Harrington Jere shows how local traditions of self-help and mutual help were incorporated into projects which benefited 160,000 people in upgrading areas and many others in sites and services projects.

No survey of upgrading programmes would be complete without a discussion of Indonesia's Kampung Improvement Programmes. In Chapter 4 Johan Silas describes how these programmes developed from *ad hoc* municipal activities into arguably the largest settlement upgrading exercise in the world, directly benefiting over 3 million people in Jakarta alone. Silas compares the approaches adopted in both Jakarta and Surabaya, and argues that the greatest success has been achieved in projects where local residents influenced the development.

All the examples described in the first four chapters have been at least partly supported by the World Bank. Chapter 5 assesses an equally ambitious programme of upgrading, completely financed by a municipality with limited powers and even more limited financial resources. Bulent Tokman explains the strengths and weaknesses of an approach in Ankara, Turkey, which enabled the majority of low-income households to obtain security and services reasonably quickly, and how this was based upon an unusual relationship between local communities and the municipality.

Although Tanzania also has a well-established upgrading programme, Chapter 6 returns the emphasis towards new development with an analysis by Joram Mghweno of the national 'surveyed plots' programme currently being implemented in five towns, including Dar-es-Salaam. The projects are based upon the realization that conventional sites and services cannot always be afforded or developed quickly enough, and that a programme which provides cheaper but initially unserviced plots may sometimes be more appropriate. Mghweno charts the evolution of the programme and its presently disappointing progress, which he demonstrates is due largely to unrealistically rigorous building regulations and a shortage of skilled staff and survey equipment.

Chapter 7 combines sites and services and settlement upgrading in a recently designed project in Ismailia, Egypt, which is currently being implemented. The Ismailia scheme is one of the largest to be found anywhere, and on one site alone will eventually benefit about 90,000 people, including a cross-section of all income groups. Forbes Davidson describes how the proposals were developed to meet a wide range of local needs, and how the projects have been able to stimulate the production of affordable new housing plots to the extent that the city's total demand is now being satisfied.

The final case study takes the policy theme one stage further. Peter Ward explains the limitations of sites and services in Mexico City (and by implication, elsewhere) and argues that concerned state intervention in land will achieve far more. He urges planners to adopt different approaches to meet these needs and explains some ideas currently being considered in Mexico.

Part Two also contains eight chapters. Four of these are concerned with the roles of major actors in the housing process, while the remaining four focus upon various factors of critical importance to sites and services or settlement upgrading initiatives. It begins with an assessment of political and administrative factors, since these probably exert the greatest influence over the success or failure of *any* policy. Francis Amos adopts an insider's view of the way in which decisions over housing policy tend to be made, and the way bureaucracies and political interests allocate resources. He illustrates his argument with evidence from a number of countries, including some of those discussed in Part One, and offers several suggestions for improving the methods and quality of decision-making.

Chapter 10 examines the influential role of international agencies, particularly The World Bank. David Williams reviews the Bank's involvement in the urban housing sector and the focus of its current activities. He outlines some of the limitations of focusing upon projects and the attempts of the Bank to encourage reform in national policies and institutions active in housing and land development. He also gives a personal view of the directions in which national and local responses to housing need could most profitably be channelled.

In Chapter 11 David Walton assesses the role of international consultants. Speaking from a personal viewpoint, he explains the changing demands that have been placed upon consultants by government and funding agencies as well as local community groups, and the changes which these have induced in consultancy practice. He concludes that, despite considerable improvements in local expertise, there are still situations in which the consultant can make a useful contribution and outlines some of the changes in policy and procedure which he believes would strengthen the approach.

Chapter 12 discusses the role of the individual households and community groups in sites and services or settlement upgrading activities. Kirtee Shah examines some of the issues which have to be tackled when working with or for low-income communities. He examines how attitudes towards public participation have changed in recent years and illustrates several projects initiated by local authorities, NGOs, and agencies such as the World Bank. He concludes with a sobering but challenging outline of what remains to be achieved.

Chapter 13 shifts the focus from actors to some of the critical factors in housing programmes. Roger Tym discusses the thorny issues of finance and affordability and examines various policy and technical issues which have to be considered in determining the most appropriate package for any specific context. He concludes with some suggestions for improving financial management and expanding the scale of existing programmes.

Chapter 14 deals with another constraint to the expansion of sites and services or settlement upgrading programmes, namely land and land markets. Roger Zetter clarifies their nature and impact and some of the options available to government. He illustrates his argument with examples from the case studies and many other countries where new policies or techniques are being evolved.

The final two chapters deal with factors which are often relegated to a peripheral role, yet which are of major importance to the eventual users of housing projects. In Chapter 15 John Kirke examines the problems involved in selecting the most appropriate on-plot and on-site[14] utilities services and infrastructure for initial development and subsequent improvement. He attacks the unrealistic standards frequently applied in low-income projects and shows how to develop affordable and acceptable solutions for both new and existing settlements.

In Chapter 16 John Parry illustrates the ingenuity that has been applied to developing new building materials and construction systems appropriate to schemes in which the user is expected to play a major role. Many of the ideas he discusses are, in fact, rediscoveries of traditional methods re-applied in an updated form, whilst others are still at the experimental stage. He shows how building technology is at least as important as cultural values in determining the way materials are used, and explores some of the implications raised by his recommendations.

There can be no simple conclusion to this book, since the approaches it describes are in many respects still in their infancy. What can be said with some confidence is that individual projects, no matter how well planned and executed, are unlikely to make a significant or sustained contribution to housing supply unless they are matched by positive intervention in land and property markets. Only then will urban low-income groups be able to gain access to land, materials, and services in locations and at costs which are realistic. In terms of achieving this there is still much to learn and much to do. The following chapters indicate some of the lessons learnt and paths to be explored.

NOTES AND REFERENCES

1. 'The task ahead for the cities of the developing countries.' World Bank, Staff working paper No. 209; IBRD, 1975, p.3.
2. The World Bank, 'Housing sector policy paper'; IBRD, 1975, pp.62–3.
3. See for examples, C. Abrams, *Housing In The Modern World: Man's Struggle For Shelter In An Urbanizing World; Cambridge Mass.:* MIT Press, 1964, J. F. C. Turner, 'Barrios and channels for housing developments in modernizing countries', in Mangin, W. (ed.) *Peasants in Cities.* Boston: Houghton-Mifflin, 1970, pp.1–14.
4. C. Ward, and D. Hardy, 'Plots of freedom', *Built Environment,* **8** (1), 1982, pp.35–45.
5. United Nations, *Improvement of Slums And Uncontrolled Settlements.* New York: UN, 1971, pp.65–67.
6. United Nations, 'Physical Improvement of Slums and Squatter Settlements'. Report of *ad hoc* Expert Group Meeting in Nassau, 1977, p.6. Nairobi: UNCHS.
7. J. F. C. Turner, *Housing by People.* London: Marion Boyars, 1976.
8. J. E. Hardoy, and D. Satterthwaite, *Shelter Need and Response: Housing, Land and Settlement Policies in Seventeen Third World Nations.* Chichester: John Wiley & Sons, 1981, p.254.

9. P. Crooke, 'Sites and services, settlement upgrading and the urban housing market'. Mimeo, 1981.
10. L. Peattie, 'Some second thoughts on sites and services,' *Habitat International*, **6** (1/2), 1982, p.137.
11. For example, see R. Burgess, Self-help housing advocacy: a curious form of radicalism. A critique of the world of John F. C. Turner, in P. Ward (ed.) *'Self-help housing: a critique'*. Mansell, Alexandrine Press, 1982. H. Harms, 'Historical Perspectives on the Practice and Purpose of Self-Help Housing', in P. Ward *op. cit.*, p.37.
12. This was the subject of a series of studies carried out at MIT and used as the basis for the design guide published by H. Caminos, and R. Goethert, *The Urbanization Primer for Design of Site and Service Projects*, IBRD, 1976.
13. A. Rapoport, 'Culture, site layout and housing', *Architectural Association Quarterly*, **12** (1), 1980.
14. In this context 'on plot' refers to provision on individual plots and 'on site' refers to provision within the project site generally.

Part One

Low-income Housing in the Developing World
Edited by G. K. Payne
© 1984 John Wiley & Sons Ltd.

Chapter 1

Nairobi: Dandora and Other Projects

T. S. Chana

NAIROBI—URBAN CONTEXT

Nairobi, the capital city of Kenya, is growing at a rate of about 7.5% per annum with a population almost reaching the 1 million mark, making it the only city of that size in the whole of the East African region. All this growth has taken place since 1899, when the city was established as a railway stop between Mombasa on the coast and Kisumu on Lake Victoria.

In Kenya all settlements above a population size of 2000 are considered to be urban. According to 1979 population estimates the urban population is around 2 million, which is 12% of the total population of about 16 million. Forecasts indicate that at an annual growth rate of 6.2% the urban population can reach 7.1 million by the year 2000 or 9.7 million if the annual growth rate is 7.2%.

Most of the urban population is concentrated in two major cities, Nairobi and Mombasa, while the remainder is spread over several smaller urban centres, especially Kisumu and Nakuru. In 1979, Nairobi accounted for about 45% of the total urban population.

The three largest urban centres, Nairobi, Mombasa, and Kisumu, dominate the urban shelter problem and therefore the implementation of the urban housing policy in the country. Moreover, these cities are also relatively more suited institutionally to undertake large-scale implementation of housing programmes and projects within their own local administrations. Nairobi, as the capital city, forms the centre of major economic, social, political, and administrative activities both at the national and international level. It accounts for almost 40% of 'modern' sector jobs in Kenya and about 45% of modern sector incomes, which makes it the main natural attraction point for rural-urban migration.

Recent international economic events, especially the oil crisis and recession, have had adverse effects on the Kenyan economy in general, and this has caused a significant decline in Nairobi's economy.

Employment trends in Nairobi according to 1974 estimates of labour force participation show about 76% in modern sector employment, 12% in informal sector employment, and 12% unaccounted for or unemployed. The informal sector has been growing at a higher rate than the modern sector employment in the past decade.

Income distribution and growth in Nairobi cannot be very accurately assessed due to lack of reliable data. Different trends have been shown by different surveys and reports. According to 1977 estimates, the household income distribution for Nairobi is as shown in Table 1.1. This pattern is unlikely to change drastically by 1985 and

Table 1.1   Nairobi household income distribution, 1977

Cumulative percentage of families	Monthly household income range	
	K.Shs	US$*
0–20	0–500	0–66
21–40	551–1050	67–126
41–60	1051–2000	127–240
61–80	2001–4000	241–482
81–100	over 4000	over 482

* 1 US$ = 11 K.Shs, September 1982 exchange rate.

the minimum wage in Nairobi in 1983 was K.Shs 480 per month. With the increasing cost of living in Nairobi many households in the lower-income groups will continue to experience financial constraints, especially the lowest two quintiles. For example, in 1977 the cost of a newly built two-roomed self-contained dwelling of about 42 m^2 and of minimum infrastructure standard (water supply, sewerage, street lighting, and roads only) was about K.Shs 33,500. The monthly repayment was about K.Shs 290 and with about 20% of income being spent on housing, the monthly income required to make such a repayment would be about K.Shs 1400. This puts such a dwelling beyond the reach of about 50% of the population in Nairobi (see also Table 1.2).

Existing housing available to the low-income groups is provided through the public, private formal, and private informal or popular sectors. The informal or popular housing activities in the uncontrolled and squatter settlements are a response to the failure of the public and the private formal sectors to supply enough housing at affordable prices to meet the needs of the low-income households. These low-income settlements, which are located mainly in the eastern and western outskirts of the city, provide shelter for over one-third of the city's population.

The public housing supplied by the Nairobi City Council (NCC) and the National Housing Corporation (NHC) similarly provides for about one-third of the city's population. However, the majority of the public housing, especially that built in the 1960s and early 1970s, caters for the medium- and high-income groups. The private formal sector provides the remaining one-third of housing for these income groups, including staff and servants' quarters provided by the employers for the low-income workers and rental tenements in some of the low-income settlements.

The cost of services and buildings is directly related to the affordability of housing by the lower-income groups. Table 1.2 shows a brief comparative cost analysis of the Dandora Community Development Project and other public housing estates of the Nairobi City Council (NCC). The table indicates that in the higher-density areas, where the plot sizes are small (e.g. Dandora and Biafra) the cost of services and building is lower than the lower-density areas, where the plot sizes are large (e.g. Ngei, Loresho). The levels of services in Dandora are in accordance with the Grade II Building By-laws of the NCC, whereas in Ngei, Loresho, these are in accordance with Grade I Building By-laws. However in both the situations there is the provision of individual waterborne sewerage, individual water supply, roads and street lighting. The target population in Dandora includes households earning up to about K.Shs 575 per month, whereas in Ngei it is households earning up to about K.Shs 7200 per month.

Table 1.2   Comparative costs of Dandora and other NCC projects (1977 figures)

Project	Plot size (m²)	Built area (m²)	Cost (incl. services) (K.Shs)	Monthly payment (K.Shs)	Affording income per month (K.Shs)
Dandora	120	60	12,800	115	575
Biafra (Pumwam)	102	36	32,500	290	1400
Kimathi	210	70	78,000	700	3500
Kibera	150	110	109,000	980	4900
Ngei	700	130	160,000	1440	7200
Loresho	2500	200	242,000	2100	10,500

Future housing needs in the city for the various income groups have been outlined by the NCC in the report on the Nairobi Metropolitan Growth Strategy by the Urban Study Group in 1973. According to this study 14,500 units are needed every year up to 1985, of which about 6700 are specifically for low- or lower-middle-income groups. This need is expected to almost double from 1986 to 2000, resulting in a projected total need of about 348,100 housing units and an average annual rate of about 23,000 units.

The performance of the public and private sectors since 1973 has only resulted in a supply of about 2000 units per annum, each sector providing about 50% of this amount. Such a poor performance has resulted in high annual housing deficits, especially for the lower-income groups who have continued to live in unauthorized settlements. The majority of public sector housing has been in the provision of sites and services units. There are several reasons for this poor performance in the past, including a lack of commitment at policy level; inadequate provision of funds; inappropriate and unaffordable building standards; slow acquisition and provision of public land; and delays due to inefficient and bureaucratic procedures in project planning and implementation. Such problems cannot be overcome without a radical change in housing policies and increased efficiency in the administration, planning, implementation, and management of housing development programmes and projects.

Major groups of actors in the existing housing process range from the users to various international agencies. Their role and activities within the process vary depending upon the different stages in the project cycle of the housing projects, especially site and services schemes and upgrading projects, play a major role in house consolidation and shelter improvements using self-help or aided self-help methods of construction. They are assisted in their efforts by the various divisions of the Housing Development Department (HDD) of the Nairobi City Council (NCC), especially the Technical and Community Development Divisions. The HDD is the major implementing agency of the local authority to provide low-income housing in the city.

The NCC is guided by the urban development and housing policies outlined by the Ministry of Works and Housing (MOWH), which is the overall national operational ministry of the Government of Kenya. The Ministry of Local Government (MLG), which is responsible for the local authorities in the country, also plays a major role in the planning and programming of housing development projects in the city through the Housing Development Committee of the NCC. The National Housing Corporation (NHC), which is the national executive agency of the MOWH, directs the public finance from MOWH to the NCC. The Housing Finance Corporation of Kenya (NFCK), which is a para-statal agency of the Government and the Commonwealth Development Corporation (CDC), provides mortgage finance to private developers, mainly for middle- and high-income groups. Of these, the MOWH and the MLG have a powerful influence on the allocation of funds both from local and international sources. Both these ministries play an important role in the decision-making process affecting housing projects in the city. The political opinions, as expressed by the national members of parliament and the local councillors and chiefs, have a strong sense of direction on the technical views of the housing implementation agencies, especially in the case of the Nairobi City Council.

The Housing Research and Development Unit (HRDU) of the University of Nairobi, which is funded by a grant from the MOWH, plays a major role in research, development, and training for housing and community planning in Kenya and has made useful contributions to the housing sector both at national and local levels, including the housing programmes and projects in Nairobi. The HRDU has provided policy inputs in the formulation of site and services and squatter upgrading programmes during the past 15 years since its establishment in 1967; carried out over 100 research studies in socioeconomic, technical, and administrative aspects of housing, building, and planning; implemented several demonstration projects on various local low-cost construction methods using indigenous building materials and self-help community participation; participated in various training programmes for architects, planners, and other para-professionals both in the University and other training institutes; and disseminated information to public and private institutions involved in housing and human settlements development both in Kenya and overseas. Similarly the Faculty of Architecture, Design, and Development and various other faculties of the University of Nairobi train professionals involved in the housing process. Technicians and para-professionals for the building industry are also trained by the Kenya Polytechnic, various institutes of science and technology, and village polytechnics.

Private professional associations, such as the Architectural Association of Kenya (AAK), and private consultants provide consulting services to the MOWH and the NCC for public low-income housing projects, e.g. the various urban development projects funded by the World Bank, USAID, EEC, etc. Other private voluntary agencies and non-governmental organizations, such as the National Christian Council of Kenya (NCCK), the Institute of Cultural Affairs (ICA), the Undungu Society of Kenya (USK) are also actively involved in the improvement of low-income settlements in Nairobi, e.g. in Mathare Valley, Kawangware, and Kibera, with varying degrees of success.

DANDORA PROJECT OBJECTIVES

The Dandora Community Development Project is an example of a large-scale attempt by the Nairobi City Council (NCC) assisted by the Government of Kenya to programme, plan, and implement a low-cost housing solution for households earning as little as K.Shs 280 per month in 1975. The project will, when completed, provide 6000 serviced plots over 7 years (originally over 4 years). In comparison to the annual housing needs, this is a 'drop in the ocean'. However, the project has been the major supplier of low-income public housing in Nairobi since the construction started in 1975, especially for the households in the lowest 20th percentile income group. At that time there were about 26,000 applicants for the 6000 plots advertised for allocation.

The Dandora project is the first in a series of urban housing projects in Nairobi and other urban centres in the country. It is therefore crucial that the public and private sectors identify the problems of housing the urban lower-income groups in the right context and develop appropriate strategies to overcome these problems, especially for the ongoing series of the second urban housing project and the future series of the third urban housing project covering Nairobi and other secondary towns in the country.

The Nairobi City Council established the Dandora Community Development Department in 1975 as part of the loan agreement between the World Bank, International Bank for Reconstruction and Development (IBRD), International Development Agency (IDA) and the Government of Kenya (GOK). The Dandora Community Development Department was renamed and expanded to the Housing Development Department (HDD) within the NCC in 1978 to implement the Dandora project and all similar low-income housing development projects in Nairobi.

The implementing agency (HDD) had to meet the following stated objectives as outlined in the project agreement between the relevant agencies:

(a) To prepare and service 6000 residential plots of 100 to 160 m² each, with individual water and sewerage connections, access to roads, security/street lighting, and refuse collection services at an estimated total cost of K.Shs 211 million.
(b) To construct the following wet cores and demonstration houses for the services plots:
    (i)   option A: 3870 plots with wet cores (toilet and shower) on plot sizes of 100, 120, 140 m²; at estimated capital cost ranging from K.Shs 6200 to 7100 per plot;
    (ii) option B: 1800 plots with wet cores and one kitchen and store on plot sizes 100, 120 and 140 m²; at estimated capital costs ranging from K.Shs 9800 to 10,600 per plot;
    (iii) option C: 300 plots with wet cores, kitchen, store and one room on 160 m² plots; at an estimated capital cost of K.Shs 16,500 per plot; and 30 demonstration houses to illustrate housing for option A and B plots. The option C plots to be sold at market prices;
(c) To operate and administer a materials loan fund amounting to K.Shs 30 million to enable plot tenants for options A and B to borrow appropriate amounts for building materials required to expand such plots to have two rooms through self-help or contracting.
(d) To construct community facilities including six primary schools, two health centres, two multi-purpose community centres with day-care facilities, one sports complex, and 400 market stalls; the capital cost of these facilities estimated at K.Shs 7.9 million, to be recovered through user charges and site value rates.
(e) To construct trunk access roads to the project site; the capital costs estimated at K.Shs 22.9 million, to be recovered through annual site value rates from the users.
(f) To ensure impartiality in the selection of prospective plot tenants, who must meet at least the following eligibility requirements:

(i)   The total income at the time of application of the tenant and his household has to be between K.Shs 280 and K.Shs 500 per month for option A plots and K.Shs 450 and K.Shs 650 per month for option B plots;

(ii)   the prospective tenant has to have lived in Nairobi for at least 2 years immediately prior to his application for a plot and not own any residential property in Nairobi;

(iii) the tenant's family (spouse, if any, or children) at the time of application, and upon allocation of a plot have to reside with the tenant; and

(iv)   prospective tenants have to pay NCC the appropriate fees for sewerage and water connection and a deposit of K.Shs 400 within 60 days of notification that they have been allocated a plot.

The Dandora project was therefore intended to benefit low-income households earning between K.Shs 280 and K.Shs 650 per month by allocation of option A and B plots, which accounted for 5670 plots (95% of the plots) while option C plots were intended to benefit all other income households through sale at market prices and the derived surplus used to cross-subsidize about 50% of the plots, all in option A.

The planned monthly charges were to range from K.Shs 73 to K.Shs 153 for option A and B plots. Based upon the assumption that expenditure for shelter and services was about 25% of monthly household income, option A plots (65% of the total) would be affordable by households as low as the 20th percentile in the city's income distribution curve in 1975. Option B plots (30% of the total) would be affordable to households in the 30th and 40th percentile. Furthermore the plot and materials loan repayments terms were made favourable by charging an interest rate of 8.5% per annum, and 30- or 20-year repayment periods for option A and B plots respectively. In order to encourage faster house consolidation, allottees of option A plots were granted a grace period of 5 years on the building materials loans. The project was therefore planned on the basis that all the capital costs of the project will be recovered from the allottees and the Council.

The formulation of the project proposals was done within the framework of the national housing policies and programmes for urban low-income housing and the Nairobi Metropolitan Growth Strategy up to the year 2000. The Nairobi City Council (NCC) prepared the proposals in close consultation with the relevant national agencies. The NCC's Nairobi Urban Study Group (NUSG) prepared the Metropolitan Growth Strategy during the period 1969 to 1973 while the Interim Urbanization Task Force prepared the detailed project proposals for the Dandora project as part of the overall eastern area extension development during the period 1973 to 1975. The World Bank sent several reconnaissance, project preparation, and appraisal missions from 1970 to 1975 before the project agreement was signed in 1975.

Since Dandora was the first major large-scale urban project to be funded by the World Bank in Nairobi, the project formulation and preparation stage took over 6 years. However, this period was considerably reduced to about 3 years during the preparation of the second urban project (1975–78), which includes similar large-scale site and services and squatter upgrading projects not only in Nairobi but also in Mombasa and Kisumu. Preparations are also being finalized for the third urban project, which includes similar projects in the secondary towns in Kenya, excluding Nairobi, to be funded by the

Government and the World Bank, the United States Agency for International Development (USAID), and the Overseas Development Administration (ODA) of the United Kingdom.

The second GoK/World Bank urban project, presently being implemented, covers Nairobi, Mombasa, and Kisumu. A total of about 11,700 serviced plots; upgrading of about 10,000 households (536 hectares); 2500 surveyed plots with minimum infrastructure; 3240 services sites for market sale; related community facilities; and employment generation programmes are to be provided in these three towns at a total estimated cost of K.Shs 576 million.

The third urban project, presently at the project planning and appraisal stages, will be a series of joint projects between the GoK and the three international financing institutions mentioned above. It is anticipated that a total of about 38 secondary small towns in the country will benefit from these projects, which will include serviced plots, community facilities, and employment generation programmes, amongst other components. Precise details on the scale and costs of the project will be known once the negotiations between the GoK and the funding agencies have been completed.

PROPOSALS AND MEANS OF IMPLEMENTATION

The Dandora project site is located 10 km east of the city centre and is easily accessible to existing and proposed employment centres near the site, city centre, and the industrial areas. It forms part of the overall proposed development plans of the city of Nairobi as outlined in the city's growth strategy by the Nairobi Urban Study Group.

The project has been carried out in two phases — namely Phase I, which consists of Residential Area I, and Phase II which consists of Residential Areas II, III, IV and V and the central spine of community facilities to be originally developed over a period of about 4 years.

The overall structure layout plan of the site has been designed to minimize public land and infrastructure investment per serviced area and to maximize individual responsibility in the development of the serviced plot. The elongated shape of the site and the Nairobi and Gitathuru river valley slopes along the northern boundary determined the physical planning of the area. The major access road is from the Komo Rock Road, which forms the western boundary of the site, and links Dandora with the city centre. This access road is connected to the central spine roads, within which are located the community and commercial facilities. The residential areas are located on the northern and southern sides of the central spine, which runs from west to east of the site. Two existing electricity power lines with land reserves cut across the Phase II area of the site.

Phase I of the project consists of a total of 1038 residential serviced plots, with 704 option A plots, 273 option B plots, 5 unserviced plots, 56 option C plots (including 21 demonstration plots), 3 community facilities plots for daycare; 6 commercial plots for corner kiosks; 1 primary school; 2 markets; and 1 pilot workshop cluster for small-scale industries.

The planning and design of Phase I was done by the Interim Urbanization Task Force of the NCC during the project preparation stage. The construction was started in October 1975 and all the 1038 plots were handed over to plot owners in November 1976. Almost all the plot-owners within the next 18 months completed two rooms; in the case of option A and B plots with the aid of the materials loan fund and technical and community

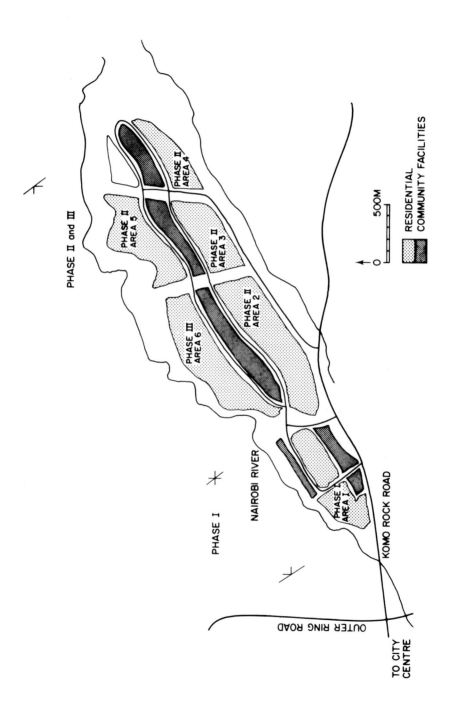

Figure 1.1   Dandora project layout plan

development assistance. The experience gained in the execution of Phase I was an asset for the implementation of Phase II. Some of the details regarding these experiences, problems, and issues are discussed below. In order to incorporate these experiences and avoid problems in the subsequent stages, Phase I served as a demonstration phase.

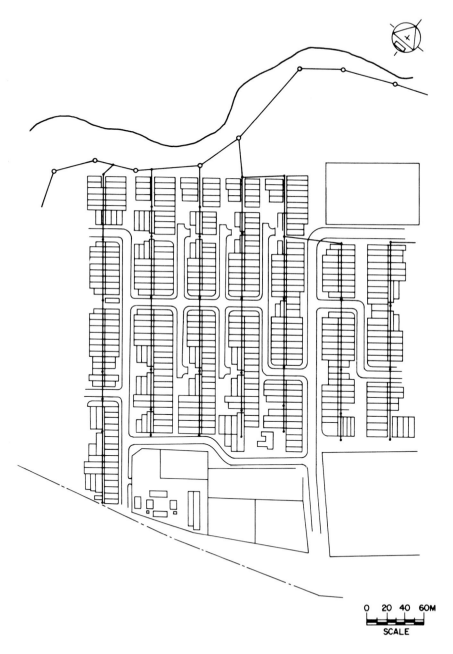

Figure 1.2   Dandora Phase I: segment layout plan

Phase II of the project consists of a total of 4971 residential serviced plots, with 3180 option A plots; 1536 option B plots; 246 option C plots; and 9 demonstration plots. In addition it has 5 primary schools, 4 markets, 2 multi-purpose centres, 2 health centres, and a sports complex. The detailed planning and design of Phase II was done by

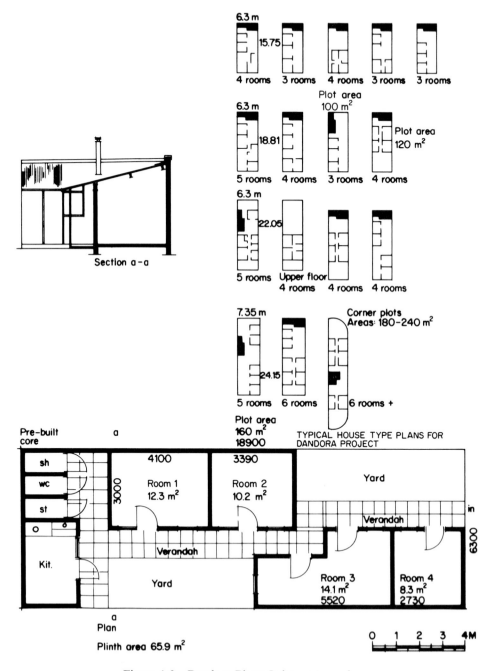

Figure 1.3   Dandora Phase I: house type plans

a local firm of consultants. The construction, anticipated to begin by the end of 1977, actually began in the middle of 1978 and was completed by the end of 1982. The preliminary planning of Areas II & III was done in-house by the project staff.

A further Phase III of the project, which will consist of about 1000 serviced plots of 200 m² each within 25 residential blocks of 1.5 ha each, will be developed as part of the second urban project. Small local developers and cooperatives will be offered these residential blocks at market prices.

The trunk sewerage, which includes the construction of about 20 km of trunk sewers and stabilization ponds, was completed in 1979. The costs for this component were recovered from the general funds of the NCC. A temporary stabilization pond was built in 1976 to provide for the treatment of sewerage from Phase I of the project. This trunk sewerage was developed in accordance with the proposals on the First Stage Programme for Sewerage and Drainage for Nairobi as part of the long-term sewerage needs of the city. This component of the project was implemented by the Water and Sewerage Department of the NCC in consultation with the Housing Development Department. The following on-site infrastructure standards were used:

(a) Roads/paths—Main roads tarmacked, 20 m reserve: 7 m carriageway;
                    —Secondary roads murram, 12 m reserve: 6 m carriageway;
                    —Parking area murram; footpaths and bicycle paths murram;
(b) Water supply—Individual water-supply to each plot;
(c) Sewerage—Individual water-borne sewerage facilities for each plot; and
(d) Street lighting—Street lighting provided; electricity available on site.

The Housing Development Department (HDD), as the implementing agency, consists of the following three divisions and two support units, which are all located under one roof on the site in Dandora:

(a) Technical Division;
(b) Finance Division;
(c) Community Development Division;
(d) Administrative Support Unit; and
(e) Legal Support Unit.

The total number of staff in the HDD is about 60 professionals, para-professionals and support staff. The major functions of the three divisions as regards the Dandora project are as follows:

(a) The Technical Division to:
    (i)   supervise detailed planning, engineering, and preparation of tender documents for site infrastructure, wet cores, and community facilities;
   (ii)   ensure proper supervision of construction;
  (iii)   provide technical staff with specific building skills on site to show allottees how to perform technical skills; and
   (iv)   illustrate the techniques of housing construction by erecting demonstration units on the site.

(b) The Finance Division to:
    (i)   keep all project accounts involving expenditures related to the project;
    (ii) develop an accounting and management system;
    (iii) prepare quarterly financial reports, and annual project accounts audited by an independent auditor; and
    (iv) operate and administer the materials loan fund.
(c) The Community Development Division to:
    (i)   publicize the project;
    (ii) solicit and process applications for the residential plots;
    (iii) orient and train allottees prior to the occupation of the plots;
    (iv) work with families during the construction phase; and
    (v) assist residents in developing institutions and programmes to enable them to create a genuine community.

In addition, the three divisions of the HDD also work with other local and international agencies such as UNICEF, UNEP, UNIDO, EEC, NCCK and others, which have similar objectives to the NCC and are interested to participate in enhancing the quality of life of the Dandora community.

The Administrative Support Unit of the HDD functions as the executive and administrative part of the department while the Legal Support Unit provides the necessary legal advice and carries out the legal tasks involved in the operations of the HDD. In order to ensure co-ordination of the functions of the HDD with other departments of the Nairobi City Council and relevant national agencies, a Housing Department Committee has been established as a standing committee of the Council. This Committee consists of representatives from the Government (the Permanent Secretaries of the Ministries of Urban Development and Housing, Local Government, Finance; the National Housing Corporation; and the Provincial Commissioner of Nairobi), chairpersons of all other standing committees of the Council, the Mayor and Deputy Mayor (as ex-officio members), and the chairperson of the committee. This structure was aimed to provide fast decision-making since all the chairpersons of all standing committees, and all the relevant agencies of the central government, are represented, which ensures linkages with the national housing policies and programmes. However, this has not always been the case since delays have occurred due to problems being referred back and forth between various committees.

There were a series of related components of the Dandora project, which were implemented simultaneously by different agencies and consultants, as part of the project agreement between the Government of Kenya and the World Bank. These included:

(a) Monitoring and evaluation of the Dandora project;[1]
(b) Joint Government of Kenya and International Monetary Fund Study on the Municipal Finances;
(c) Housing Operation Study of the Nairobi City Council;[2]
(d) Nutritional Needs Survey in Nairobi; and
(e) Low Cost Housing and Upgrading Survey for future sites and services and upgrading projects in Kenya (which now forms the basis of the second urban project).[3]

Similar studies have also been carried out as part of the second GoK/World Bank urban project[4] and some of these include:

(a) Study of the National Housing Corporation (NHC);
(b) Study of the Low-Cost Housing By-laws in Kenya;
(c) Study on the Institutional Strengthening of the Ministry of Local Government; and
(d) Study of the preparation of the third urban project to be funded by the GoK and
     the World Bank.

The monitoring and evaluation of the Dandora project, which was a new feature of
housing development projects in Kenya, was carried out by a team of local consultants
under the co-ordination of an inter-ministerial/inter-agency steering committee of the
Ministry of Finance. The team has prepared a number of Monitoring and Evaluation
Data and Interpretation Statement (MEDIS) reports during the implementation of the
Dandora project from 1976 to 1980. The eight MEDIS reports have provided feedback
on the implementation of the project with respect to the stated objectives as agreed upon
in the project agreement between the Government and the World Bank. The feedback
includes both the short-term and long-term issues facing the project and similar large-
scale housing development projects. Some of these issues, consequences, and implications
of the Dandora project are discussed in more detail below.

   All the above-mentioned studies and other research studies, such as the Evaluation
of the Sites and Services Programmes in Kenya[5] undertaken by the Housing Research
and Development Unit (HRDU), are aimed at improving the overall housing process
not only in Nairobi but throughout the country. The relevant ministries, especially the
MOWH and MLG, are already acting on some of the recommendations from these
studies. The MOWH, for example, has now appointed a Chief Building Inspector to
follow up on the drafting of new building and planning by-laws for low-cost housing.
However, greater use of these studies can be made in reformulating housing policies,
programmes, and projects in the future.

CONSEQUENCES OF THE PROJECT

The Dandora Community Development Project, as the first large-scale site and services
scheme in Nairobi, and especially Phase I of the project, offers a number of relevant
experiences gained during the planning, programming, and implementation stages. These
experiences deal with the economic/financial, technical, community development, and
administrative aspects of such projects and also broad policy and programme aspects
of housing and urban development.

   Phase I of the project has been completed with the majority of the houses built by
the allottees either through self-contract or self-help methods of construction. There
has been no major problem in the development and repayment of loans of the houses,
even by the poorest allottees, resulting in almost 100% cost recovery. This experience
has confirmed one of the main objectives of the Dandora project and shown that low-
income households in the urban areas can repay loans and organize adequate housing
through the sites and services approach. This significant outcome of the project was
one of the major contributing factors to the replicability of the project in other urban
centres of the country in the second and third urban projects.

   The first phase area has an estimated population of about 13,000 resulting in a plot
occupancy of about 13 people per plot as compared to the planned occupancy rate of
about 10 people per plot. About 45% of this population are tenants while the remaining

Figure 1.4   Paid labourers building a house for an allottee

Figure 1.5   Contractor-built wet core, shower, store and kitchen

are the owners/allottees. The increase in population of 30% as compared to the originally planned population of about 10,000 people has created stress on the community facilities, especially the schools, health centre, and recreation areas. The actual costs of Phase I compared very favourably with the estimated costs of the project in 1977. Without the materials loan the actual capital costs for option A plots ranged from K.Shs 7600 (K£380) to K.Shs 14,800 (K£740) and from K.Shs 15,600 (K£780) to K.Shs 23,300 (K£165) for option B plots depending upon the plot area, which ranged from about 100 to 140 m². The monthly payments for the capital costs, excluding the service rates and materials loan, ranged from K.Shs 72 (K£3.6) to K.Shs 86 (K£4.2) for option A plots and from K.Shs 144 (K£7.2) to K.Shs 160 (K£8.0) for option B plots. However, according to the data from the monitoring and evaluation reports, almost half of the allottees were paying over 30% of their income for housing as compared to the anticipated figure of 25% at the project planning stage. But in spite of this higher figure, the default rate on the repayment of the capital costs was reported by HDD to be negligible.

One of the interesting experiences has been the rate of house construction or consolidation by the allottees. Option A plot allottees in Phase I were given a total of K.Shs 5760 as a materials loan to build two rooms at different stages of construction in addition to the existing wet core of WC and shower, while option B plot allottees were given K.Shs 2880 to build one room in addition to the existing wet core of kitchen, store WC and shower. Option B allottees occupied the kitchen and built their houses faster than the option A allottees, who in most cases built a temporary structure in order to occupy and build the rest of the house. The Public Health Department of the Nairobi City Council had earlier objected to the construction of these temporary structures, which in most cases were demolished at the end of the 18-month period allowed for

Figure 1.6   Temporary shelter takes care of housing needs during the construction period

house construction in accordance with the approved type plans provided by the implementing agency.

Both option A and B plot allottees completed their additional rooms within the 18-month period while the others were given an extension of time and the remaining allottees completed their structures within 24 months. Having completed the additional rooms, the allottees were allowed to sub-let part of the completed house in order to supplement their incomes. According to the monitoring and evaluation data occupation surveys showed that about half the occupied plots in Phase I were rented out fully to non-allottees by the absentee allottees. Rents ranged from K.Shs 150 to 200 per month per room and the allottees had a good rate of return on their investment since in some cases up to 3 rooms on a plot were rented out. In a few cases plots, either developed or undeveloped, were also sold. Both the selling of the plots and the complete renting by the allottees were violations of the plot agreement. But due to various constraints, including interferences by the local councillors, it was often difficult for the implementing agency to take any actions to correct the situation. There is a possibility, of course, that the high rate of tenancy could lead to the deterioration of the physical environment in Phase I, since the absentee allottees/landlords could lose interest in the improvement and maintenance of the properties.

In terms of the technical aspects of the project, one of the significant experiences in Phase I of the project was the issue of the applicability of the existing building by-laws and the Public Health Act rules, which are enforced by the Public Health Department of the NCC, in relation to the minimum requirements for site and services projects in Nairobi. After detailed analysis during the project preparation stage, long before the implementation commenced, the Grade II by-laws of the Building Code were adopted for the project area, which was zoned as a special high-density zone using the infrastructure standards as outlined in the project agreement (see above). However, once the construction of Phase I had started the development control and law enforcement officers of the NCC, especially the Public Health Department, did not approve the plans of Phase I and II. This led to a long controversy regarding infrastructure design standards, especially sewerage layout design and standards, which were finally agreed upon after 6 months of discussions and meetings. This led to delays in issuing house type plans to Phase I allottees and also in the construction of Phase II. The plans of Phase II had to be amended and resulted in cost overheads both due to the design changes and increased cost of construction due to inflation and price escalation.

The total additional costs of the various design changes was estimated to be about K£1.38 million. After about 4 months of discussion between Council officers, Council members, Government officials and IBRD/IDA officials, a compromise was reached. The location of the sewer mains in relation to the wet-cores was changed to provide for a 3 m way-leave at the back of one of the two rows of the back-to-back plots. This also affected the design of the wet-core blocks, which were originally in groups of four with two shared walls, and were changed to groups of two with one shared wall (see Figure 1.2). The estimated additional construction costs and design fee was about K£190,000. These additional costs, however, were not recoverable from the plot owners. These discussions resulted in delays of about a year in the execution of Phase II. Furthermore with the increasing cost of construction due to the various delays and inflation mentioned above, it gave an opportunity to the income groups above the specified target income groups to occupy the plots, especially in Phase II.

With respect to the community development and technical assistance provided to the plot allottees, one of the innovative features of the project was the participation of the allottees in the construction of their houses. Three methods of house construction were predominant, namely (a) self-help building by the allottee; (b) self-help building using subcontracted labour; and (c) self-help building by the building groups. Of these three methods, the second was the most popular. The Community Development Division together with the Technical Division of the HDD assisted the allottees to form building groups in order to help individual members to build a room or rooms. By the end of 1978 there were about 15 such building groups in Phase I of the project. These groups, consisting of about 7 to 16 members, had completed about 194 rooms for their respective members by 1978 using the materials loans and the monthly contributions of the members. In several cases the building groups also hired subcontracted labour to complete the rooms. In all the three methods of construction the allottees received assistance from the staff of the two divisions of the HDD. One building foreman and one community development assistant worked as a team to assist a group of 250 plot allottees.

From the administrative and political point of view, the project experienced several delays, mainly because of the full acceptance by the City council of the various principles involved in the project, especially regarding the infrastructure standards as mentioned above, use of temporary structures, plot allocation procedures and enforcement of the plot agreement. There were often misunderstandings between the local political councillors and the senior technical officers of the HDD, mainly due to lack of adequate appreciation of a large-scale project involving innovative and demonstrative components, which have not been used in the conventional housing projects of the council, including the role of the new executive agency to implement the project which evolved incrementally over time. Having implemented Phase I of the project with reasonable success, most of these problems were overcome and the co-ordination between the various city council departure and the HDD has been increased in the implementation of Phase II of the project and the similar projects to be implemented as part of the second urban project. Such problems are, however, often associated with such large-scale, low-income housing development projects in Third World cities.

Another major consequence of the Dandora project has been the impact of the project on other low-income housing and urban development programmes of the government. The project is now a reality and a visible fact. It has by its presence removed some of the stated and unstated fears about large-scale sites and services projects at the policy level. Furthermore, the success of the Dandora project as the first major project has had a useful political impact since there is relatively more support for similar projects from some of the councillors and officers of the city council. The lessons learnt from the project will hopefully be incorporated and applied in the implementation of similar projects in the future.

IMPLICATIONS OF ANALYSIS

Apart from the feedback on the Dandora project the Ministry of Works and Housing (MOWH) also requested the Housing Research and Development Unit (HRDU) to carry out an evaluation of the sites and services programme in Kenya in 1978–79. The draft study has looked into the problems facing both the large-scale and small-scale projects in various urban centres in the country and made several recommendations for overcoming them. These recommendations are presently being studied by the various agencies at the national level, especially the MOWH and the National Housing Corporation.

The recommendations for future action related to the low-income housing policies and programmes, with special reference to sites and services projects, can be grouped into the following four areas:

(a) institutional and management resources;
(b) financial aspects;
(c) technical performance standards; and
(d) community development programmes.

(a) Institutional and management resources

It has been pointed out in various studies and reports that the institutional and management resources of the major agencies involved in the housing process are inadequate and need to be strengthened in order to ensure more effective and efficient planning, programming, implementation, and management of the sites and services projects, or for that matter any type of housing development project. The existing administrative, financial, and organizational structures of the implementing agencies urgently need to be reviewed and strengthened accordingly. The formation of the Housing Development Department (HDD) within the NCC as a result of the Dandora project is a good example, which has now been replicated to establish HDDs in Mombasa and Kisumu.

Apart from creating the necessary institutional infrastructure, there is a shortage of trained professional and para-professional staff to plan and implement sites and services projects both at the local and national levels. Hence there exists a tremendous need for various training programmes, i.e. short-term courses for mid-career development and long-term courses for new staff requirements, especially for those involved in the technical, financial, and community aspects of housing development projects, e.g. architects, planners, engineers, financial analysts, and community development workers, amongst others.

The on-site project management approach, as in the case of the HDD in Dandora, was successful from the point of view of being close to the community, but not so successful from the point of view of being far away from the policy-makers and other operational departments of the NCC, which play a significant role in the overall urban development of the city.

(b) Financial aspects

The funds presently allocated to the sites and services projects are grossly inadequate to cope with the immense urban housing task. By and large the financial allocations are a 'drop in the ocean' and do not correspond with the actual financial needs of the programme. Yet the success of the programme, to a great extent, is determined by the volume of the available financial resources, which means that the programme needs to be given a much higher priority in the overall economic and financial planning at national and local levels. Similarly, more effective utilization is needed of the existing financial resources by the local authorities.

The financial base of most local authorities is weak, especially in the smaller secondary towns, while there has been poor financial management in the major urban centres including Nairobi. In order to correct the situation, a lot more effort needs to be put into finding and implementing ways to improve financial management.

Project costs can be further reduced if the existing high standards required according to present bye-laws are critically reviewed and discarded so that the houses are affordable by the lowest-income groups; greater emphasis is placed on joint public and private sector investments in low-income housing; use of locally available and manufactured building materials, such as stabilized soil blocks, timber, etc., is promoted; and community participation is further consolidated and organized through the formation of building groups, housing co-operative societies and other local organizations. These and other measures are critical in order to increase the present low annual supply of housing units from the formal housing sector using existing bye-laws, especially when compared to the high annual supply of units from the informal housing sector using no bye-laws.

(c) Technical performance standards

Apart from the often-stated need for appropriate technical performance standards, there are often problems related with physically inefficient designs, especially regarding the more capital-intensive components such as roads, water supply, and sewerage. Tremendous cost savings can be achieved by ensuring that the site layouts in terms of land utilization and subdivision are such that the cost of infrastructure services is minimized at the design stage. Similarly, house type designs often do not respond to prevalent environmental, social, cultural, economic and political conditions; and inadequate forward planning fails to ensure that land is available well ahead of the project preparation stage.

Furthermore, there is need for more research and development in the areas of non-waterborne sanitation, rainwater utilization, road construction and maintenance, local materials and alternative forms of energy amongst other things, in order to demonstrate more innovative and cost-effective solutions, which have to be socially acceptable. Research studies related to these areas are presently being undertaken by the Housing Research and Development Unit (HRDU); the Appropriate Technology Centre at the Kenyatta University College; the Faculty of Engineering at the University of Nairobi; the Kenya Building Research Centre; and the NCC in collaboration with USAID, amongst other institutions working in the fields of housing, human settlements, environment, and energy. Additional funds need to be made available to execute demonstration projects resulting from research studies so that the findings of these projects can be implemented and replicated in large-scale projects by the various implementing agencies.

(d) Community development programmes

In many of the existing sites and services projects the role of community development is either minimal or almost non-existent. It is only in the recent planned housing development projects in Nairobi, Mombasa, and Kisumu that emphasis has been placed on the role of community participation and development in the sites and services projects. Even though the major intention is to build the housing units through self-help, the local authorities and the national executing agency do not have adequate manpower to provide both technical and community development assistance to the people.

Community participation at the planning and project preparation stages is almost non-existent or supposedly left to the elected councillors in the local authorities. It is anticipated that community participation may be enhanced through the formation of co-operative housing societies and building groups (e.g. as in Dandora) to overcome this problem. In addition, there is often no or inadequate provision of other basic community and employment facilities, such as health centres, refuse collection, schools, markets, and workshops. This problem was also experienced during Phase I of the Dandora project. When the allottees moved to occupy the plots there were no community facilities on the site. However, these were later built and in Phase II their construction was simultaneous with the construction of the residential areas.

A part from the provision of physical facilities for community development, there are other related activities which are equally important. Some of these activities and programmes include family planning, nutrition and urban small-scale farming; community-based organizations to assist tenants and allottees in dealing with local authorities and to ensure adequate communication and information flows. Some of these programmes are currently being developed in Dandora and are planned to be implemented in the Second and Third Urban projects. In some of the existing low-income uncontrolled settlements, such as Kawangware and Mathare Valley, local voluntary organizations such as the Institute of Cultural Affair (ICA) and the Undugu Society of Kenya (USK) are promoting such community development programmes and activities.

The above-mentioned aspects of the urban housing projects, and particularly the sites and services projects, are by no means exhaustive. There is now a growing amount of information and documentation which looks into the various aspects in depth. However, this chapter has highlighted some of the important aspects.

REFERENCES

1. Senga Ndeji and Associates, MEDIS 1–8. Unpublished mimeos, Nairobi, Kenya, 1977–80.
2. Nairobi City Council *Nairobi's Housing Needs: Meeting the Challenge.* Nairobi, Kenya: Coopers and Lybrand, 1976.
3. International Bank for Reconstruction and Development (IBRD). *Kenya: Appraisal of a Site and Service Project.* Washington, DC, USA, 1975.
4. IBRD. *Kenya: Second Urban Project.* Washington, DC, USA, 1978.
5. T. S. Chana, G. de Kruijff, *et al.* Evaluation of the Site and Service Programme in Kenya. Unpublished draft, 1979.

Low-income Housing in the Developing World
Edited by G. K. Payne
© 1984 John Wiley & Sons Ltd

Chapter 2

Can Shelter Programmes
Meet Low-income Needs?
The Experience of El Salvador

*Michael Bamberger
and Alberto Harth Deneke*

ABSTRACT

The purpose of this chapter is to describe and evaluate the experiences of a shelter programme in El Salvador which was able to successfully reach the low-income urban population while at the same time achieving one of the highest cost recovery rates of any World Bank-financed urban shelter programme.[1] Since the inception of its first pilot project in one of San Salvador's squatter areas in 1969, the shelter programmes of the Fundacion Salvadorena de Desarrollo y Vivienda Minima (FUNDASAL), a private non-profit Salvadorean foundation, have been based upon the concepts of community participation, progressive shelter construction, and financial accessibility to the low-income population. By the late 1970s the FUNDASAL production of about 1400 units a year (7000 units completed by 1975 and 1980), represented almost half of the total annual production of new 'formal' housing (i.e. units complying with all legal and planning requirements) in urban areas.[2] More importantly their programmes represented virtually the only type of housing programme accessible to the poorest 50% of the urban population.[3] FUNDASAL's ability to design and implement very low-cost, largely unsubsidized units, carefully tailored to the needs of the urban poor, enabled the organization to mobilize substantial support from foreign sources, among them two World Bank loans and grants from various US, Canadian, and European agencies.[4]

The shelter programme described in this chapter differs from most sponsored by national and international agencies in two fundamental aspects: first, FUNDASAL is a non-governmental organization, although it reached the scale and impact normally achieved by public sector agencies and was operating in six major cities. Second, the shelter programme is seen as a part of a broader institutional commitment aimed at achieving community social awareness through community participation. The principal objective of the Foundation's shelter programme is to overcome the restraints on formal and informal housing supply by producing[5] a wide range of serviced sites and basic dwelling units.

In order to assess the impact of its approach to low-income shelter, the Foundation set up an evaluative research programme, sponsored by the IDRC and the World Bank. It was part of a

---

* The views expressed in this chapter are those of the authors and do not necessarily represent the opinions of the World Bank.

comparative study of similar programmes in Manila, Lusaka, and Dakar, during the period 1975–80.[6] This chapter summarizes some of the insights gained from this extensive evaluation exercise in El Salvador.[7]

SOCIOECONOMIC BACKGROUND

Located on Central America's Pacific Coast, El Salvador is the smallest and most densely populated country on the American continent. With a land area of only 21,000 km^2 and an estimated population of about 5 million, it has a population density of over 230 persons per km^2, roughly equal to India.

About 41% of El Salvador's population in 1980 was classified as urban. Prior to the military–civilian coup of 1979,[8] there were about 2000 large (over 100 ha) coffee and cotton plantations and about 250,000 smallholdings producing basic grains. The main crops provide employment for only 5 months of the year and during the rest of the year as much as half of the rural labour force could be unemployed. Unstable employment, insecure rural land tenure, and lack of basic services have all contributed to rural migration in El Salvador.[9] Although there is much seasonal migration, increasing numbers of families have remained in the cities or migrated to other countries. This process has been exacerbated by the political conflict that began in 1980.

Despite these problems, gross domestic product grew at an annual rate of 5.3% between 1960 and 1977. However, since 1979, GDP is estimated to have fallen substantially due to the political conflict, though natural population growth rate has remained at over 3% per annum.

Prior to the military–civilian coup, El Salvador had an estimated per capita gross national product of only $660 in 1978. The effects of poverty were worsened by the highly skewed income distribution and the negative growth rates after 1980. In 1982, GDP per capita was estimated to have fallen below the 1972 level. In 1977 it was estimated that whilst the top 5% of households received over 21% of the total income, the poorest 10% of families only received 2.1%. One consequence of this skewed distribution is a high level of urban malnutrition, which affected three-quarters of all children between the ages of 6 months and 5 years. Another result is the high infant mortality rate, with 120 of every 1000 rural babies and 85 of every 1000 urban babies dying in their first year. Diarrhoeal diseases, nutritional deficiencies, pneumonia, and perinatal diseases—nearly all related to problems of environmental sanitation—have been the main causes of early deaths.

URBAN SHELTER AND SETTLEMENT SUB-MARKETS

According to the 1972 census, 55% of the existing housing stock needed replacement or improvement, and of these, about two-thirds were occupied by households earning less than the equivalent of US$100 per month. Although most urban homes (84% in 1975) had electricity, only 31% had individual water supply and only 38% had sewerage connections. In addition, low-quality materials and poor construction methods contributed to the physical deterioration of the housing stock. Poor-quality construction, however, tends to be concentrated in the squatter or invasion areas, where the provision of land titles has encountered legal complications.

A study conducted by FUNDASAL in 1975[10] divided the national urban housing market into several distinct sub-markets, each operating with a different rationale, serving different demand structures, and with different policy implications.[11] For many of the poorest urban households, the only available options were three principal types of informal settlements: the invasion-type squatter areas (locally called tugurios), the extra-legal land subdivisions (or colonias ilegales), and the rental rooms in tenement houses (or mesones). The study estimated that population growth in these areas exceeds that of the city as a whole, reaching 15–20% per annum in some of the municipalities comprising the San Salvador Metropolitan Area.

Tugurios are shanty towns which have been typically built in areas not suitable for other construction, including ravines and railroad right-of-ways (see Figure 2.1). These areas tend to be located near centres of urban employment or public transport routes. The FUNDASAL study estimated that in 1977, 38,000 people, or only 4.8% of San Salvador's total population, lived in squatter settlements. Few shanty towns in San Salvador have more than 1000 families and many have less than 100. Most tugurios have no individually supplied sanitary services, though in the well-established ones conditions are generally better. Water is sometimes available from public taps or from private individuals who sell water. In many of these settlements the national or municipal Government has constructed communal latrines.

Mesones (see Figure 2.2), the local term for tenement, generally consist of 5–50 rental rooms clustered around a central patio. In most cases a family rents a single room and has to share water and sanitary services with other families.[12] In most mesones, residents receive water and electricity for no payment beyond their monthly rent. Mesones are usually located in the centre of the city. In 1977 it was estimated that 23.4% of the San Salvador total population lived in mesones. Access to water is usually controlled by the manager and can be as little as 2 hours a day. The number of inhabitants per toilet and shower averages 15–16 persons. Electricity is more readily available in most tenements. In 1975 80% of the tenants had incomes which placed them between the 17th and 39th percentiles of the city's income distribution.

Colonias Hegales consist of peri-urban subdivisions sold without the installation of basic services or official subdivision standards. 'Sale' is normally through the system of 'rental with promise of sale', whereby the purchaser assumes title with the final rental payment. If the purchaser defaults on a rental payment all his equity in the property can be lost as he technically only has a rental agreement. Colonias ilegales may be actually considered extralegal for either of two reasons. First, they have not been presented for approval by the landowners and, because they lack basic services, they have no legal recognition as subdivisions. Second, the 'rental with promise of sale' system, under which families pay monthly instalments for 5–15 years before getting title, is no longer legal. Despite these factors, colonias ilegales housed 20.5% of San Salvador's total population. Plot sizes ranged from 80 to 200 m², with an equally wide variety of building materials and construction systems, mostly built by their occupants. Lack of adequate utilities is the main drawback to residents, and the majority buy water from tank trucks, while some use communal taps. Typically, electricity is more readily available from the private distribution companies, which do not require legal tenure before providing the connection. Many of the original occupants of colonias were very poor, though the increasing land pressures and time have transformed most of the oldest colonias into consolidated middle-class type settlements[13] (see Figure 2.3).

Figure 2.1   Footpath into a hillside tugurio

Figure 2.2   View of typical mesone in San Salvador

Figure 2.3   Colonia Ilegale, San Salvador

THE FAILURE OF CONVENTIONAL APPROACHES
TO URBAN SHELTER AND SERVICES

Shelter policy in El Salvador has typically suffered from four major weaknesses. The first is that total housing production and finance has been inadequate in relation to need: formal housing construction averaged only 2600 units per year during the 1960–70 period, while 10,000 new households were formed annually in urban areas. Second, even the limited commercial and public finance which was available for shelter and services has only been accessible to the middle- and upper-income groups. This has forced most of the urban poor to finance housing out of personal savings, thus requiring extraordinarily long periods of construction, or to resort to informal usury credit sources charging very high interest rates. Third, government has not faced the urban land supply problem and its impact on urban shelter and services. Finally, there is no explicit policy towards the upgrading of the bulk of the informal housing supply system: the mesones and colonias ilegales.

Not unlike most Latin American countries, El Salvador's public policies have faced the shelter problem by creating a series of institutions and finance systems: the public housing authority (IVU) in 1950, the development of a savings and loan system (FNV) in 1965, the creation of a national community development organization (FOCCO) the same year, and the compulsory salary tax system (FSV) in 1973.[14]

The national housing authority, IVU, was financed principally through central government transfers and, initially, through loans from the Interamerican Development Bank. In its first 28 years of existence, IVU built about 23,000 conventional family units in walk-up blocks. However, the bulk of its programme has been affordable only to middle-income groups, although it carried out several pilot projects for low-income families that did not become part of its regular operations.

The second approach, the savings and loan system under FNV, was established as a means of channelling private savings towards housing construction through the specialized banking system. During its first 13 years the system financed 26,600 complete, one-family dwellings at an average unit cost of US$20,000, benefiting families from the top 30% of the urban income distribution. By 1978, however, it had lifted its price ceiling further and was financing condominium apartments for up to US$48,000.

The third, and perhaps the most valid, approach as far as reaching the urban poor, was the creation of a community development organization to provide for facilities in low-income urban areas. Although FOCCO did not finance shelter itself, it did extend community facilities and services to many unserviced squatter and colonia ilegale areas in El Salvador's main cities. More than any other agency, it was subject to political influences and its potential role in urban policy was never fully realized.

The last approach, the Social Housing Fund (FSV), designed as an extension of El Salvador's social security system, was modelled after similar examples of Mexico and Brazil in the form of a payroll tax earmarked for housing. Its automatic source of funds made FSV the most financially stable housing agency in the country. The heads of household covered by the system were earning in 1978 less than US$280 per month. During its first 4 years FSV financed about 5000 conventional one-family dwellings at a unit cost of US$4000 to US$10,000 which made them only accessible to about the wealthiest 30% of families participating in the social security system and supposedly eligible to benefit from the FSV programmes. In addition, the self-employed and heads of household working in establishments not linked to the social security system are by definition not eligible. Early in 1978 the FSV also announced that it was going to double its ceiling prices.

As is also the case with many Latin American countries, the aspect most overlooked by urban policy has been the land supply problem, and to date, El Salvador has developed no specific and effective approach for urban land *per se*. This has exacerbated shelter supply problems due to the country's overall land scarcity, and has generated substantial profits for the owners of land—small and large—on the urban fringe, where land value is increased by proximity to public infrastructure.

FUNDASAL'S PROGRAMME OBJECTIVES
AND EXPECTED BENEFITS

The Foundation's shelter programme was one of the first sites and services approaches to be supported by the World Bank, as early as 1973. Given the increasing supply constraints in land, services, and shelter as well as the inability of existing formal housing programmes to supply new units affordable to the low-income population, the Foundation's shelter programme objectives are defined as follows:

(a) to demonstrate that a serviced site approach with partially built core units is a viable alternative to conventional, fully built Government housing programmes, the costs of which have been beyond the means of nearly 60% of the urban households;
(b) to ease the severe shortage of low-cost urban shelter by providing units affordable to families earning US$40–100 per month, reaching down to as low as the 17th percentile of the urban income distribution scale;
(c) to demonstrate the potential role of the informal and non-government sectors in providing self-financing low-income housing, thereby easing the burden on Government resources;
(d) to encourage provision of adequate community facilities as an integral part of low-cost shelter development;
(e) to generate employment through labour-intensive construction methods and the organization of small commercial cooperative enterprises;
(f) to actively involve the households in building both the shelter units and in developing community organizations;
(g) to ensure approaches are tailored to their needs; and
(h) in general to create neighbourhood groups capable of developing socially and economically viable communities.

The Foundation's programmes were designed to provide the minimum package of services which would both permit the evolution of stable communities with standards acceptable to the target population, and satisfy the planning standards required by the Government. The standards and design evolved over a number of years and involved continual discussion with Government planners to permit lower, and hence more affordable, standards of water supply, plot size, and land use. By 1978, a typical unit was being offered with 20-year financing at about 6.5% interest for the purchase of a serviced plot, with 12-year financing at 8% for a materials loan to complete the construction of a basic living unit.

The Foundation's programme was carried out by providing the following interrelated components:

(a) serviced plots with individual connections for water, sewerage and storm drainage, optional electrical connections, unsurfaced footpaths, public lighting, and a minimal semi-surfaced access road;

(b) sanitary core units and optional expansions to the level of an unfinished basic dwelling unit of 36 m^2;

(c) off-site water distribution and sewerage mains as well as upgrading of existing off-site access roads;

(d) financing for construction materials, designed to induce self-help extension of core units;

(e) the construction and equipping of health clinics, multi-purpose community centres, sports fields, and markets;

(f) the provision of loans for small-scale industries; and

(g) short-term technical assistance for training, studies and the evaluation of the socio-economic effects of the programme.

It should be stressed that the Foundation's shelter programme was not intended to completely cover the urban housing need of the low-income groups, but to demonstrate that the serviced-site approach, combined with progressive shelter development through family and community participation, was effective, viable, and replicable on a national scale. In fact, it was estimated that the shelter programme would meet the demand of only one-third of new household formation within the target income group limits. It should also be pointed out that the shelter programme was accompanied by other social programmes aimed at the same target groups, often considered by FUNDASAL as more central to its objectives.

As designed, the shelter programme was expected to provide the following benefits:

(a) improve the living conditions and community facilites for about 15,000 households;

(b) increase the employment of households through mutual-aid and self-help construction techniques, including increased earnings from the various co-operatives organized through the programme.

(c) demonstrate an approach to shelter problems which would enable government to keep pace with housing needs throughout the country;

(d) expand the construction capacity of the non-governmental sectors for very low-cost shelter and services; and

(e) improve Government policy formulation for low-income illegal settlements.
    In addition, a number of positive externalities from the programme were anticipated, particularly (f)

(f) a substantial redistributive effect in the provision of low-cost serviced shelter units to low-income families who were paying excessive prices for mesón rental rooms, or for unserviced plots in quasi-legal subdivisions of land;

(g) net external economies to help reduce uncontrolled urban growth;

(h) benefit families in adjacent urban areas through the provision of off-site infrastructure;

(i) improve the chances of the urban poor finding stable employment through training in self-help and mutual aid construction; and

(j) in general, increase the quality of life of the households included in the programme.

The World Bank estimated an internal rate of return of 20% for the programme, when all of the estimated costs and benefits were discounted over a 30-year period.

IMPLEMENTATION APPROACHES

The programme was implemented by the Foundation, and contained a number of organizational and design innovations designed to ensure a high level of community participation and at the same time to reduce costs, thus making it accessible to low-income households (see Figure 2.4). In terms of organization, emphasis was placed on developing a high level of community participation in the programme's implementation and in the building of the shelter units. This was achieved through the requirement that one member of each participating household take part in mutual-help construction to complete the major part of the shelter unit.

It was explained during the initial selection process that participation in the mutual-help construction groups was a requirement for acceptance to the project. Except in the case of one project site in which there was a lack of demand, (Usulutan) this requirement was strictly adhered to. It was explained to the families that mutual help was both a way of eliminating the need for a 10% downpayment and also a means of teaching construction and organizational skills which would prove useful in the completion of the house and community facilities, as well as preparing households for assuming later control of the management of the community. Although there was some variation from one project to another, in general it was found that groups worked best if formed by between 20 and 25 families. In some cases the number was determined by the number of plots surrounding a park, but in general this size range seemed to permit sufficient specialization within the group without becoming so large as to be unmanageable. Each group met together during the week to plan the work and to discuss problems, and during the weekend for the construction itself. Evaluations conducted during the mutual-help phase suggested that the process of working together effectively created a sense of community solidarity and responsibility. Although rigorous evaluations were not conducted on this issue, it is believed that this sense of solidarity was one of the main factors contributing to the programme's long-term success: firstly, by creating responsibility for maintenance—almost all sites are well maintained by the communities themselves; secondly, by contributing to one of the best rates of cost recovery (under 2% default rate) with the community in some cases being directly responsible for collection of payments;[15] and thirdly, because in several cases the community was able to organize demonstrations and other forms of pressure to ensure the installation of water and other services which public authorities were responsible for installing but which were suffering long delays. There are a number of significant design differences between the Foundation's programme and traditional shelter projects in El Salvador. The following are some of the most important:[16]

(a) Considerable efforts were made to learn from the experience of the earlier projects and to tailor the projects *to the needs and priorities* of the families who would live there. This was reflected in plot sizes, width and quality of streets, levels of

Figure 2.4   Community participation in house and site development

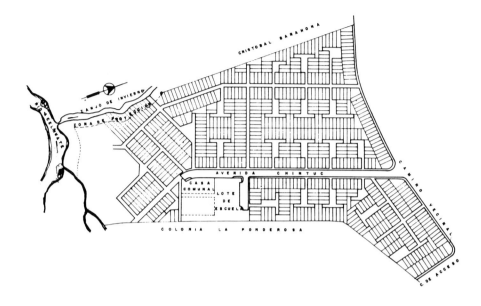

Figure 2.5 Layouts of sites and services projects. Chintuc site in Apopa, north of the San Salvador Metropolitan Area (720 units)

    infrastructure, construction around open spaces, etc (see Figure 2.5). Considerable economies in *land use* were obtained (principally by reducing vehicular access) whilst, at the same time, a more livable environment was produced.

(b) Individual family units were not completed but were sold at various stages of their development to be completed by the users. Families had the option of receiving a serviced plot with only a sanitary core, or a serviced plot with 18 m² of additional construction, or 36 m² semi-completed shelter unit. The provision of options has proved to be important as all families (of different income levels) tend to have different preferences.[17]

(c) Grouping of houses around common open spaces, which provided plot access and semi-private recreation areas.

(d) Priority was given to the provision of public spaces which occupy a higher proportion of total land areas than is the case in most shelter projects.

(e) Significant reductions in the proportion of land assigned to vehicular traffic and parking.

    Even though most project households had monthly *household* incomes of less than $100 it proved to be a long battle to gain approval of more realistic levels of vehicular roads.[18]

    In order to respond better to the needs of different socioeconomic groups and to reduce costs, the Foundation has continued the experiment with a number of new design innovations, of which the following are important to single out:

(a) Provision of two-storey single-family rental units near community facilities. In this way it is possible to locate projects on higher-cost land nearer to the city centre and place of work at affordable costs. Plot sizes have been reduced to 4–5 m frontage by 8 or 10 m deep (instead of about 125 m² in other projects) whilst still providing 45 m² of living area. In this way it has been possible to achieve densities of 140 units per hectare as compared with only 94 in conventional four-storey walk-up apartments in the same location at one-fifth the cost.

(b) Renovation of existing tenement rental houses and their conversion into co-operative condominiums. Because a significant proportion of the low-income population live in mesones, the Foundation has conducted experiments by acquiring a meson building and renovating it through mutual help and offering co-operative or condominium ownership to the families. This is a potentially important approach to upgrading centrally located rental housing at a cost which is affordable to most low-income families.[19]

EFFICIENCY OF DESIGN AND EXECUTION

A comprehensive review of the physical, economic, and social design of the Foundation's programme has been presented in other FUNDASAL, IDRC, and World Bank-sponsored studies,[20] but a number of indicators can be mentioned briefly. First, the units have proved to be affordable to the target population (see summary below), despite the very high rates of unforseen inflation. Second, participants have indicated a high level of satisfaction with most aspects of the project. The main areas of dissatisfaction were related to provision of public services such as lighting and garbage collection which were not part of the Foundation's responsibility. Third, a comprehensive comparison of Foundation and public housing on a wide range of indicators including plot density, provision of communal areas, and efficiency of services layouts shows that FUNDASAL projects compare very favourably. For example, the proportion of land area devoted to plots has steadily increased over the years; FUNDASAL sales prices are much lower, as is the proportion of land devoted to vehicular traffic; and the newest FUNDASAL project (Conacaste) has been able to achieve densities 50% higher than any other project.

SUMMARY EVALUATION: ACHIEVEMENT OF OBJECTIVES, IMPACT ON PARTICIPANTS AND ON NATIONAL HOUSING POLICIES[21]

In general, all of the 6600 shelter units co-financed by the first World Bank loan were produced in 5 years, although with delays of more than 2 years in some cases due to problems in land acquisition, a problem which still has to be faced by policy-makers.[22] Water supply and sewerage construction progressed reasonably well, but by late 1981 many of the community facilities still had not been provided by the appropriate government agencies.

When the programme was designed the target population was defined as households falling between the 17th and the 65th percentiles on the national urban income distribution curve. This objective has been largely achieved as it is estimated that at least 85% of households had incomes which placed them below the upper income limit. In the original affordability estimations it had been assumed the households would not be willing to spend more than 20% of their monthly income on housing. It was found, however, that families were sometimes prepared to invest twice this proportion, and substantial assistance was received in the form of transfers from relatives not living in the households.[23] A small number of families come from below the 20th income percentile, showing that the programme can reach down on to the minimum target levels (17th income percentile), but the majority come from the 3rd, 4th and 5th deciles.

The programme's ability to continue being accessible to the target group despite sharply rising costs is even more impressive when compared with highly subsidized public housing, or projects which in most cases are not accessible to families below the median income.[24]. The extremely low drop-out rates once the units are occupied also shows that families are able to continue meeting both mortgage and loan repayments to the Foundation and the additional costs for the completion of the unit.

In 1982 the Foundation had one of the best loan repayment records of any shelter programme financed by the World Bank. As of July 1980 total repayments in arrears represented only 2.3% of the total loan portfolio, and of these, only a fifth were overdue by more than 90 days (three payments).[25] The impressive cost recovery performance is due to a number of factors, including: the active involvement of the community in the collection process, an efficient record-keeping and billing system, loan collectors who visit each household every month, the threat of eviction for defaulters, and a careful selection of project participants.

The cost recovery situation has deteriorated, however, during the past 2 years due to the present severe political and economic constraints. Although the evaluation did not detect any clear pattern of impact on the overall income and employment situation of participants, there were, however, a number of indications of ways in which the programme might be affecting the economic situation of certain sub-groups. It was found that between 1976 and 1980 the total family income of poor participants in the shelter programme was increasing more, relative to the control group families, than the income of wealthier programme families. This is due in part to income transfers received from the extended family. It was also found that during the very difficult economic climate, labour force participation rates for secondary workers in participant families declined less than for the control group families. The reasons for this are not fully understood. This was particularly true for spouses where there was a significant reduction in the number of working spouses in the control group but almost no change among participants. In addition to the approximately $2000 paid by each family to the Foundation for mortgage payments and material loan, the average family also invested an additional $1000 of its own resources to purchase additional materials or to pay labour. It was estimated that these additional investments generated about $500 of wage employment, equivalent to about 6.4 man-months of employment, per unit.

The evaluation also found that there did not seem to be any overall negative effects of participants' investment in housing on consumption of basic necessities such as food and medicine.

Most programme participants previously lived in tenement houses (mesones) located in the city centre. In comparison with their former dwelling, the move to the project sites meant an increase of 4.8 m^2 in the living space per person and a reduction of 2.2 in the number of people per room. From the health point of view these improvements can be viewed as very significant. Studies in several interior cities did not reveal any significant increase in transport costs, though information is not available from the capital city where distances, and hence travel costs, are greater.

When compared with the control group, in 1978 there was a slightly higher proportion of participants who felt their conditions had improved over the previous 2 years. The differences were greatest with respect to income (63% considered they were better off, compared with 52% of the control group), and health (37% considered their conditions had improved, as compared with 28% from the control group).

The Foundation considers the provision of housing, in addition to being a good in itself, is a means for developing community organization and social awareness and participation among project participant families. The house construction process is believed to provide an effective means to achieve this goal for several reasons. First, the completion of the house is a tangible and very significant goal, the achievement of which provides positive reinforcement to continue with other activities. Second, the process of planning the construction exposes the group to a wide range of social, economic, and political issues such as the problem of disciplining members who do not participate, negotiation with public and private agencies involved in the project, resolution of political and other rivalries among members, etc.

The objective is to have developed, by the time the houses are completed, a well-functioning community organization which will be able to assume the responsibilities of community government. To achieve this objective, representatives are elected from each 25-family work group to participate in a central community board, the functions of which expand as the project develops. Once the houses are completed, the project is designed so that a number of relatively simple physical projects remain to be completed (parks, sidewalks, etc.) by the community on their own initiative. The more active community groups then begin to become involved in non-physical projects such as co-operatives and social and cultural activities.

By 1980 there were a number of indications that many of these organizations were developing into effective community governments. For example, in several projects the community board assumed responsibility for the collection of loan payments. In other cases they mobilized sufficient support to pressure government and private service agencies to comply with their commitments to install services such as electricity and water. The boards have also organized a large number of physical, economic, and cultural activities on their own initiative. None of this evidence is by any means conclusive, but it does suggest the strong potential of these organizations, and hence the apparent validity of the general strategy followed by the Foundation.

From the point of view of the development of a national urban shelter strategy, it is essential to compare the Foundation's approach with alternative housing options. Cost comparisons show that the Foundation's programmes are accessible to families down to about the 20th percentile, whereas most public housing programmes are not affordable to families below the 5th or 6th deciles, with some only reaching the top 30th percentile. A good-quality completed FUNDASAL unit costs perhaps less than half of the cost of the cheapest standard government dwelling. A cost–benefit analysis, in which the FUNDASAL projects were compared with the main shelter options in the formal and informal sectors, showed that the FUNDASAL project had the highest economic rate of return, suggesting that it offered more benefits per dollar than any other shelter project.[26]

Although the units offered by FUNDASAL are far cheaper than any other public housing programme, they are not the cheapest form of shelter available to the poor. Squatter units (usually made with cardboard materials) and the poor- to medium-quality tenements and subdivisions are cheaper than the Foundation's basic units, although these do not provide secure land tenure, and are not fully serviced, nor do they have access to long-term financing.[27] As the Foundation must provide a minimum standard of housing and services in conformity with planning regulations, it is inevitable that in a very poor country the lowest-income families will not be able to afford this package.[28] In practice this means that about the poorest 20% of families have been excluded because of affordability.

For families above this minimum cut-off point, the question arises as to how the Foundation compares for a given monthly payment with the alternative shelter options available in the informal housing market. It was found that the quality of construction of the FUNDASAL house is usually superior to that of all the main types of informal housing.[29]

The level of water and sanitary services of FUNDASAL projects is also much higher in most cases. However, the colonias ilegales are more attractive in terms of individual plot size, although they have no community and open spaces. The mesones on the other hand, have the advantage of greater access to public services and to places of employment.

A cost–benefit analysis was conducted[30] to provide a more systematic way of comparing the package of benefits obtained for a given amount of money.[31] Using the internal rate of return and similar economic indicators, it was found that FUNDASAL had a superior benefit–cost ratio[32] to any other shelter options in either the formal or the informal housing sectors. It was found that rates of return for both FUNDASAL main shelter options were significantly higher than the 20% estimated in the World Bank's Appraisal Report.[33]

SOME IMPLICATIONS FOR
AN URBAN SHELTER STRATEGY

Although the Foundation's research on the demand structure for informal shelter, as well as the evaluation of the serviced site approach, demonstrate that even in a country as poor as El Salvador, with the exception of the lowest 17%, income is rarely the only limiting factor in the provision of minimum shelter. In fact, families would be prepared to pay more for shelter if better housing was made available. One may ask why, then, so many households live in inadequate housing in El Salvador and so many developing countries?

Whilst effective demand for adequate shelter exists, experience also suggests that the main issues in shelter are not in fact restricted to the demand side. The failure of the various systems that influence the structure of supply can be equally important. These issues fall under three general headings: supply of land, the supply of urban infrastructure, and the supply of mortgage finance.

The Foundation's approach of providing financing for serviced sites is one way of facing the three main supply issues, especially for new households and for those living in the non-tenured rental sub-markets. Therefore, an aggressive policy for increasing the supply of affordable serviced sites is one key shelter strategy. Such programmes have to be designed and implemented so that they at least keep pace with new household formation.[34]

A national policy for sites and services would not, however, be sufficient in most countries because they already have significant proportions of low-income families in squatter areas, mesón type rentals or in quasi-legal land subdivisions such as the colonias ilegales in El Salvador. A parallel policy for upgrading these shelter sub-markets is necessary. What is more, the experience around the globe in the 1970s indicates that secure tenure, adequate infrastructure and shelter improvements can frequently be provided at half the cost in existing settlements as compared to the provision of new serviced sites, because the latter requires the acquisition of land and the meeting of official standards.

The approach in both strategies is similar and based on the following principles:

(a) agile mechanisms for securing land tenure as a first step towards stabilizing or consolidating shelter;
(b) integrated provision of urban infrastructure (water, sewerage, drainage, lighting, and access roads) on a staged schedule according to affordability and preference criteria;
(c) financing schemes that are replicable on a larger scale, and which emphasize cost recovery and the restriction of subsidies, if they exist at all, to the lowest income percentiles;
(d) the involvement of the community in the planning and implementation of both sites and services and upgrading approaches; and
(e) in general, the improvement in the quality of urban management.

The management issue is in fact an extraordinarily difficult and critical task, because many of the supply constraints identified are essentially institutional issues. To improve the supply of affordable adequate shelter for low-income households in the appropriate location with varying service levels, tenure arrangements, and financing schemes, requires a high degree of planning and coordination at the national and local levels, especially if the objective is to expand shelter programmes beyond the pilot scheme stage.

In the long run, success in meeting basic needs in urban shelter will depend, in large part, on the improvement of urban management to plan and execute land, services, and housing schemes for the huge numbers of low-income households who are currently excluded from urban housing programmes, as well as an overall national policy focusing on the basic needs of the urban poor.

NOTES AND REFERENCES

1. The two main sources used in the preparation of this article were: Alberto Harth Deneke, 'Towards a Distributional Urban Policy: A Critical Analysis of El Salvador's Urban Land, Shelter and Services Policies', Ph.D. Dissertation, Dept Urban Studies and Planning, Massachusetts Institute of Technology, Cambridge, Massachusetts, 1978; and Michael Bamberger, Edgardo Gonzalez-Polio, and Umnuay Sae-Hau, 'Evaluation of the First El Salvador Sites and Services Project', *Urban and Regional Report No. 80–12*, Urban and Regional Economics Division, The World Bank, 1981.
2. In 1970 the annual production of urban housing was estimated at about 2600 units. More recent figures are not available, but assuming some growth of production it is likely that

the FUNDASAL production figures may represent close to 50% of total housing production (see M. Bamberger *et al.*, Chapter 1, cited in Note 1).

3. A study conducted in 1977 showed that none of the public housing programmes were accessible to households below the 48th income percentile (M. Bamberger *et al.*, cited in Note 1, Table 13.1).

4. Among the principal granting agencies were IDRC of Canada for research, Interamerican Foundation of the US for sector and community development, and the European agencies MISEREOR, CEBEMO and NOVIB for the social programmes. The World Bank loans were signed in 1974 and 1978 for US$8.5 million, and for US$10.7 million, respectively.

5. In addition to the shelter programme the families selected by the Foundation participated in savings and loan co-operatives, employment and production enterprises, community education programmes, etc., not described in this chapter.

6. The results of these evaluations have been reported in more detail in publications prepared by FUNDASAL, IDRC, and the World Bank. Some of the more important are listed in these Notes and References.

7. The activities and the evaluation research described herein took place prior to the period of political violence initiated in El Salvador in 1980. The Foundation's activities after this period have diminished considerably due to its lack of ability to mobilize private grants and international loans, as well as the difficulty of carrying out community organization activities in urban areas. At the time of writing, its institutional and financial viability was becoming more critical.

8. The principal findings of the evaluation described herein were obtained from research carried out before the coup.

9. After the 1969 military–civilian coup, El Salvador initiated a series of structural reforms, among them an agrarian reform which expropriated the largest land-holdings and has been the subject of considerable debate, a financial reform in which government assumed the country's financing system, and an export reform which centralized in government the sales of the three primary exports: coffee, sugar and cotton.

10. This section is largely based on that study. See: Alberto Harth Deneke, *et al.*, FUNDASAL, *La Vivienda Popular en El Salvador*, Vol. I. San Salvador, 1975.

11. The results of the study were further analysed by one of the authors and several policy implications drawn. See: Alberto Harth Deneke, 'Towards a Distributional Urban Policy: A Critical Analysis of El Salvador's Urban Land, Infrastructure and Shelter Policy', Ph.D. Dissertation, Massachusetts Institute of Technology, Cambridge, Massachusetts.

12. Although there is, at least in theory, rent control, families have no security of tenure and live in constant fear of eviction.

13. See paper written by Alberto Harth Deneke: 'Quasi-legal Land Subdivisions in Latin America: A Solution or a Problem for Low-income Families', UN Experts Meeting on Housing Policy, UN, New York, 1978, published in *Development* (Journal of the Society for International Development), No. 2, 1982, pp.50–54.

14. This section is in part based on the publication: 'Housing Built by Mutual Help and Progressive Development: To What End?' by Mauricio Silva and Alberto Harth Deneke, in P. Ward (ed.) *Self-Help Housing: A Critique*. London: Alexandrine Press, 1982.

15. Obviously many other factors such as efficiency project design to reduce cost levels also contribute to the good cost-recovery position.

16. Designs are discussed in detail in a two-volume study by the Foundation, *Analisis del Proceso Evolutivo y Soluciones Autónomas*, which compares FUNDASAL projects with public housing, and in M. Silva, *Evaluación de Proyectos Habitacionales en El Salvador*, forthcoming.

17. Contrary to initial expectations it was found that some higher-income families preferred plots with services and no construction, whereas some poorer families preferred to receive a higher level of construction; the reason being that higher income groups can afford to have labour and buy materials to build according to their own design, whereas poorer families cannot mobilize financial resources, and prefer to receive a unit which they can occupy with minimal additional investment.

18. When the first loan began, city planning norms required one parking space per house, even

though only about two families in the whole project owned cars! Reduction of the number of roads also reduced the cost of installation of water and sewerage lines.

19. Aida Herrera and Francisco Altschul, *Proyecto Experimental de Rehabilitation del Mesón El Progreso*. FUNDASAL, 1979.

20. For examples: FUNDASAL, 'Analisis del Procesco Evolutivo y Soluciones Autónomas'; Bamberger, González Polio, and Sae-Hua, 1981, cited in Note 1.

21. Most of the data in this section are taken from Bamberger, González-Polio and Sae-Hau, 1981, cited in Note 1, parts II and III.

22. The impact of these units in relation to total housing demand in El Salvador is not large; however, if one related this output by city and economic strata, the impact is great. For example it is estimated that in Santa Ana, the second-largest city, total population is about 100,000, equivalent to 18,200 families. The Santa Ana project is aimed at the bottom 30% of income distribution, or 5450 families. The first site in that city supplied 1200 units, or 22% of the demand of that strata. Similar impact can be assumed in the five secondary cities in which the Foundation had projects. In San Salvador, however, with a metropolitan area of about 800,000 hectares, the impact was much smaller.

23. Kaufmann and Lindauer, *Basic Needs Interhousehold Transfers and the Extended Family*. Urban and Regional Economics Divisions, World Bank, 1980.

24. The precise amount of public housing subsidies is very different to estimate, as subsidies are not documented.

25. The political instability during 1980–81 has increased the arrears to about 5% of the loan portfolio.

26. Bamberger, González-Polio and Sae-Hau, 1981, Chapter 13, cited in Note 1.

27. A house could be constructed in a squatter settlement for about 1200 colones (one-third of the FUNDASAL cost), and in a tenement for about 2200 colones (about 60% of the FUNDASAL cost), excluding land. These units are not comparable, however, since standards vary.

28. The norms require, among other things, individual water and water-borne sanitation for every unit.

29. Bamberger, González-Polio and Sae-Hau (cited in Note 1), Chapter 4, 'Project Impact on the Quality and Value of Housing'.

30. Marisa Fernández Palacios and Michael Bamberger, *Economic Analysis of Low Cost Housing Options in El Salvador*. World Bank (forthcoming).

31. This is a method for quantifying and comparing the 'streams' of costs and benefits throughout the life of the project. A number of different methods exist for quantifying these flows, of which the two most common are the internal rate of return and the net present value.

32. It should be emphasized that these techniques only compare benefits per dollar invested. The issue of affordability is a separate question, and it was pointed out earlier there are other shelter options.

33. Bamberger, González-Polio and Sae-Hau, 1981 (cited in Note 1), Table 13.4.

34. For a broader discussion of these issues see: *Shelter*, Washington, DC: World Bank, 1980 and *Urban Land Policies*, World Bank, 1978.

Low-income Housing in the Developing World
Edited by G. K. Payne
© 1984 John Wiley & Sons Ltd

Chapter 3

Lusaka: Local Participation in Planning and Decision-making

Harrington Jere

INTRODUCTION

Zambia is one of the most urbanized states in independent Africa. The establishment of the copper mining industries in the 1930s led to its early urbanization. In 1971, over 30% of the Zambian population lived in urban areas, and it was projected that if the trend continued 50% would be urbanized by 1990. During the early years of urbanization, African migration was carefully controlled by European settlers and regarded by them purely as a source of cheap labour. As early as 1929 there existed an Employment of Natives Ordinance which tied housing to employment, thus forcing the unemployed to return to their villages. The African presence in urban areas was always considered temporary.

On 24 October 1964, Zambia achieved its independence from British rule. The new Government removed all legal and artificial barriers of rural–urban immigration, which immediately led to the increase of urban populations. Lusaka and other Copperbelt towns had the largest share of this increasing population and in the 1960s Lusaka's growth rate was 15% a year, one of the highest in the world. For example, in 1973 the population of Lusaka was estimated at 381,000, and by 1976 it was expected to rise to well over 450,000. Of this population, close to one half were living in squatter settlements, which lacked clean water, schools, health centres, roads, and many other communal facilities.

An early act of the new Government was to create a Ministry of Housing and Social Development. The Ministry was given the responsibility of mapping out an overall housing and development policy and providing enough houses for the increasing population, through City and Municipal Councils. In addition, the Zambia Housing Board was charged with building houses for low-income workers but, given the inability to meet demand squatter housing quickly spread in many urban areas.

ZAMBIA'S POLICY OF SITES AND SERVICES

Having inherited a housing system which did not cater for the majority of Africans, the new Zambian Government had a limited number of options in attempting to alleviate the looming housing crisis. In addition to traditional conventional housing programmes the Government introduced in 1967 a new programme of 'Aided Self-help Site and Service Schemes' to be administered in parallel with many other efforts.

In the first year of the programme (1968) 2000 new units were expected to be built throughout urban Zambia. They were very successful and quite popular, yet it soon became apparent that they were only a partial solution, since lack of qualified personnel and adequate funds restricted the number which could be provided.

Other government efforts aimed at finding some affordable housing options appropriate to national needs as well as the users themselves focused upon the potential contribution of squatter housing. In 1974, squatter housing accounted for 28.6% of Lusaka's housing stock. There were, of course, many who were critical of such housing, but equally there were others who appreciated the contribution people made on their own initiative.

SQUATTER UP-GRADING

By 1972 the government had gained much experience and a better understanding of the housing problem. Rather than advocate a solution through conventional housing, the Second National Development Plan (1972–76) took a bold step and recognized that although squatter areas were unplanned, they nevertheless represented assets both in social and financial terms. It argued that the planning and provision of services to such areas was better than their wholesale demolition, and went on to state that first priority must be given to the acquisition of land when any unauthorized settlement on it was to be upgraded; strict control of any further development had to be enforced both inside and outside designated areas; and the following services must then be provided in any upgrading exercise: piped water, sewers, roads and surface water drainage, street lighting, and other communal services.[1]

PROJECT FINANCE AND OBJECTIVES

While Zambia was keen to put this new policy of squatter upgrading into practice, the resources were lacking—particularly at a time when returns on copper exports, the major foreign exchange earner, were unreliable. The only other option left to Zambia was to seek financial involvement from the World Bank. The Bank had apparently been following Zambia's sites and services projects closely, and considered the new policy of squatter upgrading as a step in the right direction. In 1973, after months of negotiations, the World Bank and Zambia concluded an agreement for a loan whereby the Bank would finance up to 47% of the project, at that time estimated at US$41.2 million. The Zambian Government contributed 48.5%, whilst contributions from the American Friends Service Committee (AFSC) and UNICEF amounted to 4.5%. The loan was repayable at 7–8% interest over 25 years, with participants paying 7.5% over 30 years. Both Government and the AFSC were involved in preparing project proposals, training Community Development workers, organizing Pre-school Teachers' courses and, in the case of AFSC, providing experienced Community Development Staff who spearheaded local mobilization.

In October 1979 the appraisal report estimated that the costs would be as follows: sites and services preparation and servicing 13.2% squatter upgrading 6.7%;

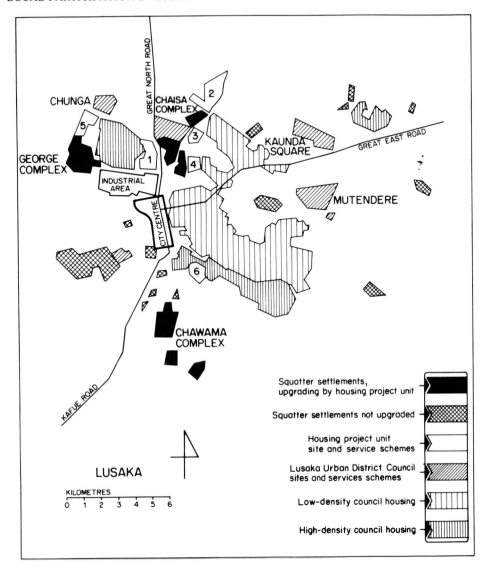

Figure 3.1   Location of sites and services and squatter upgrading projects in Lusaka

building material loans 22%; the provision of primary infrastructure 11.5%; community facilities 9.7%; technical assistance 13.7%; land acquisition 0.5%, and various other contingencies estimated at 22.7%.[2]

The new Lusaka sites and services and upgrading projects were designed specifically to benefit low-income groups. They were also intended to improve the quality of life of people in the project areas and develop a set of housing strategies which could be used to provide the urban low-income population with access to adequate housing. The following major squatter settlements were chosen for improvements: Mwaziona Complex (formerly George Compound), with 7361 houses being improved on existing sites and a further 3028 redeployed on new plots next to Mwaziona. These new extensions are referred to as over-spill areas. Chawama Complex had 5528 houses to be improved on existing plots, with Chaisa/Chipata Complex 7437 houses to be improved on existing plots and 2675 redeployed on new plots.

Briefly stated, the main objectives of the Lusaka squatter upgrading and sites and services projects were basically:

(a) To upgrade and service 17,000 dwellings in four large squatter settlements, by creating enough incentives for the improvement of the existing housing stock.
(b) To prepare and service 7600 plots in overspill areas, to facilitate the resettlement of the families affected in the exercise of major infrastructure provision and in reducing overcrowding in the existing areas.
(c) To make available 4400 fully serviced plots in six sites and services projects.
(d) Provision and administration of building material loans for improving existing houses and the construction of new ones.
(e) Provision of schools, community centres, health centres, improved markets, roads and piped water, street lighting, and security of tenure; also making available technical assistance.

Of the 29,000 households who owned existing houses in upgraded areas, it was planned to improve 20,323 such units. For the project to provide surfaced tarred roads, pipe-borne water, schools, and markets, it became necessary to resettle nearly 7600 in overspill areas where services had already been provided. These required the construction of entirely new core houses to replace the old dwellings which were demolished to make way for the installation of physical infrastructure. The only addition to the housing stock were the houses built in the section of sites and services which formed part of the Lusaka Project. There were six locations for the sites and services (see Figure 3.1), which made available 4238 plots. For the owners of dwellings in the existing squatter settlements, occupancy certificates for a period of 30 years were issued, whilst residents in the sites and services projects were granted 99-year leases. Within these periods it was accepted that residents would be able to sell their houses and transfer ownership without difficulty. Implementation of the projects began in 1974.

PARTICIPATORY MANAGEMENT

During the negotiations between the Zambian Government and the World Bank, both saw the question of citizen participation in the planning and implementation of the projects as extremely important, since it was agreed that upgrading was a social as well physical exercise. Careful planning and much care therefore had to be exercised to secure the trust, approval, and cooperation of the affected residents if the projects were to succeed. This called for a sensitive approach with respect to their existing leadership and aspirations. The National Housing Authority (which prepared the Government request to the World Bank), planned to achieve this by emphasizing the importance of local involvement, in line with constitutional amendments emphasizing Zambia's one-party participatory democracy. It therefore spoke broadly of a division of responsibility between the community and authority in which local authorities could support and reinforce the residents' own efforts to improve their environment, rather than take over from them. It had to act as a stimulus to the investment of popular savings, skills and initiative, and was therefore to be seen as a phased programme of development in which authority and the community determined at each stage the type of input that would help residents achieve their aims.[3]

The answer to these stated objectives was seen as the training of a special type of Community Development Worker, who would be sympathetic to this approach. AFSC and UNICEF were selected to help in training these workers. On many occasions it was being urged that programmes of this nature involving large investments, tend to have a negative impact on communities which in the past had taken care of most of their needs and enjoyed independent direction. It was feared that 'big daddy' with big money, bringing all the answers to their problems, would quickly destroy such independence. If squatter upgrading was to be a means of countering this approach, the contribution of the Community Development Workers was vital. Although programmes to train them had already been conducted in Zambia, the skills acquired were not suitable for the new squatter upgrading projects, and a new approach was considered necessary. Books on Community Development Techniques by T. B. Batten[4] were used in the training programme to help stimulate a process of self-determination and self-help within the projects. The strength of the methods is that they encourage trainees to develop their own capabilities to respond to the varied needs by thinking and acting for themselves. The expectation was shown to be justified, and graduates from the training programmes performed extremely well in promoting participation.

The Government, Lusaka City Council, and the World Bank agreed on the need to set up a separate Housing Project Unit within the City Council, which would specifically carry out the sites and services and upgrading projects. This was because it was believed that the project team would find it difficult to implement their objectives within the City Council's Department of Housing and Social Services. At one stage there were some doubts about this approach, as it was considered that problems would arise when the time came for handing over completed projects to the responsible Council department, especially as day-to-day operations were carried out in isolation from the main City Council departments responsible for housing. However, others argued in favour of a separate unit to avoid being caught up in the usual local government bureaucracy and to increase the chance of giving these communities an experience of participation. In the end a separate Housing Project Unit (HPU) was accepted, though it must be acknowledged that not all the problems involved have been solved, since there is an inevitable tendency for participation to be interpreted in ways that suit project management rather than residents.

LOCAL PARTICIPATION

In Zambia, the political system is defined as a one-party participatory democracy, so that community participation and grass-roots involvement in decision-making is an integral part of national policy. The Party has sought to achieve this by decentralizing all political institutions. Under this policy the village is considered the most important and effective unit for self-expression and action, whilst in urban areas the basic unit is the section.

Squatter upgrading in Lusaka has therefore been executed in close conjunction with the ruling Party organization. This has had the benefit of providing project administrators with the fullest co-operation of Party leaders at all levels. In sites and services schemes, where new communities were being created, the community development staff, in conjunction with the Party organizers, also allocated plots in groups of 25, to conform with Party Section and Leadership patterns in existing areas. However, this type of leadership was seen as temporary. Sooner or later, as people got to know each other better, it was assumed that other forms of leadership would emerge.

The Community Development Workers were responsible for community mobilization and for informing residents about the projects through briefing meetings to explain project organization, financing, and all physical aspects of the project. Although Community Development Workers often worked closely with individual households, community-wide concerns were decided upon through the local leadership, as in the Road Planning Group.[5] This was largely composed of Party leaders and each complex had its own. Working with these committees, the Community Workers organized section meetings at which each section of 25 households participated. Only those issues and decisions affecting the community at large were left to the Party leadership in the Road Planning Group meetings. Importantly, all those decisions which affected individual households, individual sections, and branches, were made by these groups alone. On the other hand, all field workers in each project area formed their own field team committees, composed of accountants, engineers, surveyors, community development workers, and construction advisers. The teams acted as brokers between the Housing Project Unit managers on the one hand and the Road Planning Group and the people themselves on the other. The field team was one group whose influence was felt in both directions of the community down to the individual household as well as in the project administration up to the Director. Because the teams acted independently their advice was listened to on both sides, and acted upon.

The other important committee was the weekly management meeting held at the main administrative office. These meetings were chaired by the project director and attended by senior project staff who represented their own sections. However, as the influence and the importance of the field teams became apparent, attendance at these management meetings was extended to field team leaders. This greatly strengthened the link between the residents and the policy-making body and in return project administrators were also invited by the field team leaders to attend some of the Road Planning Group meetings if the need arose. Naturally, all this was possible due to the flexibility of the HPU management, in responding to the implications of local participation. This created an atmosphere of mutual trust which was essential for efficient implementation.

The creation of the Road Planning Group resulted from a rejection by residents of early attempts to encourage participation. Before this is explained, let me point out the common fallacy found in many projects which claim to be participatory. What is popular participation? Is it informing the residents about a planned project in their area? The Lusaka projects did not completely escape this danger and a typical example concerned the planning of road layouts. It was initially the project planners who drew up routes for possible roads. These were taken to the residents saying that the sketches only represented rough ideas and must be considered as provisional. They were labelled 'Green' or 'Temporary pegging'. When approval was given by the residents they were painted with red paint and considered accepted, permanent, and ready for grading.

This 'green pegging' system failed to involve residents in physical planning, and many complained at public meetings that they were simply being asked to rubber stamp officially prepared plans.

Engineers, planners, and other elites resisted any compromise when this was suggested, but those within the management committee who supported flexibility and compromise won in the end. This happened soon after the project started in the John Howard area of the Chawama Complex in 1975. Inexperienced management had to acknowledge that the Housing Project Unit was not a control power to dictate what people must do, but rather a service organization to assist people in developing their own institutions in a manner acceptable and affordable to them. Management therefore sought to find an acceptable way of getting the residents properly involved in planning and the Road Planning Group was born out of this dialogue. It resulted in a local leader winning a majority in the Planning Group and achieving a direct form of community participation in the decision-making and planning process. This victory was won by residents and, as a result, project staff found themselves acting as consultants to the groups.

By this time project management had become more experienced and realistic. Rather than impose external solutions they sought to strengthen the hand of local leaders by holding leadership seminars. During the seminars, residents' leaders were given more details of project financing, physical infrastructure, and the programme of implementation, with emphasis on the importance of their continued participation in decision-making and project maintenance. In addition, these seminars gave an opportunity to the local leaders to express their grievances over certain aspects of the project and to point out the wishes and expectations of the affected population. At the end of these seminars recommendations and resolutions were made. Later, these were carefully examined by the project management before recommendations and resolutions were given back to the leaders. For example, in Chawama Complex, residents were unhappy with the kind of street security lighting and demanded that lights immediately be replaced with brighter ones; on receiving this complaint, the project team immediately instructed their electrical contractors to have them replaced. There were many other cases which received immediate attention to the satisfaction of the residents.

In Zambia, there is a long tradition of mutual help in which people assist each other in building, cultivating the fields, and looking after neighbours' children. This tradition survives undiminished throughout the country's squatter settlements. Most squatter residents in Zambia are rural people who greatly value their rural traditions and it is interesting that at a time when governments throughout the Third World are spending vast sums trying to bridge the gap between urban and rural areas without much success, migrants have successfully integrated their rural living systems with urban conditions.

At an early stage in the life of the projects, management formed a self-help co-ordination committee chaired by the Deputy Project Director. This writer was privileged to be its secretary and self-help co-ordinator. As a result of the committee's work, four collective mutual self-help trench digging projects were successfully undertaken by residents in Nyerere Compound in the Chawama Complex during the months of May and June 1976. Residents there decided to dig the water trenches themselves and as a result earned themselves a credit of K1813, which was paid into an account in the name of Nyerere Compound. The residents used the money to construct a clinic which is used for community health education as well as other community needs. In Desai Compound of George Complex during the months of August and September 1977, the residents successfully undertook another water trench-digging exercise at the end of which K1150 was credited to their account. They used the funds to build a day-care centre. In January to March 1978 the residents of Garden Compound decided to dig the water trenches in their area, earning credits of K2500 which was used in building a clinic and making improvements to their self-help market. The people of Chaisa too, took part in digging water trenches and had their accounts credited with an amount of K3088, also to build a clinic. In Paradiso, residents even undertook successful individual house water connections, including the supply of required pipes and labour. The project staff only assisted with a plumber, tools, and the services of a project co-ordinator. In Jack Compound, Chawama, Paradiso, and Chaisa many self-help markets were built in a similar manner. All these works, which were additional to those provided by the Housing Project Unit, had originally been budgeted for execution by the general contractor.

At the start of squatter upgrading the level of house improvement was low, as expected. It is quite important at this point in time to explain the reasons for this:

(a) At first the project had hoped to issue a K100 building material loan to those wanting to improve their houses. Unfortunately this never materialized as a result of high inflation on building materials. Only very few benefited from this arrangement.
(b) The Housing Project Unit could only allow the purchase of building materials on loan to the families being resettled in the overspill areas and restricted cash purchases to them as the materials were getting hard to obtain for the overspill builders. The majority of them lived in temporary shelters on their new plots and needed to have their core houses built and occupied before the next rains.
(c) Until the existing houses were given a number and assured of an occupancy licence, very few were willing to commit their scarce resources to improving a house which may later be chosen for re-allocation, particularly when the time came for reducing overcrowding in the existing areas.

However, by 1978/79, once this was done, improvements to existing houses took an upward trend. At the time of writing, figures showing the progress of house improvements were as follows: Chawama Complex, with existing houses numbering 5525, had 1569 houses completed and 310 under construction; Chipata and Garden Complex, with 7437 old houses, of which 1542 were improved, and 296 receiving attention; and George Complex, where there are 7361 existing houses, the progress report, as of 31 December, showed 6721 improved houses, 163 receiving general extension and 345 houses receiving improvements about foundation level. However, all these reports from the individual complexes do not include widespread action in stockpiling building materials, such as river sand, cement, and cement blocks or bricks. As one drives around, the impression and estimates suggest a 50% general house improvement rate. In the overspill areas, where 7628 plots were allocated, 5335 core houses (some with full extension) are completed. The remainder consists of houses at various levels with only a few undeveloped. In the site and services projects, out of a total 4238 plots allocated, 1343 core houses are completed, 691 fully expanded houses, 275 being developed, and 1285 still underdeveloped.

From the outset, the Lusaka projects sought to stimulate the production of good, affordable and legal housing for the low-income groups in a way which provided residents

Figure 3.2   Improved house in an upgraded project

with ample opportunity for participation. So far, over 160,000 people in the upgraded areas now enjoy the services of clean piped water, the use of schools and community centres, as well as new tarred roads and the availability of building material stores. The development of appropriate housing strategies was achieved by avoiding the enforcement of unnecessarily high building standards, and permitting a more flexible attitude. Although the projects were planned so that residents could afford to pay for services, this has not, however, generally been achieved and for many, even token service charges have remained a burden. There is more scope for optimism in assessing the degree of participation in that what was initially termed shared responsibilities between authority and residents in the end came out reasonably well. The formation of the Road Planning Group, which had wide powers and greatly influenced project decisions, was composed jointly of officials and residents. The rejection of some plans and the favourable responses from management constitute a real success in terms of local participation. As to self-help and mutual collective self-help, participation in various works and the building of family houses stands out as a good, if qualified, effort and a former deputy director of the project has stated that although, from the perspective of the comparatively junior staff, the extent of 'bottom-up' decision-making appeared small, there was substantially more than in any other bureaucracy in Zambia and that this was formalized to some degree. He claimed that this was the only project in which the tail of the organization (which is what Community Development Workers usually are) had the power to wag

Figure 3.3   Making bricks for extension or rebuilding

the dog of engineers, accountants, administrators, and the rest.[6] However, local participation was not brought into action at an early stage of planning and when it was, all the financial details and expected objectives had been worked out in the board rooms of Lusaka and Washington. The excuse advanced was that at that stage it was difficult to know which of many squatter areas would be upgraded and it was therefore difficult to say which local leaders should be brought in. As a result, local participation was restricted to decisions on physical layouts and on-site decisions and less in terms of where to raise funds, how much was needed, and what conditions were acceptable. Today, a further difficulty has emerged in the upgrading areas over the decision to form a separate Housing Project Unit to administer the projects. When completed projects are handed over to the main Lusaka Urban District Council Department of Housing, the Council has found it difficult to improve or even maintain services because it has

Figure 3.4   House on a sites and services scheme

inadequate funds and cannot recover costs from residents. Also a separate section, known as Peri-Urban, which was created specifically to supervise the upgraded areas, is experiencing difficulties due to inadequate transport and staffing, and a lack of co-operation and co-ordination with other relevant Council Departments. However, it has been argued here that, because some of the people who helped to plan the project in the early stages had close touch with the realities of life in squatter areas, and had the chance to discuss with local leaders tentative plans for upgrading the settlement, projects have in general been successful. The Lusaka experience in squatter upgrading represents some useful lessons in community participation in decision-making and planning which are lacking in many other projects of this nature. Considering all the problems of cost and co-ordination involved in such a large-scale and sensitive project, I believe the results are most encouraging.

POLICY IMPLICATIONS FOR THE FUTURE

Early Government attempts to formulate a policy which would replace the elitist colonial approach with one which would cater for all people in Zambia could hardly achieve this objective immediately. In an attempt to meet increasing housing demand, interest in sites and services schemes increased and by the 1960s the Government had introduced aided self-help and sites and services projects.

By 1974 the number of houses completed in sites and services schemes was 18,579, representing 7.2% of all total houses of the formal urban housing stock in Zambia. Lusaka alone recorded 7908 completed and occupied houses in sites and services schemes, which represented 10.6% of the city's housing stock. The major schemes in Lusaka were Mtendere, Kaunda Square (Stages 1 and 2), and, in 1971, Chunga. Whilst this represents a creditable achievement, the proportion of Lusaka's population living in squatter settlements was 45.8% out of a total of 413,000.[7]

At the time of writing, the population of Lusaka is estimated to be 650,000 and continues to grow rapidly. Despite their small numerical contribution to total supply needs, the experience gained in these projects at last appears to offer a ray of hope. In 1980 the National Housing Authority, which greatly influences Government Housing policies, introduced six sites and services projects in provincial areas. Initial signs are that the Lusaka projects will be guided examples with necessary modifications to suit each project situation. Official pronouncements in support of continued self-help and self-reliance have increased enormously and indicate widespread official support which is matched by the Zambia National Building Society; which recently introduced small but significant loans for low-income home-builders, particularly in sites and services schemes.

LOCAL PARTICIPATION IN TERMS OF
COSTS AND COST RECOVERY

Projects involving local participation are often regarded as costly because of the extra administrative procedures and possible delays. However, a former Field Director for the AFSC has argued that

> the fear of delays resulting from community involvement is often exaggerated, especially by contractors. Nevertheless, community participation does introduce an additional element of uncertainty into project planning. Where disbursement schedules and inflationary pressures are such that failure to spend quickly at the front end will result in rapid cost escalation, community participation both in decision making and civil works is a real financial risk. It is a practical decision for those negotiating and planning a project to determine the extent to which they are willing to take such a risk.

However he goes on to say:

> the limited amount of community participation which existed in the Lusaka project has not, in fact, caused any major delay or resulted in financial loss.

There have been many delays due to various factors, but community participation has not been one of them.[8]

In my view, investment in community involvement should be considered as a long-term, rather than a short-term investment, especially since the projects only give sufficient assistance to encourage the users to take responsibility for the planning, provision, and management of their own shelter. This was the position in Lusaka when the Government proposal to the World Bank stated that

> in order to ensure that it is compatible with the life-style requirements of the population in each settlement, the process of up-grading must stimulate the investment of popular savings, skills and initiative, and enable authority and the community to determine at each stage the type of input that will help the residents achieve their aims.[9]

Cost recovery in low-cost housing remains a major source of concern throughout Zambia, and the Lusaka squatter upgrading and sites and services projects are no exception. Although the plans were to keep the charges as small as possible repayments are beyond the reach of many households. Officials involved in the early planning stage had assumed the residents would be willing to pay up to 25% of their monthly income towards housing costs. Now, it appears that the question of affordability and willingness to pay were not studied with sufficient care. A number of reasons are given for the poor level of cost recovery, including inadequate debt collection machinery; the inability of some residents to pay even if they wanted to; poor maintenance of the services by authorities; non-delivery of certain services which had been promised; lack of continued community education and ineffective sanctions against defaulters. However, serious attempts are being made to provide the promised services, adequate debt collection arrangements, and increased community education. Also service charges are being examined with a view to adjusting them to the correct levels as the conditions permit today.

RECOMMENDATIONS AND SUGGESTIONS

From my own involvement with the Lusaka project a number of observations and recommendations may be offered. First, the funding of community development aspects was underestimated. Second, time schedules for project development did not recognize that participation by residents *can* be time-consuming. If funding organizations such as the World Bank continue to take an interest in similar projects, they should therefore allow flexible time schedules for meaningful local participation. Countries and their planners should be able to identify the target community in time for local leaders to be involved in project preparation and possibly early involvement in negotiations for funds to be used in their areas. Self-help building should not be organized by project administrators, but allowed to surface naturally after the major infrastructure is installed. In Lusaka, an early attempt at self-help encouragement proved futile and those concerned with project evaluation made a premature conclusion that self-help was a failure. Yet, after the dust had settled, we saw widespread and unprecedented self-help work in block-making and house construction in all upgraded areas.

In relation to community organizations and briefing, the project staff in Lusaka were too enthusiastic and created expectations which were later difficult to satisfy. In addition, key staff were moved off to spearhead work in new areas, so projects suffered dislocation. Continuity of staff on each project is obviously an asset in this respect.

In view of the difficulties in handing over completed projects to the City Council, greater emphasis should be placed upon working within existing institutions and reforming them where necessary to increase proper resident participation. Nonetheless, despite all their limitations, the Lusaka experience in sites and services and squatter upgrading should be viewed as a major step in the right direction, and one which makes sense in terms of shelter provision. It achieved many successes and some failures. In terms of future replicability I believe we can make good the failures and improve on the successes.

NOTES AND REFERENCES

1. *Republic of Zambia Second National Development Plan, January 1972–December 1976.* Government Printers, Lusaka, p.147, items 21, 22, 23, and 24 specifically dealing with the provision of 70,000 serviced plots, and on p.148 items 24, 25, and 26 dealing specifically with the recognition of squatter areas and the procedure to follow in upgrading.
2. Source: Project and Appraisal Report, October 1979.
3. Government of the Republic of Zambia, *Lusaka Site and Service Project*, Vol. II, p.5.50.
4. 'Evaluation report on the training programme for Community Development Officers', dated 13 April 1975 to 25 September 1976.
5. The Road Planning Group was a counterpart committee to the Project Management Committee. At the time when the project started the Party was already well organized. Locally the party structure was as follows: Constituency Committees — these supervised a number of Branches. Composition — 12 men, 12 women, and 12 youths. Below this we have Branches. The smallest Branch had 200 households and the largest could go up to many thousands. Composition — 12 men, 12 women, and 12 youths. Then came the Section Committees representing each 25 households. All these are democratically elected. The Ward Chairman is a Councillor of his area and is in charge of both Party and civic matters. The Party structure is unique in that nearly everybody has a leadership role in one way or another.
6. R. Martin, in a letter to Marja Hoek-Smit of June 1981.
7. Report of the Workshop on 'Human Settlements in Zambia', held at the University of Zambia, 12–14 September 1975, p.65, annex II.
8. Robert J. Ledogar, in 'Community Participation, Collective Self-help and Community Development in the Lusaka Housing Project', Second draft of July 1979.
9. *Lusaka Site and Services: Project Proposal*, Vol. II, p.5.50, of July 1973.

Chapter 4

The Kampung Improvement Programme of Indonesia: A Comparative Case Study of Jakarta and Surabaya

Johan Silas

URBAN CONTEXT

Socioeconomic conditions

The most recent census figures show that in 1980 Indonesia had a population of nearly 147.5 million people, making it the fifth largest in the world. Between the last two censuses the population increased by 2.32% per year, up 0.24% from the previous period of 1961–71. This population is spread over 13,600 islands which cover more than 2 million km², yet Java, which covers only 132,000 km², or 6.9% of the inhabited islands, accommodates 62% of the total population.

Problems related to population increase are inevitably concentrated in Java. At the beginning of the nineteenth century its population was less than 5 million; at the turn of this century it was 30 million and by 1960, 60 million. Another 30 million people have been added to this total within the last 20 years. This dramatic rate of population growth is largely due to the presence of the country's largest cities, namely Jakarta (the capital city), Surabaya, and Bandung.

Jakarta has at present a population of 6.5 million persons with an annual increase of 3.99%, whilst Surabaya, as the second largest city, has a population of just over 2 million and an annual increase of 2.93%. The annual increase in other cities varies between 3% and 4% a year, half of which is due to natural increase. Most cities also accommodate an unofficial population of almost 15 million and Surabaya 6 million.

In the centralized economic system of Indonesia, Jakarta provides better income and employment opportunities than other cities. For that reason, it has relatively less low-income families than Surabaya and in Surabaya, a greater proportion of family members have to work for a living. The informal sector accounts for about one-third of total urban employment opportunities. In both cities, about 80% of the population are in the 10–45 age group.

Cities in Indonesia are governed by municipal governments, under the provincial government (see Figure 4.1). Jakarta as the seat of central government enjoys the same level as a provincial government. The important differences of these levels of governments are the availability of revenue and improved access to the central government. For example, taxes on motor vehicles, plus land taxes and surtax, are all collected by the provincial government, even though most of the revenues are raised from the cities. In addition, local development projects in Surabaya have to be submitted through provincial government. These proposals are subject to review by the planning board of the provincial government so that delays and cost increases are common.

The municipal government of Surabaya consists of eleven urban districts, (Kecamatan) which are subdivided into four to six sub-districts (Kelurahan), each of which may contain one or more kampungs.[1] Further, a sub-district may be responsible for four to six neighbourhood units (RWs) and each neighbourhood unit consists of four to eight community units (RTs), which takes care of approximately 60 households. In rural districts there exist two systems: the urban system as mentioned above in villages on the fringe of the built-up areas, and the rural subdivision of hamlets, at a scale between neighbourhood and community units with populations of 1000–2000 persons.

As development activities were implemented at the lowest level of community organization, an Institute for Local Development was sponsored by the government in the early 1970s and attached to each sub-district organization. Participation and involvement is organized by neighbourhood or community level organizations, whose members are elected by and from the local population. As will be shown below, the success of the W. R. Supratman Kampung Improvement Programme (KIP), is an obvious example of the role of the RTs and RWs in generating resources and participation from the local population.

Housing conditions

Compared to most other developing countries which gained independence after the Second World War, Indonesia only formulated national housing programme in 1975. Prior to that time, housing needs had to be satisfied by individual families themselves.

The only housing construction activity outside the government service housing programme is the housing cooperatives established by the local government and assisted through long-term credits from the central government to the co-ops. The housing co-ops were first established in 1954 in 120 towns and cities throughout Indonesia. In 1964 the movement was officially terminated due to the high rate of inflation. During its existence, only about 1250 houses were constructed, though in Surabaya some co-ops continued without government assistance and by 1981 over 4000 houses had been built, mostly in the medium-size range, without any financial assistance from the public sector.

Even after the National Housing Corporation (Perumnas) was established in 1974 together with the National Housing Policy Board and the Mortgage Bank, the number of housing units constructed was still very limited and the majority of families still had to provide for their own housing needs. In cities and towns, private speculative housing construction was only started significantly after the enactment of the Investment Act of 1968–69. Between the period 1970–76, less than one housing unit per 1000 population was built annually for sale or rent. Even after the Perumnas joined forces with the private sector to construct housing, only about 20% of urban housing needs were met through

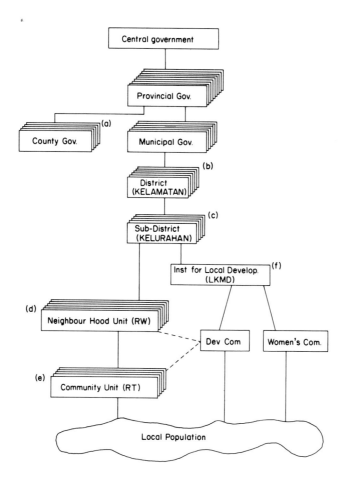

(a) Have the same structure as Municipal Government, with more emphasis on rural problems.
(b) The lowest level of government, covers a population of approximately 150,000–200,000 persons, locally known as Kecamatan.
(c) In urban areas the head of the sub-district or Kelurahan is appointed, but in the rural areas the lurah is elected.
(d) Each sub-district is divided into four to six neighbourhood units. The head of the unit is elected from among the head of the community units.
(e) Community units usually have a population of 400 to 800 persons. A neighbourhood unit consists of four to eight community units. The head of a community unit is elected among its members.
(f) Since more development activities occur within the urban population and projects require their support and participation, the sub-district organization has been supplemented during the last decade with an institution known as the Institute for local development (LKMD). The chairperson of this institution is the head of the sub-district, complemented by a vice chairperson with other staff members appointed from the local population. Again the wife of the lurah is the chairperson of the women's organization.

Figure 4.1   Levels of government and urban administration in Indonesia

this urban supply system. The remaining 80% of needs still had to be satisfied as before, by the families themselves, and for them urban kampungs or villages on the fringe of the built-up area were the best option.

Despite these problems, the physical condition of the urban housing stock in Indonesia improved significantly during the period 1971–76, when a household condition survey was conducted. In 1971, only one-quarter of the existing housing stock consisted of permanent structures, but in 1976 this had increased to over a third. There was a slight decrease in the semi-permanent housing category and a significant decrease in the temporary category from 7.5% to only 1.5%. In big cities such as Jakarta and Surabaya, however, the overall housing condition was not much better than the national average. During the period 1971–78 the owner-occupier category of tenure increased significantly, though rental housing still played an important role, especially in the supply of low-income housing within most kampungs.

Sanitation and water supply conditions in Indonesia also improved substantially after 1971, due to the development programme in the Pelitas (national development plans). Toilet facilities within individual houses were improving and it is important to note that the government is still increasing the water production capacity in urban areas. For this purpose the present Pelita has a larger budget and projects were planned in no less than 18 cities.

The Kampungs

Most Indonesian urban areas were formed by the expansion and conglomeration of existing villages or kampungs. Formally planned urban development always tended to bypass existing villages or kampungs, turning them into low-income settlement areas, though not necessarily slums or squatter settlements. During the colonial period, this policy of bypassing but replanning kampungs was adopted as a convenient way of creating a cheap labour supply within the built-up area of a city. In terms of present-day low-income housing needs, kampungs provide an attractive housing location for recent arrivals looking for employment. As an example, the overall survey, conducted before formulating the present KIP, found that Surabaya had 115 kampungs almost evenly scattered throughout the built-up area, with a further 103 villages on the outskirts of the administrative boundary. These kampungs occupied only 5% of the total built-up area, but accommodated 72% of the total population.

Most kampungs were integrated into urban areas with the provision of limited urban utilities and facilities. Although they serve mainly residential purposes, they also contain a range of cotton industries, mainly within the informal sector. Certain kampungs are known for their specific products, such as garments and sewing products, whilst others specialize in leather goods, junk and second-hand goods or 'produce' antiques. Easy access is obviously an important element in supporting such economic activities.

The density of a kampung may range from 350 persons per hectare (pph), to over 1250 pph. Although 60% of the houses are owner-occupied, rental housing accounts for at least 30–35%. Rental or lease tenure may range from one room shared by several persons, to one house per family. The size of a kampung normally varies from as little as 15 ha to over 120 ha with populations from 6000 to over 35,000 persons.

Land tenure in a kampung is not necessarily the same as housing tenure. As these settlements were originally villages, land was held under traditional tenure and inherited

Figure 4.2 A typical kampung; very dense single-storey buildings with the larger houses facing onto the main local roads

over generations. Later, as the city developed, more village land was bought by landlords or colonial companies and individual ownership was steadily reduced. When Dutch companies were nationalized at the end of the 1950s, and the Agrarian Law (Land Law) no. 5 passed in 1960, much land in the kampungs automatically came under government control, and this opened the opportunity for kampung residents to apply for a right to their land. Thus kampungs had both formal and traditional land tenure systems. In most of Surabaya's kampungs, individual land ownership covered only 20–25% of households compared to 60–80% who owned their house; on the other hand government-controlled land exceeded 60% of the total land area in kampungs. It is therefore quite common for a family to rent a piece of land and own the building on it. The building may be leased or rented by yet another family or persons creating complex tenure patterns.

A survey conducted between 1978 and 1979 indicated that half of the households had total monthly incomes of less than Rp.15,000 (US$24–79)*, with the next income group (Rp.15,000–50,000), consisting of about 30–35%. Middle-income households (Rp.50,000–80,000, or US$79–126.5) accounted for approximately 15% of the population and higher middle (Rp.80,000–120,000 or US$126.5–190) less than 5%. Kampungs therefore contain a wide range of income groups, unlike squatter settlements or typical slums.

* US$1 = Rp.430 (1977–78); US$1 = Rp.630 (1978–80).

Depending on its location, one-third of a kampung's population may be seasonal migrants. This applies particularly to those located near transport terminals. As only 35–45% of their populations have regular employment (usually in the formal sector), it is difficult to get reliable information on incomes, especially in-kind income.

Community health in most kampungs is reasonably well covered, though educational levels are poor with illiteracy at 10–20% and school drop-outs at 10–15%. Since only 3–5% of the kampung population have had any academic education, they are naturally the potential community leaders.

Indonesia's kampungs have possessed *de facto* security for many years, and there are only few cases outside Jakarta where kampung clearance or relocation programmes have been carried out. Most city masterplans drafted after the middle of the 1970s include kampungs in their allocation of land for residential purposes. The adoption and implementation of an improvement programme in the kampungs clearly recognizes their legal status and guarantees security for the people living in them.

To illustrate the physical conditions in a kampung prior to intensive improvement, certain environmental aspects will be explained here. The main problem in most kampungs is flooding. During a heavy rainstorm, flooding can reach as high as 1 m above ground and may last for several hours. Paved roads or footpaths very much depend on the locality and age of the kampung; the nearer to the urban centres the better conditions generally become.

Half of the existing housing stock has an area of less than 45 m². Only 22.5% has an area of more than 75 m² and 43.9% of building plots are less than 50 m², 25.2% are between 51 and 100 m² and the remaining 30.9% over 101 m². Nearly half of all dwellings (47.4%) have a permanent structure, 34.0% are semi-permanent and 18.6% have temporary structures. In Surabaya's kampungs, about 95% of the buildings are one-storey structures and more than 90% of them are used mainly for residential purposes. Kampungs in Jakarta have more two-storey buildings in which the ground floor is used by the owner and the upper floor leased to several families or persons. About 60% have their own toilet facilities, one-third of which are water-borne; other residents have to depend upon communal facilities. Most of the kampungs are well served with electricity, but only one-fifth are served by individual piped water. The others have to depend on water vendors for drinking and cooking and well water for washing and bathing.

OBJECTIVES OF THE KAMPUNG
IMPROVEMENT PROGRAMME

Jakarta and Surabaya first experienced *ad hoc* kampung improvement activities well before the Second World War. In Jakarta M. H. Thamrin, a member of the local council, was the main advocate of such a programme. In Surabaya the first improvement activity occurred as early as 1924, where sewerage and a storm-drain system in the kampungs were improved. In 1925 more systematic and comprehensive improvements were introduced, including roads and footpaths. However, funds from the municipal budget were inadequate, so certain parts of the works were financed and carried out by the local people; participation had already become necessary to complement the local government effort (von Faber, 1934).

Improvement activity expanded in the early 1930s and in 1938 a committee was established to investigate the problems and possibilities and to propose a nationwide kampung improvement programme or KIP, though its proposals were never carried out because of a dispute on funding between central and local government (Milone, 1966). No significant improvement works were implemented in the kampungs until 1968/69. Then, as a result of the new atmosphere in development activities, the Jakarta local government decided to improve the basic urban infrastructure in low-income settlements as part of its urban development programme. This approach enabled development programmes to benefit more areas, including those which had formerly been neglected: the kampungs.

In Surabaya, the local government faced another problem. Not only were the socio-political conditions at that time less stable than in Jakarta, but resources were still limited. As part of the government's normalization programme after the abortive coup in 1968–69, it was decided that squatters who had constructed settlements on storm-drain canals, or the fire corridors between blocks of buildings, had to be cleared. Simultaneously, however, minimal improvements were initiated in those kampungs which had to absorb the evicted population by providing building material subsidies for footpaths and drainage improvements.

In its early stages the Jakarta KIP concentrated on the provision of basic infrastructure to improve accessibility and public health. In Surabaya limited funds restricted improvements to the installation of concrete slabs and gutters for main roads, and even these had to be installed by local communities themselves. However small in scale, this first attempt received a positive response from the kampung inhabitants, and very soon footpaths were improved by the residents themselves.

The scale of these activities increased steadily, and after the first Pelita the Jakarta KIP achieved a remarkable increase in its scale of implementation when it received support from the central government and the World Bank. In the first Pelita (1969–74) 89 kampungs were improved, benefiting about 1.2 million people, but after the World Bank loan was agreed in the second Pelita, a further 242 kampungs were improved, benefiting an additional 1.9 million people. In Surabaya, during the first Pelita, kampung improvements were carried out as part of general public works, so no detailed information is available. However, a modified KIP was initiated in 1973 as a pilot project in one kampung, and the W. R. Supratman KIP (named after the composer of Indonesia's national anthem, born in Surabaya) was also improved from an 'in-kind' subsidy to 'in-cash' with more funds and greater flexibility. This approach was implemented in 14 kampungs, even before the World Bank assistance for Surabaya was received. Only after 1976/77 did the World Bank include in its assisted projects in Indonesia the modified KIP of Surabaya modelled on the first pilot project, with small additional funds made available to assist the original W. R. Supratman KIP. Thus, since the fiscal year 1976/77, two types of KIP have been implemented simultaneously in Surabaya.

The approach adopted in the modified and Jakarta KIPs was a conventional 'top-down' public works method (i.e. initiated and continued by government agencies), whilst in the W. R. Supratman type of KIP the local community had to initiate its own proposal, and then request a subsidy from the KIP budget, a 'bottom-up' approach.[2] The local government never knows, therefore, where or when a W. R. Supratman KIP project will be implemented, since it is up to the concerned community. Government agencies concentrate instead on providing information on standards and regulations which can be modified to suit local conditions.

Even before the Habitat Conference in 1976, Indonesia included the KIP in its national housing programme within the second Pelita, 1974–79. In this last Five Year Development Plan it was intended that implementation would start in Jakarta and Surabaya, and in other cities studies and preparation works for future KIP works would be carried out. The bold decision to include KIP in the National Development Plans aroused considerable interest among various international agencies willing to assist the Indonesian Government, and the World Bank, UNICEF and ILO have shown particular interest, while UNEP provided a grant for demonstration and research projects in Surabaya and Bandung (along with Manila in the Philippines). Later UNESCO, together with UIA and the Institute of Indonesian Architects, will start its own training projects in the KIP. Other international agencies assisting the KIP are The Royal Dutch Government (for Bogor) and the Asian Development Bank (ADB) for Bandung, and some central Java cities.

With the involvement of various international agencies in Indonesia, the problem arose of how projects should be handled, especially in the initial stages. Before the involvement of the World Bank, plans and programmes were formulated by local government officials, sometimes with assistance from local universities, as in the case of Surabaya. When the World Bank agreed to assist the programme, foreign consultants were invited to study, appraise, and propose a programme according to general guidelines from the Ministry of Public Works. In most cases the foreign consultants were required for work with local consultants, but in practice only minor responsibilities were actually entrusted to the local personnel,[3] and until the third Pelita no clear coordination was introduced in order to optimize the overall programme. This can be observed through the different concepts of KIP implemented in different cities by different sponsors.[4] In the third Pelita, co-ordination in concepts has been attempted, though with little success.

Formally defined objectives improved gradually through the addition of 'welfare' elements. However, the programme components and approach are still basically the same; non-physical components were proposed, but received no positive response from the decision-makers. It is abundantly clear that up till now KIP is more or less a public works affair, with slight differences in approach from area to area. The links between recent objectives and actual programmes is difficult to appraise. However, limited evaluation studies were recently carried out in Surabaya and Jakarta.

PROPOSALS AND MEANS OF IMPLEMENTATION

In the early stages of the programme it was not easy to select which of the 115 kampungs in Surabaya or the 550 in Jakarta should be improved first. The objectives initially formulated were so broad that almost all kampungs were eligible for improvement and the selection was often made in practice on personal judgement. Only later did Jakarta select its kampungs through a priority list compiled from the existing information of ALL kampungs, and according to the data collected for the master plan of Jakarta in the mid-1960s. Surabaya was not so fortunate in having complete data on all of its kampungs and so no priority list could be prepared. Only after the World Bank agreed to assist Surabaya's programme did the municipal government request assistance from the local Institute of Technology to prepare an appropriate priority list according to agreed criteria formulated by the Bank's consultant.

There are three main criteria for selecting kampungs for improvement. The most important group concern problems of flooding, drinking water, sanitation, and health facilities. The second group relate to accessibility within the kampung, community attitudes towards development activities, population density, average population, income level, education facilities, and the age of the kampung. In this respect it was assumed that old kampungs would have worse conditions, though this is not always true. The last group concern the general physical condition, building layout, and the prospective impact of the improvements. Decisions were then made by weighting each set of data according to the selection criteria.

One important feature not strictly implemented in the selection criteria was the conformity of the kampungs' land-use to that of the existing plan. It was less easy to incorporate newly developed kampungs into the programme, because of the uncertain legality of their tenure, but with certain adjustments and understanding, these kampungs were also improved. Another problem encountered later was the relationship between an existing kampung's infrastructure networks to formal plans concerning rights of way and building setbacks. This same problem was already recognized when the colonial government attempted to improve kampungs in the 1920s, and was solved by neglecting the official plan and adapting the existing pattern. The same approach was also adopted in most kampungs for improvement today.

A general evaluation on the impact of KIP was conducted for Surabaya in 1979. This showed that kampungs with a high overall priority for improvement did not always have a high priority on the individual elements used for selecting projects, whereas some kampungs which were not of a poor general standard scored high in the selection process because they were deprived of one or two elements considered important, such as roads and footpaths or school buildings.

Until the end of the second Pelita, both Jakarta and Surabaya spent most of their budget on constructing vehicular roads. Jakarta has utilized half of its total budget of Rp.72,653 million (US$115 million) for road construction only, and an extra 15% of the budget was spent on footpath construction. In Surabaya, only one-third of the total budget was used for road construction, and almost the same amount was utilized for footpath construction. The total KIP budget of Surabaya outside the W. R. Supratman KIP was Rp.8,337 million (US$13.2 million).[5] The next most expensive components were piped-water provision through public taps and the construction of education facilities which received equal funds. This ratio of expenditure may seem odd in a kampung where less than 2% of the population own a motor car, yet it seems that kampung residents consider roads as an important urban element. In Jakarta, road construction was also considered important for safety reasons, such as the prevention of neighbourhood fires and traffic accidents.

Surabaya, on the other hand, considered road improvements important for providing easy access to the city's main traffic network. The standard applied is more or less the same as that used by the Dutch during the colonial period, when it was said that 200 m should be the maximum distance between a vehicular road and the furthest house it served. Other improvement components in the KIP are the provision of public toilets and baths, health posts, and solid waste-disposal systems.[6]

A rather controversial situation appeared in Surabaya as the scale of the
W. R. Supratman KIP increased alongside the modified KIP. It may be considered
strange to have on the one hand improvement works in the kampungs which were carried
out and fully financed by the local government (the modified KIP), whilst on the other
hand, kampungs not far away implemented improvements which were initiated,
organized, and more than half-financed by the local communities themselves
(W. R. Supratman KIP). Partly because the project components of the W. R. Supratman
KIP only consist of road and footpath construction, the procedures to obtain the financial
subsidy for it are simple and only take about 1 month. Works have to be initiated by
the local community and technical assistance can be requested from the Public Works
Department to check that the improvements conform to municipal regulations, plans
and standards. With this plan, partial finance from the W. R. Supratman project fund

Figure 4.3   Concrete path in a W. R. Supratman KIP, made and maintained by local residents

can be requested from the city maintenance section of the PWD which is responsible
for implementing the programme. Priority for funding obviously depends on the locality
of the kampung, the income level of its population, and consistency with overall urban
development programmes. By and large, almost all requests have been approved, though
the amount of assistance given depends upon the level of local incomes and the scale
of the work involved. At the beginning of this programme emphasis was given to
kampungs which could contribute most towards costs. In the last 3 years, however, cross-
subsidies have been generated, balancing projects where residents can only afford a small
contribution with those where the local community can contribute up to two-thirds of
project costs. Implementation is normally carried out by registered small contractors
selected by the local community itself to ensure that work is done in accordance with
the approved plan and standards. The first part of the work consists of the portion
financed by the local community's fund and the final part of the work is then paid for
by the local government. Supervision of the work is done jointly between local community
and the municipal official in charge. Starting from the fiscal year 1980/81, the budget
for the W. R. Supratman KIP was taken over by the provincial government and the
annual amount was increased from app. Rp.80 million to Rp.300 million (US$480,000)
(see Figure 4.4).

No special agency was made responsible for carrying out improvements in the initial
stage of the KIP. In both Jakarta and Surabaya, works were prepared and carried out
by individual departments of the municipality in accordance with the existing PWD

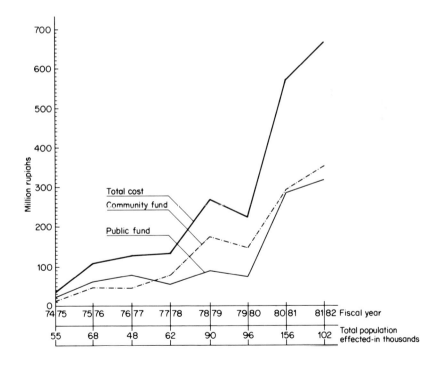

Figure 4.4   Progress of the W. R. Supratman KIP

procedure. The consequences of this have been poor co-ordination and conflicting directives to the implementing parties. With the availability of more funds through the World Bank loan, the scale and the scope of the work was increased substantially and as a result separate agencies were specially created in each city and made directly responsible to the Governor in Jakarta, and to the Mayor in Surabaya respectively. For day-to-day decisions, supervision, and co-ordination, a steering committee was established. Initially, this committee proved to be useful, but after the second Pelita, when more experience had been gained, improvement of the kampungs in Jakarta and Surabaya became a more or less routine operation.

In the event, what proved to be important and effective was the contribution of personnel within the agencies, most of whom were selected from local government and usually from relevant departments within the city government. This considerably improved the relationship and co-ordination between the special agencies and the related city departments.

The general relationship between the programme and the respective communities is not easy to describe. In the early period, at the start of a project, local people knew very little of what was going to happen in their kampung, and the result in most cases was reluctance to support it, especially if fences had to be moved back, or buildings had to be demolished. If people were, however, informed much earlier of what was going to happen and what was expected of them, it increased the smoothness of the programme, and achieved success in the sense of keeping within budget limits and time allocations. In Surabaya, ever since the introduction of the KIP, the local population were given the opportunity to be involved in the planning process. A rough plan was proposed to the people, and they were given the opportunity to comment or make changes. This approach not only informed them of the scope of the work, but also invited them to take necessary steps to complement the programme. Thus, whilst participation was initially seen in terms of residents complying with plans and making sacrifices, it later assumed a more active involvement in decision-making. For example, after a footpath had been constructed, individual households along it started planting trees and flowers, garbage cans were provided, and street lighting installed using electricity sources from individual houses. Other areas provided community meeting halls and security guard houses. Periodic communal cleaning activities were organized to maintain environmental quality after improvements. The willingness of both parties to interact in the implementation of the programme encouraged and stimulated the local people to take over responsibilities for maintenance, utilization, and further development. In Jakarta, due to the scale of the project, rigid bureaucratic procedures were deemed necessary and a strict 'top-down' approach was adopted. Obviously little significant participation was observed, and subsequent re-upgrading of the earlier work by government was necessary.[7]

In 1976 UNEP provided a grant to demonstrate a different concept of improvement. Among the objectives of the programme, it was hoped to establish a comprehensive approach for improving marginal low income settlements that gives special emphasis to population and environmental dimensions through technologies which reduce environmental degradation and promote utilization of appropriate renewable resource and organisational forms that maximise popular participation in the improvement process.[8]

The experiments in Bandung and Surabaya proved that most of the parties did not realize the problems encountered in implementing this kind of approach in the kampungs, because programme formulation was not based upon actual kampung conditions. The result was confusion and delay in implementation, and poor co-ordination and distrust among those involved. On the other hand, valuable experience and knowledge has been gained, especially in the possibilities and expectations of popular participation in co-operatives, environmental health, and women's activities. Appropriate institutional and organizational frameworks were tested to see how participation of the various parties, such as government, community leaders, consultants and university staff, could be achieved.

As the UNEP project was implemented in one kampung which was in the process of improvement by the World Bank-assisted KIP, indications of over-investment were observed. In this project, participation was only significant if the amount of funds for a project component were big enough; a 'normal' scale of investment in the KIP received less response from the population. Obviously upper and lower thresholds of investment for KIP should be considered in the future.

The experience of the UNEP project in Indonesia contributed to an understanding of the importance and possibilities of an integrated kampung improvement concept. It also proved that non-physical components of the kampung should be included and

Figure 4.5   View of an improved kampung. The local community completed the landscaping by planting trees and flowers along the public footpath

that popular participation has greater possibilities than had been anticipated in the World Bank-assisted KIPs in Jakarta and Surabaya. The experience of the health component of the UNEP project also served to smooth the implementation of the UNICEF programme which was introduced in the later stage of the KIP kampungs (from 1980 onward). The role of co-operatives has also proved useful and more knowledge has been gained on how to organize co-ops and the roles that can be expected of them.

CONSEQUENCES OF THE POLICY
AND PROGRAMME

Clearly, the experience of implementing the KIP during the second Pelita encouraged the National Government to adopt the KIP as an important alternative to other housing programmes. It has already been decided that in the third Pelita, 200 cities and towns of different sizes and locations will have this programme. What has yet to be assessed is the kind of concept that can be applied to towns smaller than Jakarta or Surabaya. By the time the third Pelita finishes in 1984, it is expected that 20 smaller towns a year in East Java province alone will have implemented their own programmes along similar lines to those in Jakarta and Surabaya; the only differences are that they are much smaller, and the provincial government has decided not to rely on outside loans for its programe. The different conditions prevailing in kampungs of smaller towns proved the need to learn more from the experience of the present KIP in Jakarta and Surabaya and a systematic evaluation is now necessary.

Another public programme for kampungs is the annual central government grant for participatory development to all sub-districts in Indonesia, which was started in the 1970/71 fiscal year. During 1980/81 this programme generated Rp.346 million (half a million US dollars) in Surabaya alone, of which 62.4% were community-generated funds.[9] This indicates yet another important resource that should be included in the overall development programme in a kampung. A comprehensive evaluation of the contribution of KIP in Surabaya is currently under way, and it is hoped that it will provide a better understanding of the role KIP can play within an overall housing policy.

At present, at least five different approaches and concepts of KIP exists in Indonesia and this has caused inefficient and ineffective use of the limited financial resources available. The picture is, however, varied. Jakarta has already included kampungs improved under the first Pelita into the present programme for further improvement. The situation in Surabaya is more favourable and it has yet to face this problem, though the extent of progress in both cities is raising questions concerning the potential of the programme in the future. Clearly the institutional framework does not conform to the formal local government organization and a dual institutional structure has evolved which confuses administrative and financial arrangements. Recently, it has been accepted in some quarters that the KIP cannot be regarded simply as a project or a final product, but more as a continuous process with the voluntary involvement of the local population and a decrease of the public sector's role from 'doer' to 'supporter'; this includes the utilization and maintenance of the result. Integration of various available resources into a single concept for improvement and development of the kampungs should be attempted soon, as part of the urban development programme within the dominant control of the local city government. Central government should provide the resources and support the programme.

In Indonesia, where the public housing programme only provides about 17.5% of the housing needed to meet annual population increase, much is still expected from the individual families at all economic levels to fulfil their own housing needs. Faced with this situation, the KIP is obviously still important as a housing programme in the future. The question is, how can we improve the effectiveness of the concept, in order to maximize results with limited resources?

Much will depend on the result of evaluations currently under way in Jakarta and Surabaya. Also important is the development of the knowledge that should come out of it by research institutes engaged in the study of this programme. This knowledge is needed to help the transfer of skill from one official to another, or from one place to another. It will also be an important tool for future evaluation purposes. However, the awareness of this need among decision-makers in the government and research workers in the universities has yet to appear. International agencies should not limit themselves to the provision of funds for implementation purposes only, but attention should also be given for research and development activities. Training centres have been established in various countries in the world on housing programmes for the poor in developing countries, including KIP. However, only a little has been learned by these centres from the experience of Indonesia which has implemented the largest and longest site improvement programme in the world. If Indonesia itself has not learned very much from its own experience, no other country or training centre can be expected to learn more from it, but encouragement from international agencies will certainly improve the understanding of the host country to do more in this direction.

In the first year of the third Pelita, 31 cities in Indonesia finished formulating their development or master plans. Fifty-five other cities and towns are in the process of formulating outline plans. However, of the existing city plans, little explicit mention has been made on the future status of the existing kampungs; neither has the KIP been given a role to play in the long-term development programme of the cities or towns in Indonesia. Very few plans mentioned the importance of the kampungs and the role they play. In Surabaya, however, the city master plan, approved in 1978, recognized kampungs as part of the overall urban settlement, and the KIP was included as an integral part of the overall urban development programme.

IMPLICATIONS OF THE PROGRAMME

The W. R. Supratman KIP, with which there is now more than 10 years' experience, has indicated the potential of small initial investment by the public and popular sectors, providing the initiative is retained by the local population. In such cases the process was continued by the people themselves through incremental improvements and at a later stage this achieved conditions equal to or better than the World Bank-assisted KIP, especially in respect of communal responsibility, care and utilization of the result. This allows the local government to save public funds normally needed for maintenance, and adds another dimension to the original improvement concept. If, after a footpath has been built, local people put a sign asking cyclists to dismount, if they plant flowers on the small strip of land along the footpath, or if they put garbage cans and lighting from a housing source, then the result of the KIP is more than the formulated objectives, especially with regard to the future allocation of both public and local resources.

At this moment it is not yet possible to present a new concept for the KIP. However, from various discussions, seminars, workshops, and articles published in news media, tentative proposals can be formulated.

According to present estimates, by the year 2000 approximately 80% of the urban population will still belong to the low-income category. The master plan of Surabaya has projected that by the turn of the century, not only will the city population be about 6 million, but the low-income population will increase from 79.7% of the total in 1974 to 84.1%, due to the influx of immigrants from the poor rural areas of East Java. If the increase in public housing construction remains at the same level as now, by the year 2000 80% of all housing will still need to be the sole responsibility of individual families, and for low-income urban families the pattern of housing provision will not differ much from the existing one. By transforming existing urban villages into urban kampungs, but in a better condition than now, it is obvious that the KIP will be the major housing option in Indonesia for the rest of the century. If the present annual economic growth rate rises from 7.5 to 9.5%, the costs of this programme can be spread proportionally between the public sector and local people's capacity. In 1982 this level of economic growth in fact declined to about 6.5%, so that the scale of public investment will be reduced, putting even more emphasis upon the need for publicly initiated and managed projects. In East Java this should present no problems, though the effect will not be the same in all parts of Indonesia.

The aim of the KIP will be not only to provide reasonable urban infrastructure in the kampungs, but to enhance their character and general development. By the fourth Pelita, *improvement* activities should already be transformed into *development* activities and the implementation of the programme should be a hostile process rather than one which emphasizes the product or project. Physical development activities should therefore be part of the total development process, with more involvement from the local population through the existing institutional framework.

Responsibility for implementation should be accepted by local government, and agencies should have the same flexibility as the present ones, but as part of the formal local government structure, as for instance, under the existing sub-directorate of village development in the present local government structure. Higher government involvement should be limited to policy formulation, budget allocation, and overall supervision and assistance only.

Research and development activities should be given a larger role in the future, especially in monitoring, evaluating, and disseminating the experience gained. Universities and research institutes, especially local ones, should be involved together with government-implementing agencies. Existing kampungs and urban villages should be given the same rights as other areas. Land should therefore be reserved by law in sufficient quantities for future kampung development to take place as part of the development plan for every city, especially since land adjacent to a kampung is traditionally owned by the local population. If these changes are made and other urban development activities are given less priority, it should be possible for Indonesia's kampungs to help considerably in easing the intense housing problems facing the country.

BIBLIOGRAPHY

Abrams, Charles (1966). *Squatter Settlements, the Problems and the Opportunity*. Washington D.C.

BPS (Central Bureau of Statistics):
(a) Population Census 1961, 1971, 1980. (In Indonesian.)
(b) Housing Condition in Indonesia 1971 (Jakarta, 1975). (In Indonesian.)
(c) Household Condition in Indonesia 1976 (Jakarta, 1978). (In Indonesian.)
(d) Living Cost Survey Jakarta-Surabaya, 1977/78 (Jakarta, 1980). (In Indonesian.)

Bouwcentrum International Education (1978–79). *Conclusions of the Seminar on Improving Low-Income Residential Areas in the South-East Asian Cities*. Bandung. Unpublished Seminar Proceeding, Bandung, 1979.

Ching, Frank (1976). 'A new life for slum dwellers of Jakarta', *Asia Magazine*.

Devas, Nick (1980). *KIP: A Case Study of Indonesia's Kampung Improvement Programme*. Development Administration Group, Birmingham.

DKI, Directorate of Physical Development (1975). *Jakarta's Kampung Improvement Programme*. Jakarta. Unpublished report Jakarta, 1975.

Faber, J. H. von *Nieuw Soerabaia* H. van Ingen, Surabaia, 1934.

Faber, J. H. von (1934). *Nieuw Soerabaia* (Surabaya 1934).

Government of Indonesia, Department of Public Works (1974). *Technical Assistance for the Preparation of Sites and Services and KIP Projects*. Jakarta.

Government of Indonesia, Department of Public Works (1976). *Kampung Improvement Programme Proposals for Surabaya*. Jakarta. (In Indonesian.)

Hofsteede, Wilhelmus (1979). 'UNEP marginal settlements Improvement Projects in Bandung and Surabaya. Report of the Consultant for the period April–September 1979. Bandung. Unpublished report.

International Development Research Centre (1972). *Low Cost Housing in Indonesia*. Ottawa. IDRC.

Jururancang Bersekutu (1978). *Feasibility Study and Detailed Engineering of Urban Development Project Surbaya-Ujung Pandang*. Surabaya. Unpublished report.

Kotmadya Surabaya, Municipality of Surabaya. (1974). *Monograph of Surabaya*. Surabaya. Published by the Municipality of Surabaya. (In Indonesian.)

Kotmadya Surabaya, Municipality of Surabaya (1976). *Masterplan Surabaya 2000*. Surabaya. Unpublished report.

Krausse, Gerald H. (1975). 'The kampungs of Jakarta, Indonesia: a study in the spatial patterns of urban poverty.' Unpublished PhD thesis, Pittsburgh.

Laquian, A. A. (1980). *Improvement and Development of Low Income Settlements in South East Asian Cities*. Prisma.

L.P.E.S. (consultant) (1981). *KIP Evaluation, Report on the Monograph of Surabaya*. Surabaya. Unpublished report. (In Indonesian.)

Milone, P. D. (1966). *Urban Areas in Indonesia. Administrative and Census concepts*. U. C. Berkeley.

Papanek, G. F. (1976). *The Poor of Jakarta*. Prisma.

Parman, S. & Co. (1977). *Kampung Improvement Programme, Jakarta and Surabaya: Final Review*. Jakarta. Unpublished report.

Poerbo, Hasan (1979). *UNEP Marginal Settlements Improvements Project*. Bandung. Unpublished seminar paper.

RMI (P. T. Resources Jaya Teknik Management Indonesia) (1979). 'Semi Annual Report and Quarterly Reports' (Jakarta, 1977–79). Final Report (Jakarta, 1979). Unpublished report.

Shubert, Clarence (1979). *Prospects for Regional and National Transferability of an Integrated Approach for Marginal Settlement Improvement*. Bandung. Unpublished Report.

Silas, Johan (1980). *Villages in Transition: A Case Study of Rural to Urban Transformation in Surabaya*. Prisma.

Silas, Johan (1979). *Contribution of Higher Education Towards Housing Demand*. Singapore.

Silas, Johan (ed.) 'KIP: The Kampung Improvement Programme in Surabaya 1969–82, Inventory and Evaluation'. Published by I.T.S. University Press, Surabaya, 1983. (In Indonesian.)

Turner, John F. C. *Reflections on Ways of Carrying Out Town and Neighbourhood Improvement Programmes*. Bandung. Unpublished seminar paper.
United Nations Environment Programme (1976). *Project Document, Integrated Approach for Improving Slums and Marginal Settlements in Indonesia*. Jakarta. Unpublished report.
The Urban Edge. **4(7)**, Aug./Sept. 1980, Washington. Published by CIUL.
World Bank (1976–78). *Project Appraisal Reports on the Indonesian Urban Development Projects (II and III)*. Jakarta. Unpublished report.

NOTES AND REFERENCES

1. The word 'kampung' in local languages can have different meanings. In areas where Malay is the base of the local language, such as in the western part of Java and most of Sumatra, the term has a rural connotation. In Javanese, as in Malay, the word also means an enclosed piece of land or even a settlement as part of a capital city. The inclusion of the Kampung Improvement Programmes in the National Development Plan has popularized and improved the positive meaning of the word and reduced its negative perception.

    Kampungs can also be classified in different ways for different purposes. Spatial classification has little significance due to the recent adoption of a decentralization policy for urban development. Grouping kampungs according to socioeconomic conditions or status can have an important meaning in directing specific development programmes. The main criteria for classifying socioeconomic conditions of the kampungs are the income level of the majority of the population, education level, type of employment, household size, residential status and population density. Other important indications are the average place of birth of the household head, housing status, duration of stay in the area, and the rate of intra-urban mobility.

2. The differences between W. R. Supratman and modified types of KIP are as follows:

Items	W. R. Supratman	Modified KIP
Scale	Small — scattered	Big — concentrated
Approach	'Botom-up' i.e. initiated and controlled by local residents	'Top-down' i.e. initiated and controlled by government agencies
Participation	Direct — balanced	Indirect — small
Project component	Simple	Comprehensive — public works
Initiative	Community	Government
Funding	Local	Plus loan from World Bank

3. Questions have been raised by local academics on the qualifications of some of the foreign consultants. In the early 1970s no significant experience was available for references, and knowledge of on-site improvement programmes for Third World countries was yet to be developed. In one city the foreign consultants charged with preparing the housing programme (including the KIP) consisted of experts of irrelevant disciplines and produced a plan more or less copying the report prepared by a local university.

4. Basically there are three elements of variation:
    (a) *responsible for plan preparation:* local government, provincial government or consultant;
    (b) *approach:* 'top-down' *vs.* 'bottom-up'; the approach influenced popular participation, and future complementary work done by them;
    (c) *standard:* strict and rigid *vs.* flexible.
    The project components are basically roads and footpaths, public toilets, drainage systems, portable water taps, and in some instances schools and health posts. In a very limited area UNICEF is involved in family welfare programmes.

5. In Jakarta, the budget of Rp.72,653 million for the period 1974–81 covered 310 kampungs of 6816 ha, inhabited by 2.3 million people. In Surabaya, the budget of Rp.8337 million for the period 1976–82 covered 45 kampungs of 1053 ha, inhabited by half a million people.

(6) (a) Footpaths should not be farther than 20 m from every dwelling.
   (b) Secondary drainage alongside or in the middle of the footpaths; and only on the side of roads. Primary drains only as required.
   (c) When possible, individual connection of water taps. Public taps to be provided approximately one per 50–80 households.
   (d) Public toilet provision depending on availability of land; if possible one toilet + bath per 8–10 households.
   (e) Primary-school facilities should cover 60% of the school-age children in the kampung. Availability of land is the main constraint to meet this standard.
   (f) Provision of health posts depends on availability of land and the overall health facilities within the city area.

7. See J. F. C. Turner, 1981.
8. United Nations Environmental Programme, project document, 1976, p.2.
9. This programme is locally known as the 'Inpres Pembangunan Desa', or 'Presidential Instruction for Village Development.'

Low-income Housing in the Developing World
Edited by G. K. Payne

Chapter 5

Ankara: Procedures for Upgrading and Urban Management

K. Bulent Tokman

In 1924 Ankara was a provincial town of about 20,000 people. By 1975 it had not only become the Turkish capital with a population of 1.7 million, but had the highest proportion of unauthorized settlement of any large city in the world.[1] Its interest as a case study therefore stems largely from the opportunity to see how such a situation emerged and the housing policies it evoked. This chapter describes why and how the authorities concentrated upon the improvement of existing informal settlements rather than directly stimulating supply. It will be argued that, during 1950–70 in particular, this form of *ad hoc* planning regulated urban growth by indirectly supporting local self-help and spreading public investments as widely as possible.

URBAN CONTEXT

Ankara is located in the middle of the Anatolian plateau and controls several traditionally important highways. The 1980 census data show a population of 2.2 million within the municipal boundaries with a further 150,000 just outside. From its 1924 level, the city increased to 123,000 in 1935, 451,000 in 1955 and 1.7 million in 1975. It has sustained a growth rate of about 7% per annum for many years and about 60% of its population are immigrants, due mostly to the better employment opportunities offered by the administrative and service sectors and the availability of public services. Almost half the population are under 20 years of age.

The city's economic structure reflects the importance of administrative functions. For example, 10% of the labour force is directly employed by the state and this figure rises to 17% when activities related to the government, such as the army, political parties, labour unions, etc. are included. When the effect of centralization and the étatist policy pursued during the first years of the Republic is considered (i.e. concentration of some cultural, social, and economic activities as a result of the city's function as a capital) 27% of the economically active population work directly or indirectly for the state. Of the rest, 10% work in construction, 11% in commerce, 13% in industry, and the remainder in transportation and in other services. The income distribution in the metropolitan area is shown in Figure 5.1.

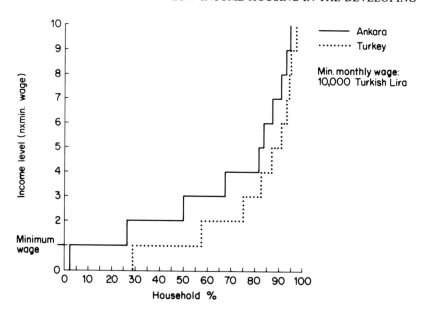

Figure 5.1 Ankara's urban income distribution. Source: Aktüre, T. *Konut Yapim Sistemlerinin Ekonomik Değerlendirme Yöntemleri*, Building Research Publication, Ankara; 1981, p.24

About 27% of households earn less than the official urban minimum wage of about US$77 P.M. Although different income groups with similar educational background may coexist in the same locality or neighbourhood, the population can be broadly divided into three main socioeconomic groups, namely low, middle and upper income groups. The social structure of the city as such is also reflected in the spatial structure. The lower socioeconomic groups are scattered around the periphery; middle and upper socioeconomic groups, however, are concentrated around the centre and in the southern part of the city (Figure 5.2).

The city centre, on the other hand, consists of two distinct parts, forming virtually two separate cities. Such a separation is usually observed in the old colonial cities as an expression of divisions between two societies — colonizers and colonized — but in Ankara it is due to the historical divisions *within* the social structure. In fact, the old centre (Ulus), part of which still retains its traditional character, is used by the lower-middle and especially by the low socioeconomic groups of the city. It also acts as a regional centre for the rural area around Ankara. The new centre (Kızılay) has developed to the south along the city's axis of prestige, near the ministries and exclusively serves the more affluent groups of the population.

Although it needed special attention during the first years of the Republic[2] the present administrative structure of the city is quite similar to other Turkish cities, and can be considered on two levels, provincial and municipal. Ankara is the centre of one of Turkey's 67 provinces that are responsible for regional administration. The province consists of 21 sub-provincial districts, four of which cover the metropolitan area. The provincial governor and district commissioners are appointed by the central government. At the local level, Ankara's municipality is responsible for the provision of services and facilities, the preparation and implementation of urban development plans, and issuing

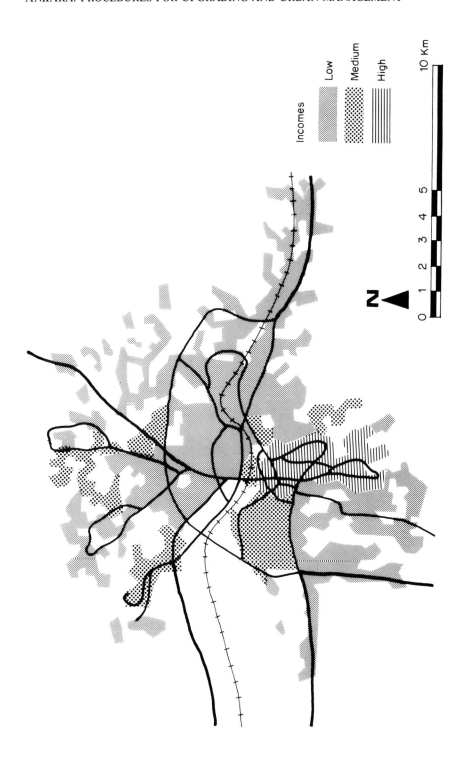

Figure 5.2 Ankara's spatial income distribution

of building licences, etc. Another aspect of the urban administrative structure, perhaps an important one as far as the low-income settlements are concerned, is the 'mahalle' system. Although the inclusion of this system into the administrative hierarchy is debatable, since it has limited official status, it serves as the first level of administration at ward or neighbourhood level and therefore justifies a place in the administrative and decision-making structure of local government.

The importance of the mahalle system for a low-income settlement is that it regulates and sometimes directs relations between the municipality and the settlement. In terms of receiving or claiming services, a settlement is only recognized by the municipality if it is part of an existing mahalle or a mahalle by itself. Formation and modification of mahalles, determination of their boundaries and names are decided by the municipal council and approved by the governor.

Under conditions of rapid urban growth the mahalles have proved an extremely flexible institution. If population growth in any single one increases to the point where it is unable to obtain its fair share of municipal resources, it may apply to be subdivided into separate units each with its own claim on city revenues. Alternatively, in areas of new settlement, residents may form themselves into an Improvement Organization and approach the municipality for registration as a mahalle.

Another feature of the mahalle system is that it enables government agencies to concentrate on those tasks for which it is best suited and enables scarce resources to be spread more widely over the city as a whole. For example, requests for new roads were often followed by the preparation of a plan for the road by the municipality. This would be obliged to follow the most efficient route within the city's transport network and involve the minimum of property demolition. However, it was up to the muhtar (the headman who is in charge of administration of a mahalle) to sell the scheme to residents of his mahalle or prepare an equally efficient alternative. If this was done the road would be approved; if not, the scheme was shelved, and the municipal resources were diverted elsewhere. One more feature of the mahalle system is the survival of the traditional rural practice of 'imece' or self-help, which was an important factor in the process of development of informal settlements. Mahalle system enabled residents to offer their labour in things like digging of trenches, laying of pipes, etc. when they requested basic services. Through such self-help methods a mahalle could obtain services in a period of 1 year which otherwise would take 4–5 years.

NATURE OF THE EXISTING HOUSING PROBLEM

Ankara is a typical example of the big cities of rapidly urbanizing Third World countries where uncontrolled urban growth and housing has been, for the last decade, one of the major problems. On the other hand, in the Turkish context Ankara occupies a special position because of its high rate of growth, as well as for the proportion of its illegal settlements.

Ankara accommodates 30% of the squatters in Turkey, known in Turkey as 'gecekondu' which literally means 'built overnight'. According to a survey of Ankara Metropolitan Planning Bureau in 1977, 51% of the total metropolitan population live in gecekondus, and squatter areas constitute 66% of the total housing area.[3] In terms of households, however, 43% of the total number of households live in illegal settlements.

The comparison of squatter population with the number of households living in squatter areas indicates the crowded dwellings (high rates of persons per room) and extended family pattern predominant in these areas.

On the other hand, the yearly housing need in the metropolitan area due to demographic growth alone has increased from 28,400 units in 1978 to 33,000 units in 1980.[4] Against this demand, the licensed production was roughly 12,500 units in 1978.[5] A large amount of this deficit belongs mainly to the low-income groups. Sectoral distribution of housing investments in the city shows that the housing market is dominated by the private sector. The public sector's share in total housing investment is only 2%. Besides, because of high profits, private sector investments are channelled into middle- and high-income housing. The housing deficit increases continuously despite the realization of investment targets every year as a result of the speculative and highly profitable character of the formal housing market in the metropolitan area. For low-income groups, therefore, the problem of accessibility to the housing market becomes a problem of income and gecekondus offer a viable solution.

Land is another critical issue. At present, the price of land in the planned sections of the city is as much as 50% of the total cost of a dwelling. High demand and inadequate supply of urban land, coupled with ineffective control mechanisms, encourages speculation which effects not only low-income groups but higher-income groups as well. In planned sections of the city, increases in density due to political and economic pressures by landowners results in the replacement of buildings before they complete their life span. Almost every 10–15 years residential areas are renewed. This process makes the services obsolete, increases the burden of the municipality, and causes inefficient use of

Figure 5.3   A view of housing in central Ankara showing early low-income dwellings in the foreground and more recent middle-income apartments beyond

Figure 5.4   A typical gecekondu settlement. Notice the apartment blocks in the background built by government to relocate the residents

resources. The trend is also reflected in the decrease of the number of houses and in the increase of the number of condominiums completed each year. Low-income groups, on the other hand, affected by urban land prices and the speculative land market, had no option other than to occupy either public land or locations which were not suitable for other groups or for other uses. Consequently, the city has acquired a form parallel to those of the metropolitan areas of other developing countries, with middle- and high-income residential areas in the centre and a belt of illegal settlements on the periphery. Recently, however, the diminishing supply of open private and public land that can be occupied, and the competition of other groups for land as a consequence of urban growth, resulted in the formation of a second informal land market, operating in gecekondu areas. Today, 70% of the gecekondus in the metropolitan area are on public land and 30% are on private land.

In general, the three-fold economic structure in the metropolitan area is reflected both in city form and in a two-fold dwelling system; gecekondus and luxury apartment blocks. These two systems are distinctly different from each other in almost every respect.

Gecekondus are usually single-storey dwellings built with less durable and relatively cheaper materials such as breeze-blocks, mud bricks etc. It is also common to use second-hand components such as pipes, window-frames, etc., that are obtained from supply yards selling materials for demolished condominiums. Gecekondus do not conform to building codes and regulations and are built without a licence. In fact, the legal definition of a gecekondu, according to Clause 2 of Gecekondu Law No. 775 (1966), is a dwelling built without a licence, on a piece of land for which the user does not have a title.

Layouts, both of the dwellings and of the settlements, follow somewhat traditional patterns. This creates a paradox which is not always observed in the metropolitan areas of other developing countries. The densities in the gecekondu areas are lower than those in middle/high-income settlements and between 52–647 persons per hectare (net) in middle/high-income residential areas.[6] Basic services (mostly electricity and water) in the gecekondu areas are provided, though inadequately, as a result of pragmatic public policies, details of which will be discussed in greater depth below. Other services, such as schools, playgrounds, and health facilities, are inadequate or completely lacking. In fact, inadequate services are a common problem for both gecekondu areas *and* higher-income settlements. In this respect the factor that determines whether an area is considered to be a lower-middle-income or a high-income area is not the level of services or the type of dwellings, but rather the social environment. On the other hand, the ownership pattern in the metropolitan area indicates that the middle income group comprises the bulk of tenants. The home ownership ratio is higher for both low- and high-income groups than it is for middle-income groups.

Table 5.1   Ownership ratio related to household income distribution

Household income	Percentage in population	Ownership ratio (%)
Low income (3 × min. monthly wage)	50	52
Middle income (3 – 7 × min. monthly wage)	40	43
High income (7 × min. monthly wage)	10	49

Source: Aktüre, T., *Konut Yapım Sistemlerinin Ekonomik Değerlendirme Yöntemleri.* Ankara: Building Research Publications, 1981, p.28.

HOUSING DEMAND AND OFFICIAL RESPONSES

1923–1950 Period

As a small town with a population of 20,000 people, Ankara faced a sudden inflow of newly appointed government employees and other civil servants immediately after its declaration as the capital of the new Republic in 1923. The housing demand thus created became one of the major issues confronting the new administration and a solution of the housing problem of civil servants who formed the new middle class in the city dominated the formulation of public responses and legislative steps throughout this period.

One of the first steps taken within this framework was to empower the municipality in 1925 to expropriate land for the housing needs of those working in the new administration, and for areas required for urban development. During the period of 2 years in which this authorization was in force, the municipality acquired 400 ha of land in the development area of the city where the new centre was located. Later, however, by selling this land stock, the municipality missed an opportunity to formulate a sound land policy supported by considerable land reserves. In a parallel development at the same time, the State Housing Bank was established to provide cheap credits for new development. The resources of the State Housing Bank, which was later transformed into the Real Estate Bank, were used in middle-class housing developments.

These measures failed, however, to reduce the housing shortage and other measures were taken by central government. In 1929 rent subsidies were introduced for government employees working in Ankara. In the Municipal Act, enacted in 1930, municipalities were given the responsibility of providing low-cost housing for ownership or for rent; but housing provision as such was listed among the secondary municipal duties. Continued growth, and the conditions created during the Second World War (Turkey did not enter the war), prompted the government to freeze rents in 1940, and with Law No. 4626 passed in 1944 the State assumed responsibility for providing housing to its employees and priority was given to Ankara. Within the framework of this law, 434 rental units were built in the city, though the numbers built were insignificant in terms of total demand.

The need for a city plan to control anticipated urban growth was obvious. Although a plan was prepared by Heussler in 1924, it was abandoned in 1927 and a new plan was prepared by Herman Jansen in 1932 through a limited international competition. The plan has played an important role in the formation of the present city structure (for example, the creation of twin poles, the main land-use pattern, etc.) but some of the guidelines provided by the municipality on which the plan was based soon proved to be unrealistic, and it was inadequate by the mid-1950s. One of the most important misjudgements in this respect was the rate of growth. Population was projected as 300,000 for 1988, but actually reached 2,200,000 in 1980. Ankara experienced its high rate of growth in the pre-war period; much earlier than the other major cities of the country. In fact, it was the only city in this period to attract migration from rural areas.

The first gecekondus started to appear in the 1930s and were built in relatively central locations unsuitable for middle-class development. The initial public response to these illegal settlements was shaped within the framework of Law No. 486 passed in 1924, which enabled the municipal authorities to demolish any building constructed on land for which it did not have legal title. However, the law was interpreted in such a way that a court order was required before any *inhabited* dwelling could be demolished. This has helped the squatters and created a process in which the shell was completed first to give a 'lived-in' appearance. Since legal procedures took considerable time, the squatters were usually safe after achieving this appearance.

While the intention of this act was to prevent illegal settlements, its actual consequence was to facilitate their expansion, and the workers quarter designated in Jansen's plan did not materialize. Municipal authorities consequently put the blame partly on the inability of providing cheap urban land for low-income housing developments,[7] which in fact, was an honest confession on their part. The decline in housing production as a result of conditions and the relaxation of controls to increase eroding political support for the existing government, were other factors which indirectly supported the development of illegal settlements in the city. In fact, by 1950 the 'gecekondu' population reached 34% of the total.

As a consequence of the strong hold on Ankara by Central Government resulting from its function as the capital and its symbolic importance in modernizing Turkey, decisions concerning the city were dominated by the central authority, and it was the municipality who had to bear the consequences of a lack of interest in the housing problems of low-income groups. Motivated by the increasing number of gecekondus and partly by the increasing political importance of low-income groups after the introduction of a multi-party system in 1946, the municipality prepared a bill (No. 5218) in 1948. This empowered municipal authorities to upgrade squatter areas and to allot parcels of land to potential builders. Around the same time a second law, called the 'Building Encouragement Law' (No. 5228) was initiated by Government. This act permitted land to be sold on a cost basis to co-operatives and assisted individuals who could prove they did not already own a house. Tax concessions and credits made available through the Real Estate Bank were the forms of assistance provided.

These two pieces of legislation were the first attempts to seek solutions to the gecekondu problem other than police measures, and they introduced new elements such as upgrading existing gecekondus, provision of cheap urban land, and financial assistance. But these two important Acts did not achieve their objectives in the process of implementation. The choice of location and conditions of eligibility (which required some capital) set by the municipality were not suitable for low-income groups. Their impact on the city was the creation of 'Yenimahalle' settlement which was a middle-income development, big enough to serve one-tenth of the city's population.

Briefly it can be said that in the early phases of the city's development, housing policies (in fact pieces of legislation, rather than a comprehensive policy) were generally aimed at helping government employees. But even for that limited section of the population, such measures have not been very effective. The number of units provided by public authorities was inadequate compared to demand; rent subsidies had a reverse effect and escalated rent levels; and the rent freeze caused the supply of housing to decline.

The exclusion of the low-income groups from these policies was the most important deficiency, though an important development was the official acceptance of their existence and the gradual legalization of 'gecekondus'.

1950–63 Period

After 1960, the effects of both socioeconomic and regional imbalances in the country, together with the increasing accessibility provided by road improvements, led to sustained rural–urban migration of a less controlled nature, and Ankara experienced a rapid rate of growth which has been maintained ever since. The introduction of a multi-party system in 1946, and the change of government in the 1950 elections, yielded some benefits to gecekondu builders and the official pressure on illegal settlements weakened. One of the first concrete results in this respect was Law No. 6188 passed in 1953, which authorized the municipalities to acquire state-owned land lacking a specific use to be allocated as housing sites. The Act gave an opportunity to many gecekondu builders to claim legal tenure and some titles were given.

In 1955 rapid development of the city necessitated a new plan, and two Turkish architects won the international competition that was launched for the project. The new plan was restricted to the existing administrative boundary and therefore excluded many gecekondu areas on the periphery. By this time the city population had reached 451,000. However, incorrect population forecasts resulted in even the new plan becoming redundant within 8 years.

In 1956 the Reconstruction Law was passed to control and to regulate urban growth throughout the country. It laid down responsibilities for the preparation of master plans for all cities. Also builders were required to obtain construction permits to ensure that development conformed to the plan and to the building regulations and bye-laws. At the same time, the increasing complexity of urban problems led to the establishment of the Ministry of Housing and Reconstruction in 1958. One of the first actions of the new Ministry was to redevelop an early gecekondu settlement in the city, by replacing the gecekondus with medium-rise apartment blocks. The scheme was intended for the original inhabitants of the area, but it acted as an incentive for growth for the settlement, since more people hoping to be eligible for the project moved in to the area and the scheme eventually had to be abandoned.

Towards the end of the 1950s, extensive areas of the city were completely occupied by gecekondus. The involvement of the political parties in the gecekondu process played an important role in the development of illegal settlements and gecekondu settlers exhibited their electoral power to ensure their security.

Achieving security of tenure or obtaining basic services in gecekondu areas was made possible by the mahalle system, since electoral potential increased parallel to the development of a settlement.

Approaches to the municipality for the provision of services were possible through 'beautifying organizations' formed in an area to pursue the interests of the community, or through the mahalle administration. The importance of the beautifying organizations was that they provided officially recognized pressure groups in areas not formally constituted as mahalles. It was necessary, however, to be part of an existing mahalle or to form a new mahalle for a settlement to be officially recognized by the municipality. The importance of a mahalle in terms of exerting pressure is that it is through the muhtar that the electors are registered. So, the formation of a mahalle is a form of confirmation of the political power of an area, but a mahalle could be provided with services only after it reached a politically feasible size. When such a size was reached the residents could trade their votes in municipal elections for services, according to whichever party promised or gave them the most. In fact, the provision of services or issuing of land titles has been exercised considerably, usually before elections. Periodic legalizations (by giving legal titles) were in fact, an incentive to develop further settlements. The high rate of growth exceeded the ability of the authorities to plan areas on the periphery and nearby villages were incorporated into the city. The population of the city reached 778,000 in 1960, and by 1963 almost 64% of the total housing consisted of gecekondus which accommodated 60% of the population. The pattern of growth was also crystallized towards the end of this period. The old city in the centre provided rental housing to new migrants; along the north and east axis of the city, 'gecekondu' areas were predominant, whilst middle- and upper-income groups were concentrated in the south and west.

After the coup d'etat in 1960 the military authorities introduced new measures to reduce the growth of new gecekondus by restricting the expansion of utilities, but this proved to be a short-lived measure. An amendment of the Reconstruction Law through Act No. 327 in 1963, in time for local elections laid down that services would be provided to gecekondus (local and national) built before the end of 1962 in areas which were declared as gecekondu areas by the Ministry of Housing and Reconstruction. Provision of services as such benefited many of the gecekondu areas in the city and added another element to the supportive role of the public authorities in the development of gecekondus.

1963–72 Period

When the planned period started in 1963, the housing sector was studied for the first time as a whole. The policy objectives for illegal settlements in the First Five Year Plan were identified as: (1) improving the existing squatter areas; (2) preventing the development of new squatter areas and, (3) clearing the poorest quality of squatter housing.

These objectives were incorporated into the Gecekondu Law (No. 775) to be passed in 1966, which was the first legislation specifically concerned with gecekondus. The Act attempted a new definition of gecekondu (as described in the previous section) and spelt out the approach to be adopted and the intended means of implementation to achieve its objectives. Responsibility for implementation was given to the municipalities on condition that the approval of the Ministry of Housing and Reconstruction was obtained.

According to the provisions of the Gecekondu Law, improvement of gecekondu areas would be realized by supplying credits to householders for house renovation and to local authorities for providing and improving services. Clearance would be applied to gecekondus in areas where the improvement was prohibitive or where the area was subject to natural disasters. To prevent further squatting, housing would be provided by the public sector within the following options: building apartment blocks on long-term, low-interest mortgages; constructing core houses with loans for completion; allocating serviced sites within prepared projects; and providing sites and credits to co-operatives.

Insufficient funding compared to the scale of the task reduced the effectiveness of the legislation. In terms of clearance, the Act stated that a gecekondu cannot be demolished unless an alternative shelter is provided. This restricted the scope of implementation and consequently gave the squatter additional security. Provision of housing was particularly affected by limited financial capability. Within the scope of this measure various housing projects were realized, the biggest of which was the settlement of Aktepe with 3760 units. When the scale of low-income housing need is considered, however, they represented a small contribution. The most important impact of the Gecekondu Law, however, was on the improvement of gecekondu areas, and in that respect legislation represents a radical change of attitude. In fact, this was the provision of the legislation on which local authorities were particularly active. By spending almost 60% of municipal housing budgets on the provision of services, such as public water supply, improvement of local roads, electrical power, street lighting, transportation, and by spreading the limited financial resources on a mahalle basis as widely as possible, Ankara municipality achieved the support of gecekondu residents.

In practice this was achieved by trying to respond to the requests from individual mahalles and to co-ordinate them as efficiently as funds permitted, rather than trying to follow a strict programme. Obviously, the increasing political power of gecekondu areas influences municipalities to adopt such an approach. An extended quotation from Payne's study on Ankara illustrates very well how this approach worked and how the mahalle system helped the residents to obtain services and how they participated in the decision-making process:[8]

> Mehmet Ali's settlement had only been officially designated as a mahalle in 1960, so that it still lacked most services and utilities. Most people had to dig their own wells to obtain water and the men usually walked to the main road each day to catch a bus for the six-kilometer ride to the city. Once its mahalle status was achieved, however, things began to move faster. The first school was built within a year, the main local road was paved a year later and, by 1963, a local bus service was provided. In 1965, when the original large mahalle was sub-divided into several smaller ones, more schools were built, the first water and sewerage mains were laid and a large water storage tank was constructed on top of a nearby hill. One factor which helped this rapid consolidation was the way in which the government encouraged the traditional rural practices of self-help. The following of conventional methods of designing and implementing infrastructure provision programmes involving lengthy procedures of acquiring legally owned properties or removing squatter houses which were in the path of a public mains network. They also involved substantial labour costs for excavating trenches in built-up areas. An ingenious solution was found to this problem. The mahalle was offered two options; either it could wait until the municipality had sufficient funds to carry out the project itself, or the work could be carried out sooner if local residents agreed to provide free labour and resolve any problems over the plans themselves. Not surprisingly, most mahalles chose the latter course and so consolidated far more quickly than would otherwise have been possible. It also brought residents and local groups into the decision-making process of urban planning. When Mehmet Ali's area was again subdivided in 1972 into its present mahalle unit, residents requested improvements to the local main road so that a bus service could be provided. On receipt of the request, the city highways department prepared a plan which increased the right of way from five to eight metres up to twelve metres, routed to involve the minimum of demolition. Rather than attempt to execute the plan directly, however, the highways department passed it back to the mahalle leaders for endorsement or to suggest a cheaper alternative. Inevitably, the greatest opposition came from those households whose homes or plots were directly affected. Although they were entitled by law to compensation for their dwelling and, if they held the freehold for their land, it was left to local

residents to accept, modify or reject the plan. Since the road was of general benefit to everyone, neighbours not affected were persuaded to modify their plot boundaries to help those whose plots were reduced and new sites were found for others forced to move. In this way, debate which would have been based upon a confrontation between the municipality and residents was avoided, time and costs were saved and local needs were met. Had the approval not been forthcoming, the municipality could have dropped the project without having committed substantial resources to it.

The Second Five Year Plan introduced in 1968 favoured urbanization as 'the vehicle for development' and in terms of approach to the housing problem of low-income groups, the framework of the First Plan was followed. In 1969, the Land Office was established mainly to provide cheap urban land for housing developments which were to be realized by Ministry of Housing and Reconstruction within the framework of Gecekondu Law, as well as to control land speculation by increasing land supply. But the attempt failed due to limited budgets. In 1969 again, Ankara Metropolitan Planning Office was established to plan, regulate, and direct urban growth, but it too had a limited effect on the development taking place on the ground.

With urban growth continuing at a high rate, the number of gecekondus increased steadily and with higher standards of construction, services provided by local authorities and with security of tenure granted in periodical amnesties, low-income groups achieved relatively higher standards compared to earlier periods. Gecekondus had become an

Figure 5.5   The provision of secure tenure, services and public facilities enabled many gecekondu settlements to consolidate rapidly. (Photo by G. K. Payne.)

accepted and dominant form of housing for low-income groups. The early 1970s, however, mark a change of character in the gecekondu process. As a result of the increasing influence of market forces on land and on gecekondu construction, the gecekondu process became increasingly incorporated into the urban economy.

Post-1972

The period starting in 1972 marks changes in the housing options available to low-income groups and in the attitudes of both central and local governments. In order to discuss the current housing processes that exist in the metropolitan area, it is necessary to distinguish between processes in the planned areas and processes in the unplanned areas, since land and its legal status in terms of the city plan is a basic determinant in the development process.

Housing options in planned areas are now very limited. The most common practice is to buy a flat either from landowners or from the builders. Generally, the builders are small contractors (small capital and organizations) operating on the scale of individual buildings. Although large building companies emerged in the mid-1970s their effect so far has been very limited. The small builders can be grouped in two types of practice, namely the 'demolish–build' type of practice and 'build–sell' type of practice. These builders usually offer some flats in the new building to meet the cost of the plot and make their profit through the sale of the other flats. The ratio offered to the landowners ranges from 45 to 58% of the total number of flats, depending on the location. In line with the nature of their practices, the 'demolish–build' practices are concentrated in the developed areas and 'build–sell' practices in either newly developing areas or on vacant plots held for speculation. The interesting point here is that the existence of the 'demolish–build' practices is made possible by density changes.

These builders and landlords control the housing market operating in the planned areas and this constitutes the major option available to middle- and high-income groups. Credit assistance is very limited in helping households to have access to the housing market. These credits are offered by the Social Insurance Agency and Real Estate Bank, and although initially developed to benefit the low-income groups, their terms ensured that the beneficiary turned out to be middle-income households.[9] The scale of their operations was even inadequate to meet this more limited scale of demand.

In the unplanned areas, access to land is possible in three ways: occupation (of both public and private land), buying the 'right of occupation' from a former occupant, and buying a shared title. Although the option of occupying public or private land still exists in some remote areas, it is not practised as widely as it used to be. Public land suitable for occupation is no longer available due to the fast rate of squatting, and there is greater control over private land. Buying the 'right of occupation' from a former occupant is more common in the occupied public land. Those who parcelled large plots earlier sell part of their plots. To buy a 'shared title', on the other hand, is the most secure option. The landowners in the unplanned areas subdivide their cadastral parcels and sell them by giving the title and at much cheaper rates than in the planned areas; but since the subdivision is unofficial, only the boundaries of the cadastral parcel are registered in the title. The owners of the subdivided plots, therefore, can only have a partial title such as $80/1000$ m^2 of land, without specifying the exact location of their plots. This, however, might lead to certain friction later, when the alignment of roads and utilities

Figure 5.6   Many gecekondu areas are being changed into middle-income localities as squatters sell their rights to developers (Photo by G. K. Payne.)

has to be done, yet the existence of a legal title makes them less vulnerable to possible intervention. In this case, although the dwelling is still a 'gecekondu', it is only the building regulations that have been bypassed. It should also be noted that the availability of relatives/friends or people from the same village in the locality is still an important factor, because it is through them that access to land is, in fact, obtained.

In terms of the building process, again three major types can be observed: self-help and hired craftsmen; self-help with hired workers, or self-help with both hired craftsmen and workers. In the building process, the trend has been parallel to those that took place on the issue of land. The more secure land tenure was, the bigger investments tended to be in the dwelling. Also, the more tolerant attitude of the public agencies gave them opportunity to build better and to spread the period of construction. While the first type of process was widely practised in the early phases of gecekondu development, it became more common to seek the help of a craftsman and even paid workers in the later phases.

These developments in the housing process led to the formation of a second land and housing market, operating in the gecekondu areas, which gave an incentive to speculative undertakings. It is now not unusual to see two gecekondu owners on a plot or to come across a craftsman working as a gecekondu contractor. Building materials used in gecekondu areas are relatively cheaper and less durable materials, compared to those used in the construction in the planned areas. Although the use of readily available materials in the locality—such as stone, mudbricks, etc.—or use of materials brought from the village, such as timber, was more common in the early phases, increasing commercialization of the process led to the introduction of new materials such as breeze blocks, and to specialization in production and distribution of these materials. Also, parallel to the development of 'demolish–build' practices in the planned areas, a recycling process started in salvaged materials such as window frames, doors, water taps, electrical equipment, etc.

These materials are available in builders' yards catering specially for gecekondu builders. They also developed a credit system for their customers in which a small down-payment is required when the materials are purchased. The rest is paid in instalments, the amount and period of the loan being negotiable. An important factor in this system is the existence of an intermediary who acts as a guarantor between the two parties. This intermediary is usually a friend, relative, or even the hired craftsman. As Payne discussed in his study on Akara,[10] some of the owners of these yards also became speculative gecekondu builders by occupying or purchasing land in their locality and offering standardized houses for sale. On the other hand, their position as financiers to households without adequate capital often enabled them to absorb any surplus materials resulting from market fluctuations and thereby stabilize prices.

With regard to the changing attitudes of central and local government after 1972, there has been an increased emphasis upon mass housing in accordance with the principles stated in the Third Plan, though this did not develop beyond the conceptual level for some time. In 1979 the 'New Settlement Areas Project' was announced by the government, aiming to provide serviced land to meet the housing needs of low- and middle-income groups, in the three largest cities of the country, i.e. Ankara, Istanbul and Izmir. The project was abandoned after the change of government in 1980.

In terms of its impact on the city, the important development during this period has been the radical change in the attitude of the municipality towards the problem of low-income housing and uncontrolled urban growth. Generally, the Ankara municipality is dependent upon central government both financially and administratively. Conflicts between local and national government tend to reduce the effectiveness of the municipality by reducing its revenues from national taxes. This inevitably reduces the autonomy of local government in decision-making.

Motivated by these facts, and with the idea that local government is directly affected by the problems in their domain and is therefore the most appropriate agency to identify and resolve local problems, the municipality of Ankara initiated a major new project known as 'Batıkent' (West City) in 1974. It was hoped that the municipality, by developing land and selling it, would generate new resources and achieve planned growth. Planned growth, in turn, would reduce the financial burden of providing services.

The objectives of the scheme, which was planned was a semi-autonomous new town development to accommodate a population of 300,000, were stated[11] as: to control and to direct urban growth in accordance with the master plan prepared by the Metropolitan Planning Office for 1990; to plan ahead of actual development; to curb land speculation by increasing the urban land supply; and to create a healthy, planned environment with adequate services and employment opportunities. Selected target groups in the scheme were low and lower-middle income groups, and in order to realize the project the municipality started to acquire undeveloped land about 20 km to the west of the city in 1974. In 1975 expropriation procedures for 200 ha were completed within the framework of the Gecekondu Law.

Further expropriation was approved 2 years later, at the end of 1976, by the Ministry of Housing and Resettlement. Shortly after these procedures started, an amendment to the Constitution made in 1977 by the Supreme Court stated that land could only be expropriated at market value and this led to rapid cost escalation. (It should be pointed out here that the amendment also limited the scope of public intervention in the land market.) By 1979 the municipality nonetheless completed the expropriation of 1034 ha of land. The project is planned to be realized in 10 years[12] and construction of 1000 units for the initial stage started in 1981.

In terms of housing systems, a variety of options are available in the scheme, such as rental housing, self-help programmes and building row housing, apartment blocks with loans from the Social Insurance Agency. Although greater emphasis was on self-help methods and sites and services programmes initially, political considerations for the 1981 elections shifted the emphasis to housing construction by the municipality. The initial cost estimates of these units, and conditions of payments, however, will probably exclude the majority of low-income groups from the project, especially those who do not have secure employment.

To finance the scheme, a credit of US$28 million was made available by the European Resettlement Fund as 'seed capital'. The remainder of development costs will be financed by credits from the Social Insurance Agency, the Mutual Aid Fund of Civil Servants, pension funds and by periodic payments to be provided by co-operatives. A new organizational system is also devised for the scheme. A union of co-operatives (Kent-Koop) is established to organize housing co-operatives which will provide access to the housing loans of Security Organizations. Kent-Koop also assumed responsibility for co-ordinating the construction carried out by different contractors. The municipality, on the other hand, was responsible for providing land and services.

The impact of the project on the city is difficult to assess at this stage because of its scale. A great deal is still uncertain and decisions to be made in the near future will determine its character and degree of success.

CONCLUSIONS

Ankara is a good example of a city expanded without an effective industrial base. The city was conceived—and planned—as an administrative centre and as a symbol of modernization. In fact, it was the first Turkish city to develop according to a comprehensive city plan. Although planned development was achieved during the first years, unanticipated growth of the city towards the late 1930s increasingly rendered it impossible.

Early growth of the city was determined primarily by the needs of the central government. With the acceleration of migration after the 1950s, however, the process of controlled growth was confined to the planned section of the city. While middle- and upper-income groups were concentrating in central areas, low-income housing occupied peripheral locations. The urban service sector, which expanded as a result of the city's administrative function, compensated to a large extent for the lack of an industrial sector and enabled the city to absorb large increases in population.

Towards the late 1960s congestion in the central areas, inadequate services, air pollution, and increased mobility led to an outward movement of middle- and upper-income groups. This, coupled with a shortage of available urban land, created a competition between different income groups for peripheral sites. On the other hand, the limited supply of suitable land for settlement and pressure of market forces created a second land market operating in unplanned areas of the city, and thus the gecekondu process became commercialized. The ambitious Batikent project initiated by the municipality was introduced when the city reached a critical stage in its development and the impact of the project on the city is yet to be seen.

In terms of housing policies Ankara presents a case in which the lack of comprehensive housing policies or an urban development policy left the lower-income groups to help themselves and find their own solutions. In order to offset the imbalances, public authorities helped them to secure their position. On the other hand the pragmatic approach of the local governments, by providing services, served well the interests of both government and residents, in the sense that while local governments gained the electoral support of illegal settlements who constituted a large portion of urban population, gecekondu residents obtained what they could not provide themselves. However, the success achieved by *ad hoc* planning methods began to erode in the late 1970s. The main factors contributing to this were commercialization of the gecekondu process and the decreasing availability of suitable land for gecekondu development. Increasing land values as a result of speculation, especially in prospective gecekondu areas, and control of the construction process by market forces, in a sense transformed the pragmatic approach of public authorities into a mechanism which started to serve the interests of the speculators. If such approaches could have been supported by long-term measures such as providing urban land suitable to the paying capacity of urbanizing low-income groups, and provision of an effective public transportation system for these areas (like utilization of minibuses if buses prove to be unfeasible, etc.), long-term success would be ensured.

Introduction of credit systems for purchase of construction materials would be a further contribution to this end.

The *ad hoc* approach to the problems of urban development and housing in Ankara adopted by public authorities both at national and local level seems to be no longer adequate as a result of changes in the nature and magnitude of the problems, and the need for long-term policies now became evident. Since gecekondus are the product of structural problems such as industrialization and unequal income distribution, the solutions call for structural measures. Unless such structural changes are realized, gecekondus will therefore continue to exist. But within the existing conditions, the recognition of the proven ability of low-income sectors to provide their own housing, thereby legalizing the process with all its implications and supporting it with comprehensive land policies, seems to be a viable policy alternative.

NOTES AND REFERENCES

1. See *Urbanization*, sector working paper, The World Bank, June 1972, Annex 1, Table 6, p.82.
2. The function of being a capital also had an effect on the political and administrative structure of the city in that some of the administrative functions of the central government overlapped with those of the city. Planning problems are only one of several examples. Until the mid-1940s, the Urban Development Authority of Ankara, which was connected to the Ministry of Interior, had the authority of approval for all the urban development plans in the country.
3. *Ankara Nazım Plan Seması Raporu*, ANPB Yayın No. 5, Ankara, 1977, p.309.
4. T. Dinc, and R. Türkmen, *Türkiye'de Yerlesme Yerleri Itibariyle Demografik Konut Gereksinimi*. Ankara: YAE Yayıinları, 1979, p.134.
5. Insaat Istatistikleri, 1978. Ankara: DIE Yayıinları, 1979.

6. *Ankara Nazım Plan Seması Raporu,* ANPB Yayın No. 5, Ankara, 1977, p.311.
7. L. Y. Tokman, *Konut Politikarları Uygulamalarinda Özel Bir Örnek: Yenimahhalle,* Faculty of Architecture, Department of City Planning thesis. ODTU, 1979, p.26.
8. G. K. Payne, 'At home in Ankara', *Geographical Magazine,* Sept. 1980, pp.805–809.
9. The housing loans offered by the Social Insurance Agency are given to co-operatives to be formed by at least 30 members who have been affiliated with the Agency for a minimum period of 5 years. This excludes the majority of low-income groups, working in the unorganized service sector. The limit of the loan is determined by the Agency's Board of Executives and with 1980 figures in is TL600,000. The cost of a dwelling in the same year is roughly TL2 million in middle-income residential areas. On the other hand, Real Estate Bank Loans require a housing deposit account for a period of 2 years. At the end of this period triple the amount of this account is given as credit for a term of 15 years. Interest rates and the credit limit is determined by the bank.
10. G. K. Payne, 'Self-help housing: a critique of the gecekondu of Ankara', in P. M. Ward (ed.), *Self-Help Housing: A Critique.* London: Alexandrine Press, 1982, p.128.
11. *Ankara Belediyesi, Batıkent Politikalar Demeti Ana Rapor.* Ankara: Ankara Belediyesi, 1979. p.47.
12. From the notes of a meeting with the planning team, July 1980.

Low-income Housing in the Developing World
Edited by G. K. Payne
© 1984 John Wiley & Sons Ltd

Chapter 6

Tanzania's Surveyed Plots Programme

Joram Mghweno

INTRODUCTION

Tanzania's current average annual population growth rate of 3.3% makes it one of the most rapidly growing countries in Africa. The population grew from 11,958,000 people (as was indicated in the first post-independence census of 1967) to 17,048,000 people in 1978. There is no reason to believe that this high growth rate will decline significantly within the foreseeable future. A number of factors, such as increased life expectancy, declining infant mortality, high fertility rates (due to the large proportion of the population in the child-bearing age group), improved nutrition, water supply, and sanitation facilities, coupled with high cultural values placed on children may, in fact tend to increase national population growth rates still further. Based on these trends, it may be reasonably assumed that the population of Tanzania will increase by more than 75% by the end of this century, reaching about 35 million people.

The urban population is currently estimated to be growing at about 9% per annum. This is not restricted to the main urban centres, but includes regional headquarters and settlements of more than 5000 people. In the 1967 census, 21 such settlements were identified, while the 1978 census identified 62. Similarly, the 1967 census classified 5.5% of the mainland population as urban and by 1978 this had increased to 12.7% of the national population. Despite Tanzania's low population base, the rates of urban growth over the past three decades have therefore been very high, especially when compared with the historical development of urbanization in Europe and North America, where rates of urban growth were always below 3% per annum. In Tanzania, as elsewhere, much of this growth is due to rural–urban migration, especially by the young. In his study of housing in Tanzania, SM Kulaba has projected that approximately one-third of the population of Tanzania will be urban by the end of this century.[1]

Urban population growth has already exceeded the creation of new employment opportunities. Regular wage employment accounted for just over two-thirds of the employment opportunities a year during 1969–76 and average real earnings for this type of employment declined slightly during this period. Informal opportunities grew at some 11% per annum, but because low-income self-employment accounted for much of the growth, average real earnings in this sector were more than halved. As a result of these changes and growth in the labour force, average per capita real earnings fell by about 50% in urban areas. Furthermore, urban dwellers' purchasing power has been sharply reduced by increases in producer prices for key agricultural goods as well as by inflation. Data for 1976 suggest that between 33 and 40% of Tanzania's urban households, (including employed and self-employed), had cash incomes below the official minimum wage (currently this is T.Shs600 (US$75) per month. A survey conducted by the Bureau of Statistics suggested that by 1978 this proportion had increased to about 65%.

Rapid urbanization has inevitably increased pressure on already over-extended urban infrastructure and services. Since the national development strategy assigns a low priority to urban areas, this has compounded the existing housing shortage. It has also created a dramatic rearrangement of national priorities and consequently a distortion of investment trends in the economy. In addition to the failure to provide adequate infrastructure and services to cater for the rapid population growth in urban areas, there has been a failure on the part of the administrative machinery to provide for a 'planned' home delivery system at a time when demand has been growing rapidly. Under the First Five Year Development Plan (1964–69), it was estimated that the cumulative shortfall for new housing in urban areas stood at about 37,000 housing units. The total demand as estimated under the Third Five Year Development Plan (1976–81) was for 250,000 housing units, and current estimates put the cumulative demand at more than 300,000 units. At the current rate of urban population growth, together with the existing deficit and the fact that quite a number of the existing dwellings will require replacement, the total demand for new dwellings in urban areas by the year 2000 is estimated at more than 2,200,000 units.

The inadequacy of national shelter delivery systems to cater for the urban population has led to extensive development of squatter settlements. Reliable data documenting the extent of urban squatter development in Tanzania are not available. However, a 1975 study of squatter housing in 13 of the major towns in Tanzania indicated that 72,500 squatter houses existed in these communities and that they had a total population of approximately 1,165,000 people. Based on estimated squatter housing occupancy rates of slightly more than nine persons per dwelling, approximately 60% of all urban residents in these towns were living in squatter settlements. Nationally, between 40 and 70% of residents in Tanzania's main towns are living in uncontrolled, inadequately serviced squatter settlements. A more alarming situation is the rate at which these settlements have been growing. For example, the total number of squatter houses in Dar es Salaam, the principal town in 1974, was about 50,000 housing units. The current figure is more than 100,000 housing units. Investigations conducted by the Housing Development Division have indicated that about 65% of all residential housing constructed in urban areas during 1980 is in squatter settlements, and that squatter developers are constructing a minimum total of 10,000 dwellings per annum in the regional headquarters.

GOVERNMENT EFFORTS AT PROVIDING HOUSING

These developments are not in themselves an indication that government has not embarked on programmes addressed to solving housing problems. In fact, the provision of decent housing for all Tanzanian citizens has long been an important objective for the Party (Chama Cha Mapinduzi) and the Government. The Arusha Declaration, the Party blueprint for national socioeconomic development, has put shelter as the third basic human need after food and clothing. Varying degrees of emphasis have been given to the issue of housing since Tanzania attained political independence in December 1961. During this period, a number of institutions have been created to facilitate the provision of housing and considerable human, physical, and financial resources have been allocated to the housing sector. Table 6.1 indicates the number of actors involved in a typical housing project in Tanzania.

Broadly, The Ministry of Lands, Housing, and Urban Development has been vested with the responsibility of overseeing all housing development in the country. The National Housing Corporation, the main institutional developer in urban areas, was established by an Act of Parliament in 1962. The main assignment for the Corporation was to facilitate and construct housing mainly for the low-income urban population. By early 1980 the Corporation had managed to construct 13,366 new dwelling units over a 19-year period which was less than 50% of the target set. Furthermore, because of prevailing circumstances, average monthly rents for the corporation house units are beyond the affordable range of a greater percentage of the urban labour force. The Tanzania Housing Bank was established in 1972 as a mortgage institution. Audited accounts for 1978 indicate that the Bank had provided about 10,500 urban housing loans with an average of about T.Sh35,000 (US$4300), yet the Household Budget Survey for 1977–78 indicated that only about 1–2% of the households who spent money on constructing their houses utilized loans from the Housing Bank and other loan sources. During the same period, total demand for new residential dwellings in urban areas stood at more than 250,000 units.

In 1972 the government realized that the provision of housing in urban areas, especially for the low-income groups, required more than just the conventional approaches. The cabinet therefore endorsed the implementation of a national sites and services and squatter upgrading programme to involve all urban areas through a phased developmental approach. In arriving at this decision, the government was guided by the understanding that the people had for a long time provided their own housing and that they were likely to continue doing so. The government therefore viewed its role as that of facilitating new house construction by the people themselves, and maintaining and upgrading what had already been constructed. This therefore called for the need to upgrade existing squatter settlements. Specifically, the government policy entailed:

(a) Legalizing squatter landholdings by providing them with leases and at the same time removing the stigma of 'temporary classification' from squatter houses.
(b) Preparing designs for squatter areas and respecting existing communities while allowing for the provision of services, including roads, drainage, water supply, electricity, and community facilities to include markets, health clinics, and education centres.
(c) Providing credit facilities to houseowners in squatter areas to improve existing houses.

With regard to sites and services, the objective has been to provide basic planned, surveyed, and serviced plots for allocation to would-be developers with preference to low-income families. In addition to the provision of services and community facilities, plot developers have been assisted with credit facilities for house construction. Unfortunately though, this approach of allowing people to build or improve their own

Table 6.1   Actors involved in urban housing development in Tanzania

Activity	1 CABINET	2 HOUSING DEV.	3 SURVEYS	4 LANDS	5 SEWERAGE AND DRAINAGE	6 URBAN PLANNING	7 BUILDING RESEARCH
					MINISTRY OF LANDS HOUSING AND URBAN DEVELOPMENT		
1. Policy formulation	●	●					
2. Land preparation							
(a) Designation of land for residential development				O		●	
(b) Acquisition of land for residential development		O		●		●	
(c) Site planning (layouts)		O				●	
(d) Plot definition (land surveying)		O	●				
(e) Plot allocation and tenure mechanisms				●			
(f) Provision of land services (infrastructure)							
(i) Designs		●			●		
(ii) Budgeting	●	●			●		
(iii) Construction		●			●		
3. Dwelling unit construction							
(a) House designs	●	O					O
(b) Housing finance							
(c) Construction standards							O
(d) Building permits							
(e) Building materials	●						
(f) Construction mechanism		O					O
4. Maintenance of residential environment							
5. Revenue structures							
(a) Establishing rates	●			●			
for land rent and service charges	●			●			
(b) Valuation of properties				●			
(c) Revenue collection							
(i) Service charges							
(ii) Utilities							
6. Sales and transfers				●			

Key: ●, Primary direct responsibility: O, Secondary responsiblity

PRIME MINISTER'S OFFICE			OTHER MINISTRIES					PARASTATAL ORGANIZATIONS				OTHERS			
8	9	10	11	12	13	14	15	16	17	18	19	20	21	22	23
HEADQUARTERS	REGIONAL ADMIN.	URBAN COUNCILS	PLANNING	FINANCE	INDUSTRY	WORKS	OTHERS	HOUSING BANK	BOARD OF INTERNAL TRADE	TANESCO (POWDER)	OTHERS	CONSULTANTS	CONTRACTORS	INDIVIDUALS	LOCAL COMMUNITY ORGANIZATION
		●	●												
	●														
	○	●													
	○	●													
	●	●													
	●	●													
	○	●				○			●	○	○				
●	○	●	●	●		○			●						
	○	●				○			●				●		
	○	●				○					○	○		●	●
			●	●				●			○			●	●
	○	●												●	
●	●														
			●	●	●			○	○	●		○		●	●
		○							○					●	
	○	●												●	●
		○	○	●											
	○	○													
●	●		●												
●	●							●	●						
	○	○													○

Table 6.2   National sites and services and squatter upgrading project standards of infrastructure services

A. *Roads*

Category	Road reservation	Carriageway	Specification
Class A	36 m	6 m	Treated macadam surface on stabilized gravel base.
Class B	24 m	4.5 m	Rolled gravel surface suitable for light vehicular traffic.
Class C	12 m	5 m	Compacted earth for pedestrian and emergency vehicle access.

B. *Drainage*

Unlined ditches along the roads with culverts at crossings. Ditches lined in steeply sloping areas.

C. *Foul water drainage*

Generally improved pit latrines are considered adequate for most project areas.

D. *Water supply*

Internal distribution system connected to off-site main. Public standpipes (four taps) for every 50 plots/houses. Consumption 40 litres per capita daily (lcd) main to be designed for 100 lcd (for 30% individual connection in 10 years and remainder 40 lcd).

E. *Electricity*

Street lighting along A and B roads generally, and electricity to community facilities. Provision for limited house connections is made.

houses as and when they can accumulate the necessary resources has been brought on more by a paucity of resources than by an appreciation of the people's ability to plan for and solve their own housing problems. Table 6.2 indicates the standards of facilities provided in both squatter upgrading and sites and services areas.

Phase one of the project started in 1974, and was one of the early projects to receive support from the World Bank. It involved the provision of about 10,000 serviced plots in three major towns including Dar es Salaam, and the upgrading of a further 11,000 houses in squatter settlements.

Phase two of the project was initiated in 1977 and also received World Bank support. It involved squatter upgrading in five towns, and the provision of surveyed plots to be allocated mainly to low-income families. The project estimated that the squatter upgrading component would benefit about 315,000 people, representing about 26% of Tanzania's urban population (1976) and providing improvement to 40% of squatter settlements in Tanzania. The surveyed plots were estimated to cover about 75% of the residential building land required up to the year 1981. In addition, it was envisaged that this approach would also assist in containing the growth of squatter settlements.

While implementation of the sites and services and squatter upgrading programme has been going on, current estimates have shown that over the span of the squatter upgrading programme (1974–80) the squatter population has increased by between

750,000 and 900,000 persons. Compared with the estimated figure of 467,000 people as project beneficiaries for both phase one and two, and the fact that the projects were planned to have covered about 75% of all squatter housing, it is clear that new squatter development has far outweighed efforts to improve existing settlements and to contain further development of these settlements.

DYNAMICS OF SQUATTER DEVELOPMENT

Before discussing the surveyed plots programme, it is necessary to discuss the dynamics of squatter development and the reasons why people choose this form of settlement as opposed to those which are more acceptable to planners. From the point of view of the squatter resident, these settlements often have unhealthy water supplies and the inconvenience of transporting potable water over long distances. Overcrowding of dwellings is common. Over-utilization or mis-utilization of the land has resulted in a lack of space for circulation routes and community facilities. Drainage is often poor, thus making it difficult to control the spread of water-borne diseases. The quality of housing is also often poor, but this situation is by no means universal in squatter settlements.

From the point of view of the urban authorities, squatter development presents numerous difficulties. The provision of public services is often difficult due to inefficient layouts. In almost all cases of squatter improvement the provision of services is initiated after the development, and developed land can only be acquired at considerable expense. This follows the national land policy which empowers the government to acquire any land for public use, but requires the new developer to pay compensation for crops, buildings, and other unexhausted improvement. Based on this policy, tentative costs for acquiring land for some project sites under phase two of the squatter upgrading project are about 50% of total improvement expenditure. The authorities have had to design transportation routes so that they remove the least number of housing structures, often at the expense of design solutions which are more efficient and effective. In short, urban authorities are faced with a situation where planning follows development, making it impossible to use planning as a management tool. In addition, the revenue collected from squatter settlements has been extremely limited and it is fair to say that to date such settlements have been a financial liability to urban authorities.

With the apparent disadvantages of settlement in squatter areas, why does the majority of urban residential development occur in these areas? It would appear that large numbers of people are consciously choosing to live in squatter settlements rather than in planned neighbourhoods which are provided with surveyed and serviced plots.

The first choice made by the potential squatter is to move to the urban area. A number of factors contribute to such a decision. It is reasonable to assume that individuals perceive of the move to an urban area as a means of improving their life situation. They may see opportunities to find employment which will increase family income or may desire access to the 'urban lifestyle' even if this has been exaggerated. Government may intervene in such decisions by encouraging or coercing people not to migrate to the urban areas. It is apparent, however, that these interventions have in the past been at best only partially successful. Other than a vigorous and perhaps harsh exercise of police power, urban authorities and the national government have few tools at their disposal with which to discourage the migration of people seeking to live in an urban environment. The issue then becomes one of how to cope with the new arrivals.

The new arrival may choose to rent, at least temporarily. The availability of disposable income will be an important consideration in making a choice regarding where to rent. If income is low—as it is in most cases—accommodation will be sought in low-rental developments, making existing squatter areas prime candidates. The existence of a strong market for such rental property is an added encouragement for people to build speculative or rent-income-producing units in squatter areas. If the migrant chooses to build a home, even after having stayed temporarily as a tenant in the squatter area, the availability of disposable income and existence of readily available land are important considerations.

SURVEYED PLOTS

Difficulties in enabling even sites and services projects to meet the required levels of affordability led to the government deciding to reduce initial standards of provision still further when confirming details of the second World Bank loan in 1977. This involved the provision of 19,000 surveyed plots in planned residential layouts to be allocated with legal titles to low-income applicants in five towns. It was hoped that this radical approach would provide a viable alternative to squatting by offering would-be squatters inexpensive plots in a planned environment.

The layouts for surveyed plots are designed for the same eventual standards as serviced sites but, except for a skeletal water supply, no services are supplied until after settlement has occurred. This approach reduces the initial capital required and is intended to enable the project to reach a greater proportion of low-income households. It affords one of the few practical options available for action before squatting occurs. The sequence of planning and implementation of the programme is as follows.

(a) Site selection

It is important that the areas selected comply with planning and zoning proposals in the development plan of the urban area under consideration. Priority is normally given to areas which are ripe for squatter development. This includes areas near employment centres such as new industrial development activities. Further, such areas should contain physical features which are easily developable (areas with high water table would not be favourably considered). Proximity to offsite infrastructure, in particular water supply and roads, is an added advantage.

(b) Basemap production and design of layouts

Figure 6.1 shows a typical layout for a surveyed plot programme. Layouts so produced have to be approved by the Urban Planning Committees of the Urban Councils and the Director of Urban Planning in the Ministry of Lands, Housing, and Urban Development.

(c) Site clearance and surveying of plots

The law of the country empowers government to acquire any land for the public interest. However, it also obliges the organization or person to whom such land will be offered after acquisition to pay as compensation the value of any unexhausted improvements

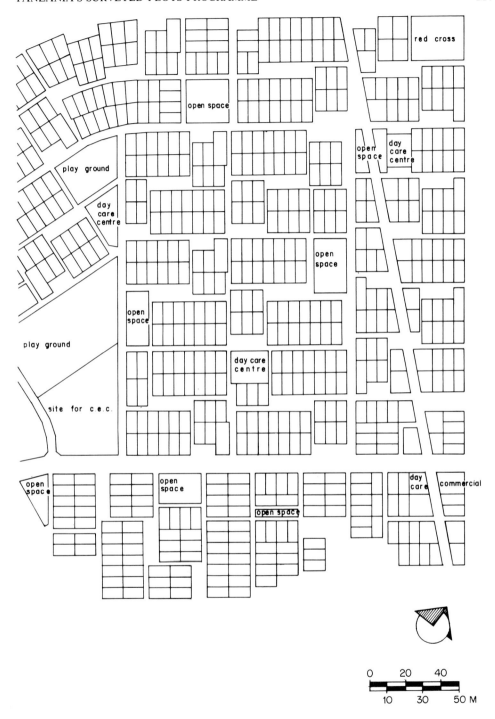

Figure 6.1   Typical layout for a surveyed plot programme. This example is in Mikocheni, Dar-es-Salaam

existing on the land at the date of his taking occupation thereof. The unexhausted improvements mean anything or any quality permanently attached to the land, directly resulting from the expenditure of capital or labour by an occupier or his agent which increases its productive capacity, utility or amenity, but excluding the results of ordinary cultivation other than standing crops or growing produce. The amount of compensation which is payable is the amount which fairly represents the value of the improvements to the incoming occupier as determined by the government chief valuer, whose decision is final.[2]

Normally the Government pays compensation to clear the land and new occupiers pay back in instalments through land rent, services charges, and other such fees. No compensation is paid for the land itself, as land in Tanzania is publicly owned.

The survey of plots entails the clear identification of each plot, public rights of way for roads, utility lines, and reserves for community facilities. Such survey plans have to be approved and registered with the Director of Surveys and Mapping in the Ministry of Lands, Housing, and Urban Development.

(d) Installation of skeletal water supply through standpipes

This work is normally done through a contractor or through direct labour by the regional water engineer.

(e) Allocation of plots

The responsibility to allocate urban building land rests with the urban council authorities which conduct the allocation exercise through urban planning committees. Committee members include the Director of the Urban authority, Councillors, and Members of Parliament residing in the area, advised by the Town Planner, the Land Surveyor, the Land Officer, and the Engineer. The Chairman is selected from among the Councillors and the Secretary is the Urban Planning Officer.

Under the surveyed plot programme, allocations are made on the basis of a points system weighted to favour households with monthly incomes below T.Sh1000 (US$120) a month. However, it is government policy to promote mixed-income committees. As such low-income applicants are given preference, but households with monthly incomes above T.Sh1000 are not excluded. Other criteria to be considered, but given lower weightings in the points system, include the number of dependants an applicant has, his employment status, and the length of time he has been on the waiting list for plots.

Following government policy on tenure, long-term rights of occupancy issued for 33 years or more are offered to all plot allottees under the programme. The right of occupancy is made after acceptance of 'an offer of a right' by the offeree. The offer normally sets out the terms of the grant such as its duration, land rents, revision periods, premium, use and type of buildings, and other improvements to be constructed. Covenants against subdivision without consent are also included. In the case of the surveyed plot programme, where the grant is for building purposes, there are provisions requiring the grantee to submit plans for approval by the area authorities, and setting out the phasing of building operations.

On acceptance of an offer, a household would be required to pay the fees for the certificate of occupancy that will be issued; registration, survey, and deed plan fees would also be payable at this stage. The allottee would then be requested to pay the stamp duty on the certificate and duplicate copy and the land rent and service charge for the first year and premium if any. A certificate would then be issued under section 9 of the Land Ordinance. This certificate is a document confirming the right to use the land and is necessary for registration of a plot. In constructing their houses, allottees have several options:

(i) They can join a housing co-operative society organized in their communities and build their houses through joint efforts or as a family venture.

(ii) They may apply for construction loans from the Housing Bank. Loans are secured by mortgages, an exercise of occupancy with the Housing Bank throughout the life period of the loan. In order to reach the programme beneficiaries more effectively, there is an understanding whereby the Housing Bank is required to establish part-time site offices in project areas for the distribution and reception of loan applications. Further, the Bank established depots for the storage and distribution of basic materials. Standard house-type plans are offered to prospective borrowers. This arrangement assists in overcoming the reluctance of the low-income borrowers who often tend to perceive the Housing Bank as a remote, somewhat aloof, and hard-nosed institution lending only for large projects.

HOUSE CONSOLIDATION

As has been indicated earlier, building activities in the housing sector in Tanzania are still to a large extent dependent upon the skills, initiatives, and resources of the households themselves. The 1977 Household Budget Surveys (unpublished) indicated that about 93% of households built their houses themselves with or without temporary labour from outside. During the same period the National Housing Corporation provided for 0.4% of residential housing, building co-operatives 0.5% and other contractors about 6%. The corresponding figure for self-built housing for the 1969 Household Budget Survey was 91%. It is therefore clear that only a very small proportion of the houses have been built by full-time professionals or contractors. No current studies have been published on the subject, but indications are that no major changes have occurred to alter the trend.

In addition to building their own houses, households provided their own house designs, usually following traditional or popular patterns. Type plans from central planning institutions or from consultant firms were only used to a very small extent. In fact such drawings were mainly used and produced for institutional housing development. Some of the ideas and details from this formal and professional sector might also be copied and used by the informal sector, but usually without the use of drawings and plot plans.

The technical knowledge guiding the household's own planning and building activities is mainly based on local traditions, common sense, long experience of locally available building materials, and the local socioeconomic situation. These are unwritten rules based on experience which are accepted by most of the people. Although building regulations under the Township (Building Rules) of 1930 apply in all urban areas, the standards applied in these rules are not affordable by the majority of house buildings and in practice most urban houses are not built in accordance with these rules. This is substantiated by investigations which have shown that about 60% of all new residential development within urban areas in Tanzania in 1980 were built in unplanned areas without regard to building regulations.

Low-income home-builders cannot avail themselves of the full range of building materials and many resort to the traditional ones of mud and pole or sun-dried mud block. Homes built of these materials would be classified as temporary or semi-permanent structures which do not meet the minimum requirements of the Township (building) rules that are applicable in most of the urban areas of Tanzania.

It is estimated that the minimum cost of a 50 m^{-2} dwelling constructed in accordance with building codes would be about T.Sh40,000–50,000 (US$5500–6200) depending upon the locality. This cost is exclusive of charges and fees assessed by the urban authorities for issuing building permits and certificates of land occupancy.

Assuming that a family can afford little more for housing than an amount equal to 25% of their income, more than half of the urban households have a maximum of T.Sh150 (US$18) available for housing each month. On the basis of current costs, plot charges alone are between T.Sh150 and 200 in a sites and services project, compared to about T.Sh150 in a surveyed plots project and a total of T.Sh100 in a squatter settlement.

Apart from the plot costs, it is clear from the above that it would require approximately 50 years to repay a construction loan for a house meeting the minimum requirements of local building codes even under favourable interest-rate conditions. Such a repayment schedule is unacceptable to both lenders and borrowers. As long as urban authorities continue to require adherence to minimum building codes for houses constructed on surveyed plots in urban areas, a large segment of the incoming population will not be able to afford to build in any area other than a squatter settlement. In effect, the municipality has made the choice for the low-income home-builder of where to build.

REFLECTIONS ON THE SURVEYED PLOT PROGRAMME

The number of surveyed plots which were to be provided in the five towns over 4 years totalled about 19,000. As has already been stated this would have satisfied about 75% of the estimated demand for building in the five towns. Furthermore, the arrangement would have assisted in checking the expansion of squatter settlements. By mid-1981 less than 30% of the intended number of surveyed plots had actually been prepared. This unsatisfactory performance is due largely to the inadequate resources in terms of personnel and necessary survey equipment. It is also a reflection on the unfavourable national economic situation which has been persisting for the last 10 years or so. On the part of personnel requirements, the estimated shortfall of land surveyors for the Ministry stood at 26 people in 1980 and is expected to shoot up to a shortage of 51 qualified surveyors by 1985. As resources for training are limited and will continue to be so, it is unlikely that this shortfall will be reduced.

The main consequence of the failure in providing surveyed plots has been of course, the continual growth of squatter settlements. As has been stated, the squatter population has increased by between 750,000 and 900,000 persons over the last 8 years and in 1980 alone a total of 10,000 squatter housing units were constructed in the main towns. It appears that estimates of demand for surveyed plots in the specified towns were lower than actual demand, so that even if the target had been met, there still would have been an unsatisfied demand.

The third factor which in a way contradicts the above-mentioned shortfalls is that in certain instances it has also taken too long for surveyed plots to be developed. Kulaba[3] suggests two main reasons for the slow development of surveyed plots. First, the target groups cannot afford to meet the initial plot charges and have a balance remaining with which to construct a house with the required permanent materials; second, the procedures involved before one can acquire a surveyed plot in an urban area are cumbersome and difficult for the low-income families to understand. It could be added here that the procedures involved in acquiring the necessary building designs and building permits which have to be provided by the plot allottee for any development over a surveyed plot are also complicated and time-consuming. Some people have also included the shortage of building materials, lack of on-site assistance, and limited financial assistance as other reasons for the slow development of surveyed plots. The fact that squatter areas are growing, and in many instances with quite attractive housing, lessens the weight of failure; in fact there appear to be compelling reasons for the continuing rapid development of squatter settlements. While writing on self-help in housing with regard to the Indian case, Kirtee Shah argues:[4]

> While the Indian metropolitan cities are growing at about 4% per annum, the slums, they say, are growing at 8%. It only shows that without intervention of any sort from formal institutions, people in need are building houses on their own. They go through almost all the processes that a normal housing agency goes through; they acquire land—albeit, in case of slums illegally; collect materials; arrange financial resources in cash or kind; put together skills; and build. It is entirely a different matter that the structures they erect don't fit into our image of a 'house'. Whatever the product, (and this is determined by the quality of the components which, in turn so heavily depends on the availability of resources), the slums and shanty towns are an eloquent testimony that people have the required motivation, desire and capacity and also some useful building skills. [He continues,] if the house comes to him not as a dole or gift, but as a step-by-step realisation of a distant dream, through his own initiative, hard work and mental, emotional and physical involvement then he feels a sense of achievement. If he thinks about it, contributes ideas in designing it, goes through processes which shape it, and continues to struggle to obtain it, then it is much more than a brick-mud structure to him. It becomes an asset which makes him realise his own work and potential. He begins to value himself, his friends and his helpers. The house, in the process of realisation, builds the man.

The surveyed plot programme was developed with this understanding in mind; the understanding that official intervention should be geared to facilitating house construction by the people themselves in the manner suited to their own situation, as has been the case with squatter development. The failures are not attributable to the concept, but the process of implementation. It is in fact a failure of the housing delivery system in the urban areas in Tanzania. Recommendations for improving the programme will be looked into within the context of improving the whole urban shelter delivery system.

IMPROVING THE PERFORMANCE

In the preceding discussion several issues have been identified. First, that urban population will continue to grow at a high rate for the foreseeable future, and that the majority of the additional population will continue to be in the low-income group. This growth will continuously increase the demand for housing and other related facilities in urban areas. Second, that the majority of the urban population will continue to provide for their own housing with or without assistance from outside the concerned families. Third, that already we have substantial housing development in squatter settlements. We recognize this investment and understand that the environmental conditions in these communities have to be improved through the provision of basic infrastructure and social facilities, but with a minimum amount of dislocation to the communities. In this way the government will have to continue to pay fair compensation to all those whose properties will have to be dislocated in the process of putting in services to squatter communities. The amounts involved in this exercise are continually growing in proportion to amounts used for actual servicing of the areas. Such amounts will soon become prohibitive. Fourth, that available resources will not allow for adequate training of the in-house professionals in land surveying. Maintaining current land survey principles and standards will therefore not allow us to meet the growing demand for surveyed plots. Shortage of the necessary equipment is also a constraint. Fifth, there are weaknesses in the shelter delivery system which have exposed themselves in cases where readily available surveyed plots have remained without development, while corresponding squatter settlements have been growing at a fast rate.

THE MISSING LINK

Realizing the inconveniences of servicing squatter areas when communities have already settled, compromising sound planning principles, spending excessively on compensation, destroying the sociopolitical fabric of squatter communities, the surveyed plot programme started off with a workable objective—that of providing land for the would-be squatters, with minimum services so as to be able to serve a much bigger demand, but also reducing initial plot development costs in order to allow for affordability.

In order to provide more plots there is a need for future programmes to concentrate on surveying at least the public rights of way for future road networks and services. Sites for community facilities should also be demarcated and preserved. This entails block surveying of new residential areas to facilitate future upgrading of services without spending on compensation or causing dislocation of the communities. Demarcation of individual plots will have to be undertaken at plot allocation stage by artisans who will have to be stationed at all sites of major residential developments. Site offices, which should be local extensions of urban administrations, should be strengthened over time to perform functions of approving less complicated building plans (which tend to be straightforward for the low-income), and assisting people to settle into their plots. In this regard urban authorities are currently reviewing regulations for approving plans and issuing building permits, and a draft building and planning code is about to be enacted. Further, conditions governing the offer of plots and issuance of certificates of occupancy will have to be reviewed, especially with regard to the accuracy of plot boundaries and development conditions.

The other aspect of the surveyed plot programme involves facilitating people's efforts to provide for their own housing. It would be improper to conclude that the vast majority of low-income home-builders desire to become or remain squatters. On the contrary, most evidence indicates that these home-builders place a high priority on settling in areas where security of tenure can be established. They become squatters for lack of other alternatives. They do not define themselves as squatters; it is we in government service, and in particular the planners, who define them as such. The surveyed plot programme should not be viewed only as a programme for making land available to low-income developers but as an attempt to facilitate low-income self-help housing. While the type of housing being built in such areas may appear to be unattractive and different from the kind of image we would like to project for our urban communities, it is the only type of housing which is realistically attainable for the majority of urban residents. The programme should assist in establishing a challenge for the review of institutional arrangements for the housing delivery system. Our housing delivery organizations and regulations—our building codes and permits and loan issuance requirements must be people-oriented. They should be equipped to recognize people's abilities and capable of involving them at every stage of the shelter delivery process. In this manner we shall manage to facilitate the construction of sufficient amounts of housing for low-income urban residents which meet basic requirements for shelter, health, safety, and social welfare, and which are compatible with the financial and physical resources of the communities within which the housing is located.

REFERENCES

1. S. M. Kulaba, 'Housing, socialism and national development in Tanzania.' Centre for Housing Studies, Tanzania—Occasional paper No. 1.
2. R. W. Jamos, *Land Tenure and Policy in Tanzania*. East African Literature Bureau, 1971.
3. S. M. Kulaba, Cited as Reference 1.
4. Kirtee Shah, 'Self-help in housing—cost reduction or change agent?' Paper presented at a seminar on Management of Squatter Upgrading Projects, Birmingham, 1976.

Low-income Housing in the Developing World
Edited by G. K. Payne
© 1984 John Wiley & Sons Ltd

Chapter 7

Ismailia: Combined Upgrading and Sites and Services Projects in Egypt

Forbes Davidson

ABSTRACT

Ismailia, a city of 175,000 population in the Suez Canal Zone in Egypt, was damaged in the Arab Israeli conflict of 1967–74, and evacuated for 7 years. The Egyptian Government resolved to reconstruct the canal cities, to promote their development, and to try new approaches to urban planning and management. The consultants, Clifford Culpin and Partners, were involved with the preparation of the Master Plan (1975–76), the detailed design of sites and services and upgrading projects (1977–78), and the provision of technical assistance to set up the implementing agencies and the training of their staff (1978–83). The projects themselves are innovative in that they are self-financing, locally staffed, and have become integrated into the local system. The chapter describes the proposals, how these have been modified in practice, and the lessons learnt.

INTRODUCTION

Ismailia is a city of some 175,000 population (Figure 7.1), situated at the mid-point of the Suez Canal about 140 km from Cairo. It receives water from the Nile by a canal which also irrigates mango and palm groves to the south and west of the city. There is a desert climate with hot summers, cool winters, and only a few days rain per year, which minimizes drainage problems. The city was established in the second half of the last century as the headquarters of the Suez Canal Authority, but rather than having regular growth, it has had a chequered history—a series of employment booms coupled with periods of relative stagnation. The boom periods did not coincide with sufficient officially controlled or 'formal' building and thus substantial 'informal' areas have developed. Approximately 50% of the total housing stock is in such areas, most of which are on Government-owned land on the desert margins. This is permitted on the payment of an annual 'hekr' rent for the use of the land which gives limited security of tenure. Lack of security and generally low incomes has resulted in construction mainly by means of traditional mud-brick. This is regarded officially and locally as a second-rate building material despite its cheapness and climatic suitability.

The two project areas described in this chapter combine upgrading and sites and services and were both examples of 'informal' development. One, in the north of the

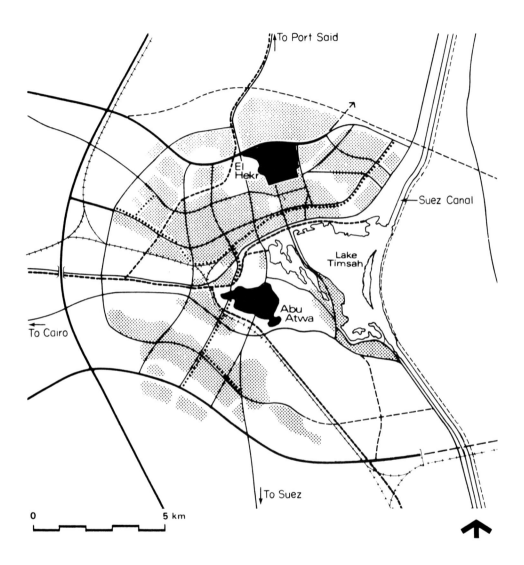

Figure 7.1   Location of project areas in the Ismailia structure plan

city, was in fact called El Hekr* and is the largest 'informal' low-income area in Ismailia. It has since been re-named 'Hai el Salam'* or 'District of Peace' in the aftermath of President Sadat's peace initiative. The other, more rural area to the south is called 'Abu Atwa' (Figure 7.1).

Ismailia today is still predominantly a service centre, with the Suez Canal Authority being the main employer. This is followed in importance by local government and canal-based industries such as small ship-building. In all, employment in Ismailia is growing at approximately 2% per annum as compared to a natural population increase of 2.5% (2.4% nationally). Table 7.1 shows household income figures for Ismailia city and El Hekr. To put these figures into context, the lowest 80% of the El Hekr population would be equivalent to the lowest 30% of the national urban population and 87% below the World Bank's urban poverty threshold of £E540/family.

Table 7.1   Income distribution for Ismailia and El Hekr (1977)

Annual household income	Ismailia (%)	El Hekr area (%)
Less than £E270	24%	60%
£E270–409	23%	22%
£E410–829	34%	16%
£E830–1400	11%	2%
More than £E1400	8%	—

Source: Ismailia Master Plan 1976, Ismailia Demonstration Projects, 1978. El Hekr figures from consultant's survey — Ismailia figures from central government CAPMAS.
1 £E = 1 US$ (1977)

The relevance of these figures to the projects was to set the broad parameters. The growth rate of the city meant that there was an annual requirement for 800–1000 housing units rising to 2500 units in the year 2000 when the city's population was planned to reach 600,000. The population of El Hekr was taken to be representative of families who could not be satisfied in the existing 'formal' housing systems. It was important that any new project should be accessible to people in these income groups, though not necessarily restricted to them. The development of the proposals was based on a thorough study of the existing situation and, in particular, on a study of the housing systems in operation.

HOUSING SYSTEMS

A 'housing system' is taken to mean all the activities and people involved in building, financing, renting, buying, living in, and controlling a particular form of housing provision. Understanding such a system requires a much deeper knowledge than can be gained from reading official statistics. In Ismailia the 'informal' sector comprises approximately 50% of the housing stock, with private 'formal' housing 30% and public and company housing together 20%. The relatively high proportion in the 'formal' sector

* 'El Hekr' will be used as the name of the area before implementation of the Project, 'Hai el Salam' after.

is due to the city's history—there was a large European population till the early 1950s and a very large public housing project was constructed after the 1967–74 war. The functioning of the housing system in Ismailia can best be understood by describing the main 'actors' involved, such as Government, private developers, and the people who require housing.

The Government's role is limited to the 'formal' sector. It involves control of the location and design of all houses in urban areas and the regulation of the supply of subsidized building materials. Government directly builds some 10–15% of the current annual housing units in the form of public rental housing, and it also controls rents of private dwellings. Subsidized building materials (cement, for example, is 50% of the free market price) are only available to those building to full standard on official subdivisions. Unfortunately, only middle- or upper-income groups can normally afford the land costs involved in this form of provision and thus low-income groups receive little or no assistance.

Central Government sets housing policy, and allocates funds to the Governorates, provincial administrations with wide delegated authority from Central Government. The Governorates are responsible for selecting sites and implementing projects, but have little freedom in how to use the funds. Since 1976 there have been changes in Government policy towards selling existing social housing, and making Government-built housing available for sale on subsidized terms. However, the problem persists of limited resources resulting in insufficient units being built.

Experiments in alternative approaches to housing on the lines of sites and services and upgrading programmes have been very limited. The first proposal for this approach was in 1976 in the Ismailia Master Plan. Shortly after this, the World Bank began working with the Egyptian Government to develop sites and services programmes in a small number of Egyptian cities. For a variety of reasons, probably mainly the lack of local conviction as to the desirability of the projects, these have moved only very slowly towards implementation. USAID have sponsored a large-scale programme with $100 million of aid for upgrading and core house development, but progress has been very slow and the heavy capital inputs and reliance on American standards is likely to limit replicability.

The contribution of middle- and upper-income groups building for ownership and rental is significant, in both the 'formal' and 'informal' sectors. This usually involves the owner of a plot building his own flat, and then building as many other flats as possible in the form of an apartment building. This type of building is known as an 'aimara'. The phenomenon of workers and professionals getting employment in the oil-rich Gulf countries and Saudi Arabia and returning with substantial savings, has led to a recent increase in this type of construction. Another result has been an increase of land prices, as the investment must be made on land which is owned, and preferably on land which has an officially approved subdivision.

The options open to low-income groups prior to the start of the Ismailia projects were: renting, either in a public housing project; in private 'formal' or 'informal' housing; or building on desert land with temporary permission through paying 'hekr' rent.

Public housing in Ismailia has long waiting lists. This is not surprising as rents are very heavily subsidized (less than 20% of the economic level) and even a low-income family will pay only about 10% of its monthly income in rent. Access to this form of housing is difficult as priority goes to certain groups, such as those born in the city.

Government workers, or newly married couples. Low-income immigrants to the city are unlikely to qualify.

In most cases the only options for rental in the private sector are the renting of one or two rooms or possibly a whole apartment or house in the 'informal' areas. In El Hekr, 25% of houses were rented to families at a rent equivalent to 20% of median family income for the area. Rooms, especially in low-quality buildings, cost about 5–10%

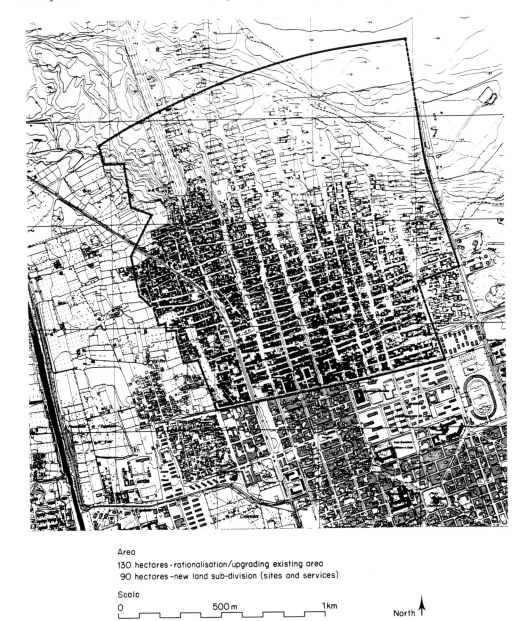

Area

130 hectares-rationalisation/upgrading existing area
 90 hectares-new land sub-division (sites and services)

Scale

0   500 m   1km

North

Figure 7.2   El Hekr: Hai el Salam project site, as existing (1977)

of monthly income and are thus a very important 'first step' in the housing ladder. The significant point is not the quality of accommodation, as it is usually seen as temporary, but rather the low level of rent which allows families to save. All the low-income families interviewed who had reached the stage of property ownership had started by renting.

For low-income families, ownership of property is only possible in the 'informal' areas of the city. A family might settle on the desert margin by building a wall and perhaps one room in mud-brick, the constituents of which are available locally. The area might be more than required, for example 300 m^2 with the idea of giving part to a relative or selling it to another settler. The alternative would be to buy land already claimed by someone else, but in a better position closer to the city. In either case, the land would not be really owned as the title would be the insecure 'hekr' lease. Investment is normally

Figure 7.3 Initial development of individual family houses in the north of El Hekr

Figure 7.4 Mixed family houses and rabaas in the middle of El Hekr

limited, partly by the incomes of the families concerned and partly by the lack of security. Where security has been given, as in the south of El Hekr, considerable investment has taken place.

The following housing types can be found in Ismailia:

Individual houses

These are the most common and about 80% of houses on the 'hekr' land are of this type. They are built on a plot averaging 100 m² and comprise rooms built round a courtyard. In 'informal' areas they are predominantly single-storey mud-brick or rammed earth; in 'formal' areas they are red brick, often with reinforced concrete frame, as there is a desire to later extend upwards. Examples are seen in Figure 7.4. Supply of this type of dwelling was restricted by lack of legally subdivided land.

Rabaas

These are also single-storey, and in many ways similar to individual houses except that they are primarily built for multi-occupancy, normally a number of single rooms and occasionally two- to three-room units. They are arranged round a courtyard or corridor, and share facilities. Occupants normally have lower incomes than those in individual

Figure 7.5   Aimaras and high density housing in the south of El Hekr

houses, and have lower levels of skills and job security. Supply of this type of dwelling depends on cheap land and building materials.

Aimaras

These have already been described. They are typically built incrementally when funds are available by the owner who normally lives in one flat and rents out the others. The majority of owners were born in Ismailia or had more than 30 years residence. This type of building is very important, as given the opportunity most urban Egyptians would build an 'aimara'. Examples are seen in Figure 7.5.

Public rental housing

Practically all public housing is of the five-storey walk-up pattern with two- to three-room flats of 30 to 50 m². Residents normally have low to moderate incomes and are mainly public employees.

   The conclusion from the Consultant's studies was that if the positive aspects of the 'informal' systems could be supported, and at the same time combined with the advantages of secure tenure and a planned subdivision, then the projects might point the way to a satisfactory and effective form of urban development.

OBJECTIVES

The objectives adopted for the projects were that proposals:

(a) must be relevant to *low-income groups* which form the majority of the population;
(b) must be capable of implementation with minimal subsidy;
(c) should be based on the best possible understanding of the existing situation in its social, cultural, economic, and physical aspects;
(d) should be able to be administered without the need for a high level of sophistication and continued support from outside experience;
(e) should be realistic; i.e. should be implementable within the existing administrative and executive structures and not require fundamental legal or organizational reform;
(f) should be implementable as soon as possible;
(g) must be capable of modification with experience and with changing external factors;
(h) should be replicable in form and content at other sites in the future.

The objectives attempted to define a project which could be the pattern for normal urban development and upgrading in Ismailia and in other cities with similar problems.

   An important aspect was that the projects should be accessible to low-income groups. This is very different from the more normal situation of designing a housing project only for the low-income groups. There are several benefits in including a wide range of income groups. New developments will not have the stigma of being 'low-income' by definition and in addition a more entrepreneurial approach can be taken to land development, increasing the income from part of the land and being better able to subsidize when desired through internal cross-subsidy. Nevertheless, it was always seen that the primary aim of the projects was to assist families with incomes of between £E180 and £E830 per annum (1977). The median household income of the 'target population' was £E290 per annum. The principal means by which these families would be able to participate was to make the costs and compulsory repayments as low as possible.

PROPOSALS

The Demonstration Projects involved the upgrading of existing low-income areas and the development of new housing areas primarily for low-income groups. Two areas of different characteristics were selected so as to test whether the approach would operate under different conditions. 'El Hekr', as has been mentioned, was an area of unplanned expansion onto the desert north of the city with adjacent open land which provided scope for expansion. 'Abu Atwa' was a collection of villages, originally rural and surrounded by agricultural land, situated 4 km south of the city. This chapter will concentrate on El Hekr, now the Hai el Salam project.

Design work started in 1977 and at the time of writing the project has been in implementation for 4 years. Abu Atwa started seriously 9 years later, thus the lessons which can be drawn from it are more limited.

The project areas of El Hekr covers some 226 ha, of which 132 ha were built up in 1976. Figure 7.2 shows the general street pattern. It can be seen that, in general, the main north-south streets are wide, respecting the street lines of the planned city to the south. The east–west streets, which had no such pattern to follow, have lines decided by the settlers themselves, similar to traditional village street patterns. The existing area has been developed over a period of some 30 years and is densely built up in the south, particularly in an area legalized by the City Council. In the rest of the area, houses are primarily one-storey and are built of mud-brick. Figures 7.3, 7.4, and 7.5 show development in the north, middle and south of the existing area in 1977, before the start of the project. They illustrate the incremental development of plots and the considerable investment which takes place, in particular when *secure tenure* is available. One of the main aims of the projects was to support and strengthen this process of incremental consolidation.

El Hekr was a relatively straightforward area. The land was nearly all owned by the Government; the ground conditions were reasonable, soft sand but with a low water-table and relatively flat. Tenure patterns were also favourable: 75% of houses were owner-occupied, a condition which is advantageous for an improvement programme as owners are more likely to invest in their own houses than are landlords. All these factors allowed the consultants to develop 'ideal' proposals which did not have to be greatly compromised in implementation. On other sites, and in other conditions, the details of the proposals might be quite different, though the approach used to develop them could be the same.

DEVELOPMENT OF THE PROPOSALS

In many ways the method of developing proposals is as important as the proposals themselves. The approach and methods are explained at length in a Manual,[1] prepared for use by the staff of the Hai el Salam and other development agencies but I will outline the main points here.

Our starting point was to try to understand the nature of the local housing system, particularly as it related to low-income families. Short 'scanning surveys' were conducted which dealt with basic elements such as family size, employment, and income and were followed by 15 household 'case studies' in each project area. Their purpose was to find out the housing history of the families; where they had lived before, where they wanted to live, what their problems were, and what were their priorities and aspirations. The number was not sufficient to be statistically significant, but provided valuable insight and information. For example, it was found that households put security of tenure as their highest priority, followed by piped water, roads, and sewerage.

The information on incomes from the scanning survey was used to define the income groups living in the project areas. These we defined as our 'target population' in the sense that we wanted to ensure that families in this income group could afford access to the project. This was vital for the upgrading areas if the existing population was not to be forced out. In the new development areas the aim was to cater for a mix of income groups, with low-income groups getting at least their proportional share. The surveys also attempted to find local representative organizations or key figures who could participate in developing the plans. However, none existed in El Hekr at that time. Later, during implementation, political groups were formed at a local level and these participated in decision-making. In Abu Atwa, large extended family groups exist and they have played an important role.

Combining upgrading and new development has many advantages. It allows relocation of families, normally unavoidable in upgrading, as close as possible to the original site. It allows the siting of social facilities, which may not be possible to install in densely settled existing areas, to be located in the new area to serve both. Utility networks similarly can serve old and new areas. New settlers can use services such as shops, builders' merchants, and skilled workers from the old areas and one agency can manage both programmes.

The population of El Hekr in 1977 was approximately 40,000 and consisted of low-income Government employees (51%), informal sector workers (30%), and small traders, as well as teachers and other professional employees who, in Egypt, have very low salaries.

For *upgrading areas* the proposals defined the street system and, within this, individual plot boundaries. The defined plot lines were then the basis for selling the land to the occupants. The price of land was set deliberately at a low level (£E2.25/m²) with repayments over 30 years to ensure that even those with very low incomes would be able to afford them. It was proposed that income from the sale of the land would be used to provide basic infrastructure, which in this case consisted of a sub-base course for roads to make them possible, water to standpipes at 150 m intervals, electricity, and street lighting. It would also pay for administration and services such as solid-waste collection and maintenance. Re-organized plot boundaries were designed to allow reasonable circulation and a minimum of demolition—less than 5% of existing buildings.

For *new settlement areas* the concept was to provide a basic level of infrastructure which could be paid for from the income derived from the sale of land. At the same time, land was priced so as to be affordable by the target income group. This meant that initially infrastructure would be limited to surveyed plots on streets which were levelled and surfaced to sub-base only. Water, power, and other services were proposed

Table 7.2   Levels of infrastructure for new settlers: total cost options and ability to pay
1 £E = 1 US$ (1977)

Level of infrastructure provision	Costs per plot (1977 £E)		
	72 m^2	108 m^2	135 m^2
	(% of families affording each level*)		
Level I (Minimum required for permanent plot occupation) administration, markers compensation, registration + pit latrines (incl. capitalised running costs) + standpipes + stage I local roads	153 (96%)	177 (93%)	194 (87%)
Level II Level I + electricity + landscaping	209 (87%)	235 (81%)	253 (78%)
Level III Level II + paved district streets + stage II local roads	247 (79%)	292 (72%)	324 (66%)
Level IV Level II (less pit latrines) + reticulated water network† + water connections + reticulated sewerage network + sewerage connections	351 (41%)	419 (30%)	469 (23%)
Level V Level IV plus: + paved district streets + stage II local roads	389 (35%)	476 (21%)	540 (15%)
Level VI Level V + trunk sewers + trunk water mains + paved access roads	502 (17%)	645 (11%)	751 (6%)
Level VII Level VI + service core	665 (10%)	808 (4%)	914 (1%)

* Affordability calculations include cost of infrastructure, land, and building.
† Excludes standpipe provision.

as in the upgrading areas. All infrastructure systems were designed so as to be capable of upgrading at a later date when resources permitted. For example, the main water lines were designed to allow individual house connections when and if mains drainage is installed. Similarly, street and plot layouts were designed to minimize the costs of utilities provision, and to maximize the proportion of the total site area allocated to individual plots. Layouts were then tested against the affordability of the target group. We attempted to get a balance between what was economic for the project in terms of infrastructure costs per square metre of plot and what was economic and socially acceptable in terms of the development of the plots themselves. The levels of infrastructure provision that we examined are shown in Table 7.2, together with the percentage of households of the target group who could afford these in addition to constructing basic shelter. The table shows clearly that without any external source of funds, only the options without water-borne sewerage were affordable. The figures were based on the assumption that 20% of gross household income was available for shelter, including land, building, and infrastructure. The future possibility of funds being available for drainage was not known, so plots were planned to use on-plot cesspits or pit latrines. It was decided that it was preferable to reduce costs by minimizing the initial levels of infrastructure provision rather than minimizing the plot dimensions. Infrastructure can be later ugraded but the plot dimensions, once fixed, would be very difficult to change. This philosophy led to the selection of the level of infrastructure provision which is outlined in Table 7.2 as Level III. This was considered to overcome the main problems of health by providing clean water; it improves access by providing basic roads and gave security of tenure.

This approach was easily accepted politically as it is quite a normal situation. Table 7.2 shows that insistence on mains drainage would have excluded 59% of the target population, and if a service core (water and drainage connections to a slab) had been provided, 90% could not have afforded to pay the full costs. Calculations were similar for upgrading areas but a smaller amount of money was estimated for the construction of the dwelling.

Proposed plot sizes and shapes were designed to allow the patterns of use observed on existing plots and, at the same time, to be economic to service. Plots can be developed with one front room as a shop or workshop, rooms can be rented, and additional floors can be built to allow residents to supplement their incomes. The number of plots in different size ranges (Table 7.3) was arrived at by assessing affordability and expected family size. The expected incremental development of plots is illustrated in Figure 7.6 and the layout in Figure 7.7.

The pricing of plots was arrived at by a combination of ensuring that they would be affordable by the target population and raising sufficient money to pay for the services. This was achieved partly by pricing according to commercial potential, as illustrated in Figure 7.7. Class A plots were located on wider streets of good commercial potential, Class B on narrower streets, and Class C on semi-private lanes or 'haras'. Corner plots also attracted higher prices. In addition, it was proposed that a limited number of plots on important roads be sold by auction as 'concession plots'. The higher price plots would allow an internal cross-subsidy.

The case studies have revealed that lack of security of land tenure was a major concern amongst the existing population. Accordingly, 'delayed freehold' tenure was proposed with freehold being given after 5 years, dependent on the project conditions being met.

Table 7.3   Hai el Salam (El Hekr) project: key figures

Project area

Population 1978	37,000
Population 2000	90,000
Improvement area	132 ha
New development area	94 ha
Total area	226 ha
Plots (total, new areas)	3181 ha

Plot sizes

Low cost (new areas)
Small: 25% provision

Dimensions (m)	6 × 12	6 × 15	7.5 × 12
Area (m²)	72	90	90

Medium: 65% provision

Dimensions (m)	6 × 18	7.5 × 15	7.5 × 18	9 × 12	9 × 15
Area (m²)	108	112.5	135	108	135

Large: 10% provision

Dimensions (m)	9 × 18	12 × 12
Area (m²)	162	144

Concession plots

Dimensions (m)	15 × 24	18 × 24	24 × 24
Area (m²)	360	432	576

Plot prices (£E/m²)

Class	Ordinary	Corner
A	10.00	12.00
B	4.00	4.50
C	2.25	2.50
Concession plots	Open market price	
		1 £E = 1 US$ (1977)

Payment terms

Class	Down-payment	Repayment period (years)
A	100%	—
B	50%	5
C	25%	5 + longer at discretion of manager
Concession	100%	—

Infrastructure	*Initial provision*	*Final provision*
Water supply	Public standpipes at 150–200 m intervals	Individual connections
Sewerage	Pit latrines	Full sewerage system
Electricity	Individual connection (optional)	No change
	Street lighting	No change

Roads: (right of way)

Arterial 20 m	Surfaced (DBST)*	Paved (asphaltic concrete)
District 15 m	Surfaced	Paved (asphaltic concrete)
Local 10/15 m	Gravel	Surfaced
Access 6/10 m	Earth	Gravel/earth

* DBST = double bitumen surface treatment.

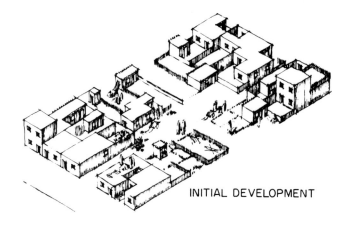

INITIAL DEVELOPMENT

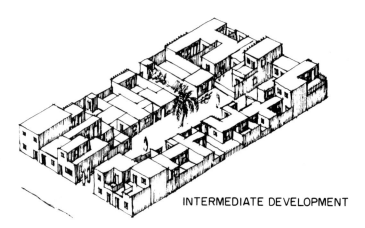

INTERMEDIATE DEVELOPMENT

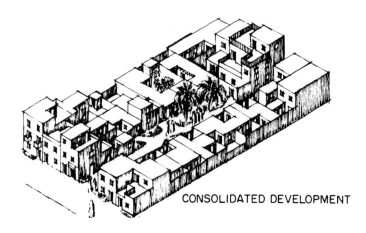

CONSOLIDATED DEVELOPMENT

Figure 7.6   Incremental development of a typical cluster as planned

This was introduced as a safeguard against speculation, which is an obvious danger when plots are sold below the market price.

Planning was based on a hierarchy of semi-private areas or 'haras' within blocks, neighbourhoods with sub-centre, and the new main centre to serve old and new areas. Sub-centres have higher order services such as health clinics and preparatory schools and the main centre has the large Friday mosque, polyclinic, social centre, and market. Shopping is mainly catered for by the ability of anyone to open a shop on their plot. Plots near the centres are, however, planned so as to be able to be more efficiently used for commerce. Only the market building includes purpose-built shop units. Small workshops can be operated on residential plots, but 'bad neighbour' uses are catered for in special areas.

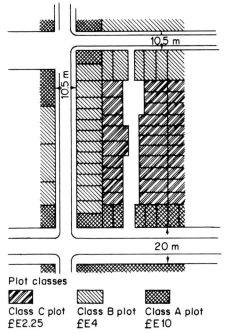

Figure 7.7   Plot layout classes and pricing

IMPLEMENTATION: THE FIRST 4 YEARS

In principle, we did not want to propose setting up yet another new governmental unit. However, there was no existing organization which could combine the range of skills necessary with the powers of buying and selling land and investing the proceeds in infrastructure. For this reason we proposed setting up a semi-autonomous land development agency. This would have a board of directors who would represent the main departments dealing with land development in the Governorate and be under the ultimate control of the Governor. The structure of the Hai el Salam Agency is shown in Figure 7.8.

The projects were designed to be self-financing, but even self-financing projects require some capital to get started. What was proposed was a modest £60,000 sterling grant for Hai el Salam (plus £40,000 for Abu Atwa), from the British Government to be used

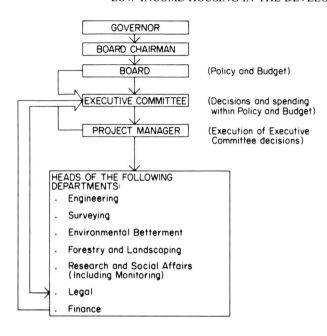

Figure 7.8   Hai el Salam: administrative structure

Table 7.4   Progress in delivery of plots in the Hai el Salam (El Hekr) project: October 1978 to March 1982

	Oct. 1978– Sept. 1979	Oct. 1979– Sept. 1980	Oct. 1980– Sept. 1981	Oct. 1981– Mar. 1982	Total Mar. 1982
New plots	314	425	950	510	2199
Plots in existing areas	356	1020	1314	310	3000
Re-location plots	196	254	12	—	462
Total	866	1699	2276	820	5661

to carry out initial site preparation and the building of an office in Hai el Salam. With this start, land sales and the raising of loans on the security of the land would allow funding of the infrastructure programme described below.

In October 1978 the Egyptian Ministry of Housing and the British Government funded us to provide a small technical assistance team to set up the proposed Project Agency. The Governorate fully supported the proposals and even before the formal agreement was signed, had carried out the legal steps necessary to set up the Agency and transfer the land. The inception capital allowed us to get work started on site, and the fact that we, as the consultants, had our own office and vehicles meant that we could move things quickly at a stage when the new Agency barely existed.

The 'vital statistics' or key figures describing the project are given in Table 7.3. Table 7.4 shows the progress that has been made in allocating new plots and in carrying out

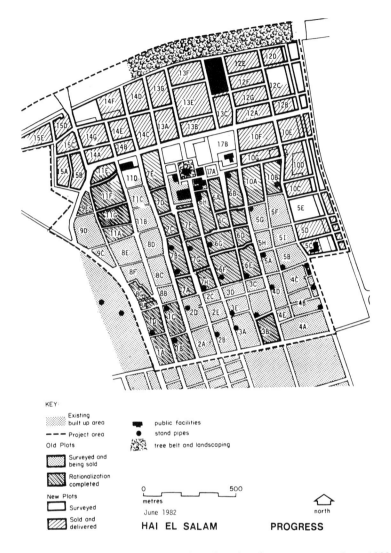

KEY:

Existing
built up area

– – – Project area

Old Plots

Surveyed and
being sold

Rationalization
completed

New Plots

Surveyed

Sold and
delivered

public facilities

stand pipes

tree belt and landscaping

0   500

metres

June 1982

HAI EL SALAM

north

PROGRESS

Figure 7.9   Hai el Salam: Community Plan showing progress to June 1982

the upgrading programme. Improving efficiency of the Project Agency is evident from
the figures. The self-financing nature of the projects is also a very important feature.
In 1980/81 the Agency's income was more than £E1 million and expenditure on capital
works, services and administration was £E700,000. Reduced income in future years will
be balanced by a change of emphasis from capital works to administration and
maintenance.

These expenditures, of course, relative only to the provision of infrastructure and
other services by the Agency. The bulk of expenditure is carried out by the settlers
themselves. A survey carried out in August 1982 estimated that investment in building
in the new areas in the first 3½ years amounted to £E6.25 million. The Agency's
expenditure in this same period was £E1.8 million. (Note: these figures should not be

used to determine average expenditure/plot as investment is much higher on the more expensive plots.)

Figure 7.9 shows the physical development that has been achieved during the period October 1978 to June 1982.

The building of houses has been by a combination of self-help, the use of skilled workers for tasks such as concrete pouring, bricklaying and carpentry and the use of small local contractors. The proportion of each depends on the income of the owner. If owners can possibly afford it, they try to build in red brick with a reinforced concrete frame, as vertical expansion is seen as future accommodation for the family or as a source of income.

CHANGES BETWEEN THE ORIGINAL PROPOSALS
AND THEIR IMPLEMENTATION

The formulation of proposals is a very important process, but what matters in the end is what is implemented. The changes which were made between the original proposals and what happened on the ground are revealing as they show the different forces at work.

Changes took place at two stages. The first was when the detailed proposals, in particular the rules for settlers, were discussed with the technical committee of the Governorate. The main change was in the application of standard building regulations which are relatively strict in Egypt (at least on paper). We were concerned that this would make it difficult for families with low incomes to comply, and we managed to obtain a concession that families could build in temporary materials, i.e. the traditional mud-brick, though final freehold title to the land would not be granted until buildings met the full regulations.

Changes were also made during implementation and the pressure for them came from many directions. They are summarized here with details of who wanted the change and the effects on the original proposals.

(a) Initial building with 'temporary' materials discouraged

The Governor was concerned that the new part of the city should not look like a slum. The desire to build in modern materials is echoed by the settlers themselves, but slowness of building amongst those with low incomes supports the original study findings that modern materials are too expensive for immediate construction without loans. For this reason, a loan scheme is now being negotiated using central government funds. Approximately, 10% of 'C' plots are still built with mud-brick and this is still permitted for special cases.

(b) Land prices increased and payment terms made harder

We originally proposed that the lowest land price should be £E1.76. This level was based on our calculations of affordability, and was considerably higher than the then current price of government land (when sold) of £E0.5 m². At the same time, the market price with freehold tenure would have been £E10–15 m², a price level which our target population could not afford. Urban land prices in Egypt are high, partly due to the desire of those who have been working the Gulf Countries to invest, and partly to the shortage of legally subdivided land. In this context the increase by the Agency Board of the lowest price to £E2.25 m^2 was not greatly significant, especially as inflation has been running at about 20% per annum. The payback period was later reduced from our original proposals of up to 30 years to 10 and then to 5 years and, with this, down-payments were introduced of 25% for 'C' plots (the cheapest), 50% for 'B' plots and 100% payment for 'A' plots. The argument was that this would give the Agency an adequate cash flow in these first years without resorting to loans—and this proved to be the case. There is a reluctance to deal with loans and high interest rates, partly on religious grounds and partly a left-over from a long period of a centrally controlled economy. The effect of these changes on the families themselves has been limited—but this is only because the purchase price for 'C' plots is low and the effect of inflation has made it lower still. For political reasons, plot prices have not been increased.

The project has been able to weather these changes primarily because the levels of compulsory payments for land purchase is low. If there had been an ambitious infrastructure programme, or if core housing had been constructed, then affordability would have been seriously affected. As it is the compulsory payments are still affordable, and there have been practically no defaulters. Greater initial payments have, however, almost certainly slowed the rate of building for poorer families.

(c) Interest rate decreased from 7% to 5%

We proposed 7% but this was reduced to 5% by the Finance Committee related to a general dislike of credit and normal Government credit of 3%. Its effects on the cash flow were minimized by increasing the proportion of down-payments and payment in cash for B and A class plots.

(d) Water and sewerage to be provided by USAID

As part of a large aid package to Egypt, USAID funded design studies for water and sewerage for Ismailia. These include a high-quality water supply and water-borne sewerage system for both Hai el Salam and Abu Atwa. The original designs of the demonstration projects allow efficient provision of these services, and they will now be provided at subsidized rates from Central Government, and USAID approximately 6 years after the start of the implementation of the project.

(e) Minimum plot width increased from 6 m to 7.5 m

Adverse comments from settlers on the ease of developing 6 m frontage plots led to the adoption of 7.5 m frontages as the minimum. The argument for 6 m had been on the basis of minimizing infrastructure costs. The change did not make a significant difference to overall costs per plot. On the other hand, it did make an improvement to the development options of the plot itself. This aspect has improved the popularity of the project further and thus also has improved its replicability, as social and political support is vital.

**(f) Irregular shape of small streets or 'semi-private
spaces' rejected in favour of straight streets**

The original layout plans had the low cost plots on lanes of 6–9 m width designed to
allow play and communal use, but to discourage through traffic. They were patterned
on traditional layouts. Agency surveyors and other staff argued that people preferred
straight streets as these seen to be legal and 'modern'. The existence of both types will
present someone in the future with an interesting research subject, though it is doubtful
if it will make a significant difference to the lifestyles of the people living there.

**(g) Selection of settlers was originally proposed to be
based on income and need. This was partially rejected
on grounds of practicality**

The selection of settlers on the basis of income was rejected by the Agency committee
responsible on the grounds that it would be impractical to check effectively. Criteria
adopted were the length of residence and a requirement that the applicant should not
own any land or property. Residents of El Hekr are given first priority, with residents
elsewhere in Ismailia second priority. Legally, it is difficult for those residents outside
Ismailia to be selected. Applicants themselves select the plot category and size and thus
the price. This is basically sound provided the criteria are reasonable, pricing is sensitive,
and there are sufficient plots. The Ismailia criterion worked against recent migrants but
priority for those living in El Hekr was a positive discrimination for low-income groups.
Monitoring is necessary to decide if an income cut-off, say for the cheapest plots, is
required.

(h) The original organizational proposals were modified

In effect, the structure of the Agency evolved, and the administrative and financial rules
were changed officially during the second year. Staffing was built up progressively from
a low initial level.

In general, the changes which have been made have not fundamentally changed the
project's ability to meet its objectives, including replicability, though some have made
it more difficult. There are a number of forces acting on the project which are probably
found in many countries. There is the desire for a new area of the city to be beautiful
or modern, which goes against an incremental project built mainly by low-income people.
Our defence has been to emphasize the fully serviced end-state. Also, our design, which
has the more expensive plots on the main streets, helps to give the project a more
acceptable appearance. As consultants, we have tried to support the use of mud-brick,
but we have also had to be pragmatic as over-emphasis on this would have had negative
results for the project as a whole. Another important point is that, from the start of
implementation, the responsibility of the project was with the Project Agency. This was
something we insisted on, as we wanted it to be a 'local' project. Thus, while we might
argue against changes, we had to accept the decisions of the Board. It was certainly
more important to get the project running in a way which could be accepted locally
than to insist that everything should be carried out precisely as we had originally planned.

EVALUATION

I would like to examine here how well the projects have met their objectives, how the Technical Assistance Programme has worked, and what lessons can be learnt. In order to avoid repetition, I will discuss here only the most important aspects — the relevance of the projects to low-income groups and their replicability.

The project has succeeded in keeping the price of land, and thus the amount of compulsory payments, low. This has been essential for low-income families as changes to repayment terms, residence conditions, and rules for building have all tended to act against their interests. Efforts are being made to introduce a loan scheme, with or without subsidy, as this will help considerably in the rate of construction. Without this there may be pressure on allocatees to illegally re-sell their plots. It is difficult to argue against the right of allocatees to re-sell if they genuinely cannot afford to build, but excessive pressure in this direction can be reduced by providing alternative possibilities for middle- and upper-income groups.

The replicability of the projects is an extremely important objective, given the concept of 'demonstration' projects. Carrying out similar projects requires: the will or desire to carry them out, the technical capacity, and the availability of land and/or finance. The development of similar projects requires that all are satisfied.

The desire to carry out the projects developed over a period of 18 months close contact with local government. It is now accepted in Ismailia that projects such as Hai el Salam and Abu Atwa are part of the means of developing the city. Local replicability thus exists. Groups from elsewhere in Egypt have visited the project, but there would be considerable advantages in wider distribution of information and a training programme to help adapt the experience. Demonstration projects require positive promotion if they are to be effective as such.

The projects were designed so as not to involve sophisticated techniques. Routines were developed with staff seconded from local government who adapted their experience from previous jobs. Where the projects differ from normal Egyptian practice is in the objective of making legal building land accessible to low-income groups, and in the use of the value of the land to pay for provision of infrastructure and maintenance. The technical assistance programme has tried to build up local staff capacity in three main ways:

(a) 'on job' training, with the consultants working with Agency staff on specific tasks;
(b) 'formal' training, the holding of a regular weekly planning seminar where the ideas behind the practical day-to-day work can be explained and discussed;
(c) the production of the 'Urban Projects Manual' which explains the process of designing of project, illustrates options, and explains relevant techniques.

The objective of implementation being possible with minimal subsidy has been met with great success. In Hai el Salam, 3000 existing plots have been given legal tenure, 2200 new plots have been sold, 18 km of roads built, 28 standpipes installed, 5 new public buildings, built, and 100,000 m^2 of tree belt planted. Employment has been created, not only in construction but also in many small workshops which have been established on plots. This has been carried out with modest 'inception capital' project preparation costs and technical assistance from the British Government and the allocation of the land by the Ismailia Governorate. This is extremely important as the limitations of current Government policies are due to lack of funds.

CONCLUSIONS

In Egypt, as in most countries, there is a considerable gap between what is desirable and thus forms a part of Government policy and what is practical, given the limited resources available. Some 80% of Egypt's urban housing is 'informal' or built outside the legal controls. We attempted to understand the operation of the informal system to see how we could build on its strengths. At the same time, we wanted to overcome the drawbacks of the 'informal' system by Government undertaking what it was well fitted to do—the subdivision of land, allocation of legal tenure, and the provision of services. In addition, we were able to use the land value to provide services, and by internal cross-subsidy could make a substantial part of the land available at affordable prices.

The projects have, in fact, 'formalized' the 'informal' sector in Ismailia within their areas. This process is inevitably a compromise. Higher standards are demanded and some flexibility is lost. However, there is a realistic acceptance by officials that the standards will be reached incrementally. There have been enormous gains in the availability of cheap legal land and in the improvement of infrastructure and services in the upgrading areas. In 1981, 1000 new plots were allocated in Hai el Salam alone compared to household formation in the same year of approximately 900 families in Ismailia. A very significant impact is thus being made in resolving the city's housing problem.

An aim of the Demonstration Projects was to give central government a working example of an alternative approach to housing. Has the demonstration had any effect? This is very difficult to answer objectively, but the probability is that it has. A number of senior government officials and politicians have visited Hai el Salam, and at the time of writing the President and the Minister responsible for Housing had recently made public statements that government housing support would concentrate on the provision of infrastructure and finance. There is, of course, considerable inertia in the system, and many more blocks of government housing will be built, but progress is encouraging.

The use of the aid funds was primarily for design, technical assistance, and training, with only limited, though vital, expenditure on inception capital. This means that the real emphasis was in building ongoing institutions. Local control of finance meant that decisions could not be dictated by the aid agency, and though this allowed the changes described earlier it had the very positive effect of making the projects *local* rather than imposed and giving the new agencies real independence.

The allocation of the land to the Hai el Salam project without charge was, of course, a considerable advantage and represents in strict economic terms a major subsidy. In terms, however, of the normal distribution of government land in Egypt, allocation at a zero or nominal charge is common and so, in these terms, subsidy was seen locally as minimal. An important aim of the project was to provide an alternative means of managing urban development to the then existing dual system of highly subsidized government housing and unserviced squatter areas. In neither of these systems was there any official pricing of government land beyond the 'hekr' lease system to squatters which implied very low land value. The project represented a position between the very low

Figure 7.10   Recent housing construction in the new development area of Hai el Salam

controlled economy official value of land and the much higher free market value of freehold land.

Where full market prices must be paid for land, are lessons from Ismailia still valid? I would maintain that they are, but that some direct subsidy might be necessary in addition to cross-subsidy to reduce the lowest-price plots to an affordable level. Much obviously depends on prevailing land costs. If the alternative to a Hai el Salam type of project was public housing — then land would still have to be purchased — and the final densities achievable (in Egypt) would be no higher.

The Hai el Salam Project included the sale of prime plots by auction and the substantial income from these has made local government much more aware of market values of land. We have now helped the Governorate set up the Ismailia Planning and Development Agency which controls development in the Governorate and promotes and carries out development in certain areas assigned to it using similar powers as those given to the Hai el Salam Agency. Projects range from money-generating high-income subdivisions to industrial, recreation, upgrading, and sites and services. Cross-financing and cross-subsidy between projects are being used as very effective tools for promoting development while meeting social objectives. The Agency is now co-ordinating development in all key growth areas, but has not tried to make its overall control water-tight — so that if it cannot meet demands effectively 'informal' development can still play a role.

The main area of financial assistance was in the provision of consultant time for the design and technical assistance for implementation. The Overseas Development Administration of the British Government financed the foreign costs and the Egyptian Government financed local costs for a team of seven for 12 months for design and three persons for 3½ years for technical assistance. This represented a significant financial input, though modest when compared with most projects of this scale.

The Ismailia Demonstration Projects and Technical Assistance Programme with modest expenditure and sensitivity to local conditions are, in my view, making a significant impact on local housing conditions and provide an example of an approach which can significantly affect national policy.

NOTE

1.   *Urban Projects Manual*, edited by Forbes Davidson and Geoff Payne for Clifford Culpin and Partners. Liverpool University Press, 1983.

Low-income Housing in the Developing World
Edited by G. K. Payne
© 1984 John Wiley & Sons Ltd

Chapter 8

Mexico: Beyond Sites and Services

Peter M. Ward[1]

INTRODUCTION

In this chapter my aim is two-fold. First I wish to present a case that conventional wisdoms regarding the provision of access to land for low-income groups via strategies such as sites and services, core units, etc., are an inadequate response for planning authorities. Yet the encouragement received from international funding agencies, the respectability accorded such schemes in the academic and planning literature, and their inherent suitability for politicians who find technical solutions to socioeconomic problems much easier to implement, have combined to elevate the role of these schemes to a level beyond which planners rarely look. This, I argue, renders them largely impotent in making any significant contribution to the housing needs of low-income groups. Second, I wish to explore possible ways in which planners might broaden their influence over low-cost land-development processes. Intervention at the level of the supply of land, even where it is only partially successful, is likely to have far greater repercussions than formal sites and services type schemes. I begin with an overview of urbanization and unauthorized settlement. I conclude that planners should be encouraged to think more widely than purely 'technical' solutions to what are, after all, invariably socioeconomic and politically induced problems.

URBAN GROWTH, UNAUTHORIZED SETTLEMENT, AND THE LIMITATIONS OF SITES AND SERVICES

In 1930 only one-third of the national population of Mexico lived in urban settlements of more than 2500 people: by 1978 this proportion had increased to 62% (SAHOP*, 1978). Moreover, the urban population was unequally distributed. In 1978, at one extreme, Mexico City with its 13.2 million contained 20% of the total population: at the other, there were 95,000 population centres each with less than 2500 people.

The 1978 National Urban Development Plan sought to integrate the national population into 11 regional systems through a range of actions to stimulate the growth of some urban areas, while attempting to consolidate and regulate expansion elsewhere.

---

* See list of acronyms at end of this chapter.

With respect to Mexico City, which grew from just over 2 million in 1950 to 8.7 million in 1970 and 13.2 million by 1978, the Plan proposed to restrict future increase through the reduction of natural population growth; by the dissuasion of would-be migrants from moving to the capital, and by actively moving people and jobs out to other cities.

The size of Mexico City and its rapid growth has meant that planners are sensitive about the promotion of new housing programmes in the metropolitan area for fear of appearing to encourage further movement to the capital. Partly for this reason, but also because of relatively high costs of land, there have been no large-scale sites and service projects in Mexico City. Rather urban policies have aimed to curtail new settlement and to consolidate and upgrade existing low-income areas (DDF, 1980).

The growth of unauthorized settlements

The majority of the urban poor in Mexico City live in unauthorized settlements, either as 'owner'-occupiers or, increasingly, as renters in small informal tenements and as 'sharers' living in plots with kinsmen or friends. The high cost of purchasing land in authorized and fully serviced subdivisions has meant that unauthorized settlement without services on marginal land provides the only affordable means to land acquisition and home ownership for the poor.

Unauthorized settlement is usually premeditated and planned by agents with clear interests in sponsoring such developments—real-estate sharks, politicians, local leaders, mafioso racketeers, even directors of housing agencies (Burgess, 1982; Connolly, 1982). In the context of this chapter, this is an important point as it is only through being aware of these interests that an accurate appraisal of the impact induced by the intervention of planners becomes possible.

Broadly speaking there are three mechanisms whereby unauthorized settlements are formed. First, and very important in the Mexican context, is the illegal subdivisions of marginal lands for the sale of unserviced plots. The failure or unwillingness of subdivider companies to provide adequate services and infrastructure meant that they were illegal and led, eventually, to residents demanding that the government intervene. It is rare for the authorities to impose legal penalties against the entrepreneurs and most have got off with their profits intact (Gilbert and Ward, 1982).

Secondly, invasions of land occur less frequently and are usually stimulated by political motives, intra-government in-fighting, or as a last resort by squatters whose claims to a parcel of land are being resisted.

Thirdly, land transfers occur when rights of occupancy are ceded to low-income residents. Especially important in Mexico is the illegal sale of community land over which peasants have use rights only. These *ejidos* (agricultural communities) were established after the Agrarian Reform of 1917, usually through a redistribution of land from large private farms. The beneficiaries (*ejidatarios*) now often find themselves controlling land the agricultural value of which is minimal but which is in great demand due to the expansion of a nearby town. Plots are therefore sold off by individual payment when the authorities intervene to legalize land-holdings through the expropriation and compensation for the 'loss' of their land.

The growth of unauthorized settlement is, therefore, a complex business and each case is likely to be the outcome of a carefully orchestrated attempt to further the interests of the agents involved, be they land-developers, vote-catchers, radicals, do-gooders,

Ministers, unions, etc. Moreover unauthorized settlements have also benefited many interest groups in addition to the developers and residents. The building materials industry has discovered an expanding market from self-builders; transporters and local retailers of those materials also benefit; government officials benefit by the proliferation of jobs and empires and may also receive bribes for condoning illegal practices and the provision of planning permission. Sometimes they derive political support from patronage links developed with residents. These considerations highlight the diverse functions that unauthorized settlement plays for a wide range of interests.

State intervention in housing

Prior to 1970 Government initiatives to tackle the problem of low-income housing needs resembled that of most Third World nations. In effect little was done. The 166,000 housing units constructed between 1964 and 1970 fell a long way below the growth in demand for that period (Garza and Schteingart, 1978). Moreover, this housing often proved too expensive for the majority of the working classes (Evans, 1974). The response to unauthorized settlement was *ad hoc*. Occasionally lands were expropriated and resold to occupants; some services were installed, usually in response to patron-client relations established between unauthorized settlements and government officials. There was no formal policy or programme.

In response to rising social unrest during the late 1960s and the growing scale of the housing problem, State intervention increased from 1970 onwards (Ward, 1981a; Connolly, 1982). Agencies were established with specific responsibilities for land legalization programmes, service installation, low-cost house-building and finance although the budgets allocated to many were derisory (Ward, 1981a). Nevertheless, the record of house construction was substantially improved by the creation of an agency (INFONAVIT) financed by a 5% levy on the wage bill, paid by employers. In only 2 years INFONAVIT constructed more than the total number of dwellings built under the earlier Housing Financing Programme. More importantly, it was at a cost that could be afforded by the majority.

Since 1976 sites and services and self-build 'solutions' have been encouraged for several reasons: (a) the natural impetus induced by a new administration under Mexico's 6-year executive cycle; (b) the rising scale of the problem; (c) the need to integrate the poor into the fiscal base as rate and taxpayers; (d) growing sophistication of expertise in the area of housing and settlement planning, encouraged by international aid institutions.

A single agency has had primary responsibility for the provision of low-cost housing through sites and services schemes. Between 1978 and 1981 INDECO constructed, or assisted in finance of, approximately 20,000 sites and services plots each year. Despite having been singled out in the National Housing Programme as being responsible for the promotion of some 150,000 sites and service plots annually, the agency never received adequate resources to make any significant impact upon total demand. INDECO estimates that it met only 10% of the demand in urban population centres of over 15,000 inhabitants. INDECO plots of 120 m² are considerably smaller than those usually acquired through invasion, illegal transfer, or sale. They come with a bare minimum of services: water, electricity, sometimes drainage, and usually with unpaved or unkerbed streets.

Limitations of orthodox site and services

Sites and services in Mexico have had only limited success generally for two principal reasons. First, they ignore the fact that processes and costs are likely to alter dramatically *once a policy existed*. In the case of sites and services schemes participants have to pay regular instalments for the land, for initial service installation, and for services consumed, as well as contribute regularly to local rates and taxes. At the same time each household is expected to invest in home-building and mutual-aid improvement schemes to the settlement. Costs are considerable *from the outset* in sites and services projects, though attempts were made by INDECO to alleviate this through a sliding scale of repayments that increased in absolute terms as wage inflation pushed up incomes. Also, the poorest groups could defer payment of a deposit. In order to make available some capital for the purchase of building materials INDECO offered credits as part of the overall plot price. Materials were usually available from a local INDECO building materials yard established specifically for the purpose of supplying project beneficiaries. Despite these efforts to ensure that INDECO participants would be able to consolidate their homes quickly, little improvement was observed (INDECO, 1982a). This may be explained by the considerable initial cost and by declining levels of real wages (INDECO, 1982a). In my opinion it also related to poor implementation procedures as the agency failed to insist that beneficiaries immediately occupy their plots. In some projects, therefore, only 50% of plots were occupied 1½ years after they were initiated. This meant that there could be no effective community participation in collaborative works aimed at improving settlement conditions.

The second reason for the failure of sites and services schemes in Mexico was the assumption that past procedures would resemble those in the future. This ignores the fact that in Mexico employment opportunities, real wages, the costs of construction materials, and the nature of the land market have changed, usually to the detriment of successful home improvement or consolidation. Evidence from Mexico suggests that sites and services 'solutions' are no longer a cheap alternative. Increased economic hardship for low-income families reduced their ability to generate a surplus which could be directed towards investment in house consolidation (Ward, 1978). In short, sites and services schemes became too costly for their target populations. Faced by this dilemma and the reluctance of the Mexican government to intervene to a significant extent in the land market the 'cloth' had to be cut accordingly. Plot size was reduced and/or sites were provided with *minimal* services. Furthermore, the cost of land in some urban centres was so high as to rule out sites and services in those locations. In 1981–82 INDECO had proposals to reduce the average plot size in some cases from 120 to 60 m². However, INDECO's disbandment in 1982 meant that the proposal was never implemented. Nevertheless INDECO's shortage of capital meant that in some projects basic services could only be installed gradually as money was recovered from residents (INDECO, 1982b). This compounded the vicious circle whereby residents did not wish to move to their plots until services had been installed.

That most INDECO projects were barely affordable by the very poor in Mexico is demonstrated by the fact that sometimes as many as one-half of the project residents earned more than the maximum target population threshold of 2.5 times the minimum salary, and that regional project staff often gave preference to regular salaried workers whom they thought more likely to be able to make the repayments (INDECO, 1982a).

In two projects for which detailed evaluations are available, more than one-half of the beneficiaries were salaried workers, despite their supposedly being beyond the remit of the agency.

Traditional approaches

Planners are generally in a weak position in Mexico, and they attempt to provide technical solutions that fail to compete with informal land development processes. The reluctance of the government to intervene directly in the land market in any significant way means that in the absence of heavy subsidy it is usually impossible to offer plots in suitable locations that are competitive with other agents, who, for one reason or another, are able to undercut the costs of government programmes. Land invasions, illegal sales, and land transfers invariably provide a cheaper alternative to land sales sponsored by housing agencies. Under these circumstances the best that planners can do is offer plots of land in distant locations or tailor down the quality of the plots that they offer. In short, planners are in a weak position because they are unable to compete with many unauthorized settlement entrepreneurs; because they are unable to apply sanctions against developers who promote land sales outside the law; and because they are usually perceived as the body responsible for picking up the bill for servicing and legalization once the land has been alienated.

A SPECTRUM OF PLANNING INTERVENTIONS

In 1978, at a time when political conditions seemed relatively favourable for a significant state intervention in the field of human settlement planning, I joined a team in the Mexican Ministry of Human Settlements and Public Works which had considerable expertise in unauthorized settlement planning. The Director and several Department heads had worked previously in government, specifically on land regularization, self-help, commercialization and cross-subsidization housing schemes. We agreed that formal technical solutions such as sites and services schemes offered only a partial answer to the housing shortage. In any case our concern was with the elaboration of urban development plans and responsibility for housing development of this nature rested outside our Department. Unauthorized settlement covered large areas of land in the specific cities in which we worked, and we collected detailed information about the processes whereby these settlements were created. Specifically we wanted to know what were the interests that underpinned such settlement, to whom they were connected, how they were articulated and, critically, what opportunity existed for planning authorities to intervene *formally* or *informally* to affect the outcome?

We began by investigating the processes of unauthorized settlement development. We complemented existing knowledge of the academic literature with case studies. Archival work in the Agrarian Reform Ministry allowed us to sketch out many of the mechanisms whereby *ejido* land was illegally subdivided and sold, usually for low-income housing purposes. In addition we investigated the legal framework (laws, statutes, regulations, dispensations, etc.) that related to human settlement issues. These included the provisions covering *ejido* lands and expropriations. Similarly, by studying fiscal legalisation for low-income settlements we began to understand the procedures of registration, cadastral assessment, tax levies, and the impact that careful manipulation of these might have.

Once we were confident that we understood the processes whereby illegal land development took place we outlined all the possible ways in which the state could intervene. At this stage no allowance was made for whether or not the action proposed was feasible (technically or politically). The idea was to generate a range of alternatives. Only then did we begin to explore the viability of each and to examine the conditions under which they might be operable. Several examples of possible intervention are outlined briefly below. They are, drawn from a range to exemplify the *types* of response which we envisaged that planners concerned to affect low-income settlement opportunities might adopt.

(a) State-sponsored land purchase

This scheme involves government acquisition through purchase and expropriation of land for residential development. In the long term 'land bank' policies are logical as land can usually be acquired relatively cheaply. The drawbacks are obvious: scarce capital is tied up unproductively and a return on the investment is delayed many years. Similarly it yields no short-term benefit to housing supply. Land reserves are also vulnerable to policy changes so that a new government may divert lands set aside for low-income housing by its predecessor to other more commercial uses.

Although land acquisition for short-term development avoids the latter drawback, it suffers because the cost is likely to be high and, by purchasing at commercial prices, it fuels inflation. Expropriation in the public interest for immediate development can provoke hostility from landholders who may, if threatened, promote the invasion or quick sale of plots, particularly if this action is likely to inflate the level of compensation that they eventually receive.

(b) Commercialization and cross-subsidization

In this case land bought by the state on the commercial market or held under earlier land reserve policies is set aside to provide dual or multiple use. As its simplest, land in one half is commercialized (for industrial, commercial or middle-income housing purposes) and the revenues obtained are used to subsidize low-cost housing on the remainder of the land. This practice has much to commend it, though as in the previous example the later-phased low-cost housing scheme is vulnerable to policy change and politically motivated attack during the (often lengthy) period of commercialization.

(c) Application of judicial and fiscal and sanctions

Although one might not expect the Mexican Government to legislate or adopt sanctions against powerful vested interests, recent investigations against such interests, and the application of stricter land-use controls, have taken place. The relative autonomy of the State offers scope for the contemplation, at least, of judicial and financial sanctions that might be applied against illegal land speculators and developers. Many sanctions already exist on the statute book and, if applied at all, fall arbitrarily upon those who are politically unprotected. Planners should not discount the possibility of pressing for penal and/or financial sanctions against those guilty of illegal land-development activities.

In Mexico, imprisonment is a theoretical possibility but is very rarely applied.

Occasionally a local leader or *ejidatario* is thrown into jail on a charge of fraud, though this is usually an outcome of inter-leader or group rivalries rather than a systematic government policy aimed at deterring others. Even the real-estate companies responsible for the vast settlement in the east of the city emerged unscathed with the bulk of their interests intact (Connolly, 1982). Nevertheless sanctions are applied. Recently landholdings in several settlements in the State of Mexico have been taken over by the Government, and the landowners have been forced to cut their losses gracefully. Elsewhere it may prove feasible for planners to impose a minimum and maximum plot size and to artificially raise the cadastral value on plots whose size falls outside those limits. Given that land taxes are assessed upon cadastral values such measures could prove quite punitive.

A tightening-up of administrative responsibility can also remove many of the loopholes that currently provide scope for illegal transactions. Large areas of *ejidal* land in the second home belt of the state of Morelos, to the south of Mexico City, were successfully disestablished by speculator developers who bought out *ejidatarios*, paid several years' land taxes, used the receipts to register their 'ownership', registered the latter in the official registry and, eventually, subdivided and sold as elite and upper-middle-income residential neighbourhoods. At no stage did the original title require verification (SAHOP, 1979, pp.134–5).

(d) Subsidies to home developers

In Mexico cash subsidies are not usually feasible. However, land subsidies might be acceptable and such a scheme was devised whereby sites and services projects could be initiated on a large scale, while being competitive with any other agent in the unauthorized settlement business. It also provides a 5-year 'grace' period in which no repayments are required. To operate successfully the basic requirement for this scheme is a reasonably inflationary land market and a willingness on the part of the state to forgo the addition to land values brought about by self-help initiatives on the part of the participants. The proposals have been written up in detail elsewhere (SAHOP, 1979; Ward, 1981b) and is not elaborated in detail here. Briefly, however, its novelty lies in two basic propositions. First, it provides the target population with twice as much land as they would normally require for a house plot (i.e. 300–400 m²). Second, the 'acquisition' cost (the amount paid to enter the project) is fixed at the rate of competitor agents who provide land in *colonias populares* (i.e. nil cost — *x* cost). Nothing is paid back over the first 5 years, during which time residents build their homes and collaborate with government authorities to install services and improve the image of the settlement. The loan that the agency has taken out to develop the low-cost subdivision (at commercial or social interest rates) is paid back by residents at the end of the 5-years period, either in a single payment or gradually over the following 5 years. This is usually done by selling the *extra half* of the plot which, after 5 years, has a massively inflated value. Residents buying in at this later stage are better-off working-class and lower-middle-income groups who were reluctant to undergo the rigours of living 5 years in a serviceless community but wish to acquire a relatively cheap lot. In essence therefore the proposal gives the poor the wherewithall to *speculate* on the land market, playing off costs of a loan and interest against the enormous increase in land values on marginal land that is subject to community-promoted improvements and 'sweat equity'.

Although we argue that the scheme potentially has widespread application it is not without its drawbacks (see Stolarski, 1980). There is a danger from 'raiding' by middle-income groups where housing demand is very high, and also a major gulf may be created between those of the poor included in the scheme and those outside it. It is also liable to be inflationary and may not be easy to replicate. Although densities are low over the first 5 years they increase dramatically thereafter, and can be increased by manipulation of cadastral values. Despite these caveats the proposal offers considerable scope for formal intervention in the land market that will compete with illegal land developers and, at the same time, short-circuit many of the economic contradictions of sites and services projects.

(e) 'Informal interventions'

Finally, it is important for planners to examine carefully the unique land tenure arrangements that exist in each country. In Mexico the widespread existence of *ejido* communities at the periphery of many cities offers an opportunity for intervention by planning authorities in land-use development. Here we analysed in detail the legal framework relating to *ejidos*. Next, we examined the informal processes of land alienation. Finally, after we were satisfied that we had gained a full understanding of unauthorized settlement on *ejido* lands we began to sketch out the range of possible actions that could be undertaken, either formally using existing legislative and fiscal machinery, or informally, via interventions to cajole, persuade, or threaten *ejidatarios* to co-operate. Several of these approaches are described briefly below.

First, in those cases where *ejidal* urban zones had been established legally our aim was to encourage an increase in the supply of plots and to install services. Two modes of intervention were proposed: indirect intervention via a manipulation of cadastral values that specifically penalized residents with excessively large plots would serve to encourage subdivision and sale; and direct actions where the state bought out whole plots or sections of contiguous plots to create substantial land areas that could be subsequently developed. Here the planning agency becomes the purchaser, speculator, and developer.

A second approach involved the very common situation whereby the request for an urban *ejidal* zone was a pretext for profitable land sales by *ejidatarios*. In these circumstances planners could not intervene formally to encourage illegal settlement. However, by using a mixture of threat and incentive several mechanisms emerge whereby the settlement processes could be firmly influenced. A clear warning to would-be buyers that planners would never authorize service improvements to plots in a specific area would lower the selling price. Conversely *ejidatarios* could be rewarded by higher levels of compensation where they preserved vacant land in prime locations.

A third alternative which we considered was rather more conflictive because it required official involvement in the invasion of lands which were under threat from illegal occupation promoted by other agents. State intervention along these lines would, inevitably generate widespread criticism and opposition and could be expected only as a last resort. Nevertheless in the course of our investigation we became aware that the practice already exists.

CONCLUSION

The approach outlined above is only one experience, and my purpose in introducing it is *not* to open a discussion about the relative merits of individual proposals nor the applicability of each to different local circumstances. Rather, the aim is to ask whether the approach has wider currency. Should planners be thinking more imaginatively along the lines I have suggested, or should they wait upon recipes drawn from the menu of international conventional wisdom? Obviously our reaction to these questions will be informed by the level of implementation that might be expected from any formal or informal proposals that are drawn up. Our experience in Mexico was mixed. The exercise was a positive one and opened up many potential avenues for intervention in land provision for the urban poor. However, that as an end in itself is not good enough. Unfortunately, to my knowledge *none* of the proposals have been implemented. It is difficult to say whether this is the result of particular circumstances relating to the group involved, or whether the proposals are unlikely to be implementing because of the benefits of conventional housing solutions to established vested-interest groups. On the first point I can say that our brief went no further than to elaborate forms that intervention might take. Our office was not responsible for policy implementation. The second point is untestable. However, our experience underscores the need to have strong institutional support from politicians who, unequivocally, wish to make a positive contribution to improving the housing conditions of the poor and who are prepared to take on those groups and individuals who have, in the past, profited from exploiting the poor. Perhaps the fact that a group such as this existed at all is a hopeful sign that in future a Mexican Government might actively attempt to initiate more subtle and imaginative schemes of providing the poor with access to land.

ACKNOWLEDGEMENTS

This paper describes some of the work that I undertook when employed by the UK Overseas Development Administration and was seconded (1978–79) to Mexico as an adviser to the Ministry of Human Settlements and Public Works (SAHOP), specifically to the General Directorate of Population Centres (DGCP). I am grateful to the Director of that Department, Architect Roberto Eibenschutz, and to the Underminister, Dr Gregorio Valner, for their support in the project undertaken. I should also acknowledge the close collaboration that I enjoyed with Noemi Stolarski, a member of the DGCP.

ACRONYMS USED IN THE TEXT

INDECO: National Institute for Housing and the Development of the Community.
INFONAVIT: Institute for the National Workers' Housing Fund.
SAHOP: Ministry of Human Settlements and Public Works.

REFERENCES

Burgess, R. (1982). Self-help housing advocacy: a curious form of radicalism. A critique of the work of John F. C. Turner'. In P. M. Ward (ed.), *Self-help Housing: A Critique*. London: Mansell Press. pp.55–97.

Connolly, P. (1982). 'Uncontrolled settlements and "self-build": what kind of solution?' In
    P. M. Ward (ed.) *Self-help Housing: A Critique*. London: Mansell Press. pp.14–174.
Departmento del Distrito Federal (DDF) (1980). *Plan de desarrollo urbano del Distrito Federal.*
    Mexico: DDF.
Evans, H. (1974). 'Towards a Policy for Housing Low-income Families in Mexico. Unpublished
    thesis for diploma in architecture. University of Cambridge, England.
Garza, G., and Schteingart, M. (1978). *La acción habitacional del estado mexicano*. El Colegio
    de Mexico, 1978.
Gilbert, A. and Ward, P. (1982). 'Low income housing and the state'. In A. Gilbert (ed.),
    *Urbanization in Contemporary Latin America: Critical Approaches to the Study of Urban
    Issues*. London: Wiley.
INDECO (1982a). *Evaluación social del programa de dotación de lotes y servicios, 'Cruz Gorda',
    Colima y El Espejo 1, Villahermosa*. International agency document, Unidad de Promoción
    Social.
INDECO (1982b). *Programa nacional de vivienda. Sistema nacional de alianza para la vivienda
    popular*. Agency publications, Mexico DF.
(Secretaria de Asentamientos Humanos y Obras Publicas (SAHOP) (1978). *Plan nacional de
    desarrollo urbano*. Versión abreviada; agency publication.
SAHOP (1979). *La incorporación de los procesos que generan los asentamientos irregulares a
    la planeación de los centros de población*. Internal agency document DGCP, Mexico.
Stolarski, N. (1980). 'Financing Land Acquisition for Self-built Housing Schemes in Developing
    Countries: Some Problem Areas Detected for the Case of Mexico. M.Sc. dissertation. London
    School of Economics and Political Science.
Ward, P. (1978). 'Self-help housing in Mexico City: social and economic determinants of success',
    Town Planning Review, **49(1)**, 38–50.
Ward, P. (1981a). 'Political pressure for urban services: the response of two Mexico City
    administrations'. *Development and Change*, **12**, 379–407.
Ward, P. (1981b). 'Financing land acquisition for self-build housing schemes'. *Third World
    Planning Review* **3(1)**, 7–20.

Part Two

Low-income Housing in the Developing World
Edited by G. K. Payne
© 1984 John Wiley & Sons Ltd

Chapter 9

Political and Administrative Factors in Low-income Housing

Francis J. C. Amos

INTRODUCTION

Political decisions and administrative[1] arrangements both precede and sustain government action in any field and the effectiveness of any programme is dependent upon the event to which these activities are complementary to each other and are consonant with the environment in which action is to be taken.

In areas of government where the tasks and practices are well charted and have withstood the tests of time, political reality and administrative practicality have been worked into an efficient piece of governmental machinery. However, in the case of urban housing the task has changed and grown so rapidly, and the needs are so urgent, that systems have not been able to keep pace with demand and performance has fallen far short of aspiration.

In part the problem lies in the political uncertainties of public sector intervention in the housing market. On the one hand issues relating to land ownership, private development interests, and the inadequate shelter of the urban poor give rise to conflicts between political ideology and political feasibility. On the other hand, economic necessity, technical practicability and administrative admissibility may either impose constraints or offer opportunities which may not have been anticipated at the time of political decisions.

This chapter considers some of the factors which affect political decisions and how these are related to administration, both at the high level of major policy analysis and at the level of routine administrative processes.

THE LOCAL POLITICAL CONTEXT

The influence of political parties

The role of political parties within the central government system is usually of considerable importance in determining housing programmes and their implementation. However, the political performance of local government has been somewhat uneven and its influence upon housing programmes has not always been beneficial. The worst abuses of devolved power usually occur where the operating agency does not have the ability or responsibility to raise its own finance. In these circumstances, functional agencies can have their priorities determined by ministerial action while local councillors use housing assistance as a means of securing popularity and public support, as shown by the example of Ankara (Chapter 5). Where two or more parties compete for political control, programmes can be subject to sudden and radical redirections and the best course for administrators and technocrats to take is to attempt to devise a programme which meets most of the primary objectives of all the contending parties.

However, the exercise of political control is seldom as malevolent as is described above, for there are checks and balances within any political system which are essential for the sustained acceptability of authority. Where the system is based on the existence of more than one party, the opposition parties' role is to challenge the validity of policy and the reasonableness of its application. In such a system the individual councillor has to support his party's policy based on predetermined political criteria and, at the same time, to sustain his local popularity. Since party and local interests are not necessarily compatible, councillors play a critical role in tempering political policy to local aspirations. Additionally, councillors in the majority party will also have to reconcile party policy with administrative and technical practicality.

These same principles also apply in a one-party system, except that there may be greater coherence between central and local party and a more private environment for the examination of difficulties and failures. However, it should not be assumed that in a politically homogeneous system there is direct and coherent administration of policy. In Tanzania, for example (see Chapter 6) the recently created urban authorities, which are responsible for housing, are regarded as the operational arm of government, whereas policy is handed down through a parallel party hierarchy. In this system the local councillors operate as a management board, making local compromises to achieve acceptable ends but always acting within the policy presented by the party.

A similar separation in policy-making from operational decision-making is not uncommon in the multi-party system. This usually takes the form of caucus meetings being held in private prior to formal meetings of council or to its committee meetings. Both in one-party and in multi-party systems, there are difficulties in getting practical considerations adequately presented to these political decision-making groups, and much may depend upon the personal relationships between key politicians and their advisers.

In relation to sites and services and upgrading schemes, one of the most common manifestations of political influence is an insistence upon standards and/or numbers of dwellings which are beyond the limit of available resources. In the period immediately after the establishment of an African majority government in Zimbabwe many of the newly constituted local authorities pressed for housing standards which were superior to those of the previous regime, and it was only with great difficulty that the government resisted these demands.

Issues of policy

The political problems of sites and services and squatter upgrading are not, however, solely confined to issues of structural relationships. Whilst the need for land for these purposes is beyond dispute, the means of making it available is another matter for considerable political argument. These matters are fully explored in Chapter 14, but it nevertheless needs to be emphasized here that political attitudes to squatting and to cheap shelter are ambivalent. Generally, squatter settlements are deplored because of the unacceptably poor quality of life which they embody, but improvement is politically hazardous.

Acquisition of sufficient land may offend powerful landowning interests, and acquisitions and servicing costs may be beyond the resources of the authority and subsequently beyond the purchasing power of the occupiers of the sites. Additionally, squatters may be reluctant to move to new serviced sites because of their need to be near to work opportunities and to neighbours with whom they may have special associations. As a consequence, although there may be a political wish to improve the situation, there is an understandable reluctance to embark upon specific courses of action which have within them the ingredients of substantial political difficulties.

But, if there is reluctance to relieve squatter conditions by the creation of sufficient serviced sites there is equivalent hesitation in adopting the alternative solution of squatter upgrading. This is largely because, in addition to the cost issue, there is a distinct uneasiness about the principle involved, for notwithstanding the squatters' absolute need for land, the fact remains that the squatter has, by force, deprived another of his legal property.

In many instances the political problems of squatting and low-cost shelter are not perceived until it is too late to contain the situation. This is because in the early stages many of the issues are only perceived as domestic property disputes between neighbours, and by the time they are seen to be of greater significance, informal systems and practices have become so well established that intervention is both difficult and hazardous.

In those countries where land is privately owned, a particular problem for governments is that it is politically very difficult to move squatters off government land unless there is an essential and immediate need for the land. By contrast, private landowners who do not depend upon political popularity adopt far more determined attitudes in deciding to remove squatters or charge them rents. Thus by a process of filtration the most impoverished squatters tend to accumulate on public land or upon areas of uncertain ownership, such as river beds in the dry season or uncultivated land on the margins of towns. In one sense this is an advantageous situation because it means that governments can embark upon upgrading schemes or re-location to serviced sites without encountering obstacles relating to land ownership and acquisition. Whilst the provision of serviced sites clearly obviates some of the problems of squatting and reduces some of the political pressures, such projects are not, however, free from political risk. In the case of squatter areas the population is an accomplished fact, but the allocation of sites involves the selection of occupiers, usually from a greater number of candidates than there are sites available. This selection process is, of course, subject to actual or alleged partiality and, since a serviced site represents a considerable asset at low cost, there is much manoeuvring to secure allocations. There is also the problem that even the low-cost sites will exclude the very poorest from access, although they may be in the greatest need of such sites.

Issues of practice

The effect of these political pressures also influences political attitudes to the practices adopted in relation to sites and services and squatter upgrading. In particular, this may be seen in a marked reluctance to quantify the needs which should be met. Quite apart from technical difficulties, the reasons for this reluctance are manifold. Civic pride inhibits public recognition of the presence of a large population inadequately housed. The scale of the problem belittles past achievement. The resource requirement thus revealed can be embarrassingly large; and there is always the risk that quantification of the problem will lead to targets for its solution which, if not achieved, make politicians vulnerable.

Similarly, if performance is not measured in precise terms it may be possible to give the impression of a successful programme, even where the original purpose has not been met. This is a common characteristic of some development or housing boards in India which have failed to meet the targets for sites and services of the economically weaker sections of the community, but which have, nevertheless, achieved a high output of sites for more prosperous groups. Careful quantitative measurement may not be popular because it could show up in sharp relief what is normally condemned as nepotism or corrupt practices. However, some of these practices should not be condemned out of hand. In some cultures there are highly developed conventions of rewards and obligations which are generally accepted as the means of getting things done and care must be taken to distinguish between such institutionalized systems and the deliberately corrupt misuse of power.

In many countries sovereign government is a relatively recent phenomenon and the nature of the relationship between the state and the individual is still being explored and charted. Under these conditions one should expect central and local governments to adopt ambitious programmes, but only embark upon them tentatively, feeling their position and committing themselves only gradually as the programme progresses. This situation is particularly observable in those programmes where, to conserve resources, heavy reliance is placed upon self-help. Such schemes depend for their success upon the voluntary participation of many people; but people will only volunteer to do things which they believe to be worthwhile and, since there is an infinite variety of human values, it is unrealistic to believe that a uniform approach handed down from government will be widely accepted and acted upon. Self-help action is dependent upon people deciding for themselves, but governments can see, in this devolution of power to communities to decide for themselves, a threat to the authority of government. Thus, while there may be a universal acceptance of the need for self-help, political systems may inhibit the development of the very institutions which could assist in improving housing conditions as well as strengthening the fabric of government. Thus, the political attitudes to providing sites for squatters are ambivalent. To maintain political popularity, both with squatters and the rest of the population, it is important to declare intentions to improve the conditions of squatters. In practical terms, however, local governments then tend to say that they can do nothing without external assistance, or to adopt schemes which are so small or distant that they are unlikely to generate political opposition — even if this means they are unlikely to meet the needs of low-income households. It is, therefore, critical to the success of upgrading and sites and services programmes that public conviction and commitment can be stimulated, so that there is sufficient political will to expand programmes from their current modest proportions to a scale which is consonant with the magnitude of demand.

It could therefore be said that one of the most common weaknesses in squatter upgrading and sites and services programmes is that, although the operational content of programmes is normally soundly devised, they make inappropriate and/or excessive demands upon the political and administrative institutions. It is of critical importance that the proposed action is, in fact, compatible with current decision systems and that politicians are not faced with culturally impossible choices.

THE ADMINISTRATIVE CONTEXT

The structure and relationships of housing agencies

The administrative relations between central and local government exert considerable influence over low-income housing programmes. These relations are largely influenced by '*de jure*' and '*de facto*' patterns of accountability. In theory, at least, the simplest systems should be found in the one-purpose organizations with a simple hierarchical command and accountability structure. However, even in these organizations there are cleavages and alliances which make '*de facto*' control far more complex than might first appear.

First, there is the inevitable tension of the centre seeking to maintain consistency and a planned distribution of resources, being challenged by field units seeking variations and extra funds to meet local conditions. Such tensions cannot and should not be avoided for, in essence, they maintain the dynamism of the agency in question. However, there may be negative effects in this relationship, since the centre seldom presents itself as a homogeneous entity. For well-justified reasons, central organizations frequently operate on the basis of specialist functional divisions, such as personnel, finance, procurement, research and development, all of which have legitimate interests in the field operations.

In some organizations the centre attempts to control field units by channelling all communications with the field through one office. This has the advantage of avoiding conflicting communications, but can lead to bottlenecks, delays, and distortions in relaying information. Conversely, other organizations overcome this problem by a substantial devolution of authority to strong field officers who are expected to reconcile whatever conflicting approaches may come from outside their area.

In those countries where local political administrations exist, the problems can be far more complex for a variety of reasons. Except in those rare cases where there is complete local autonomy over a particular programme, central/local tensions can be heightened by the employment conditions and career prospects of the local staff. If these staff are employed by the local agency, their immediate responsibilities are clear and central/local tensions should be contained within the political field. However, even in these situations employees may have professional commitments to integrity and competence which may be incompatible with the policies or practices of the employing agency.

Where the staff of a local agency either form part of a larger public service cadre, or are employed by central government, there is the additional problem that, because they have two masters, staff are seldom sure to whom they owe their ultimate loyalty. This can present particularly acute problems where there are central/local differences of a political nature and where career prospects may be affected by the managerial decisions which staff have to make. However, it should not be assumed that staff are always the victims of such situations. Within staff structures there are often powerful alliances of administrative and professional cadres who may not be above using situations to their own particular advantage.

Some aspects of central/local differences are also to be seen in the task of ensuring that all elements of an upgrading or sites and services programming move forward in step with each other. It is sometimes simplistically believed that such problems of co-ordination could be overcome by making all the requisite operations the responsibility of one agency, but this is unrealistic for three reasons.

First, if it were possible to place all the operations within one agency the scale and diversity of the tasks are so great that the only effect would be to translate the problem from being an inter-agency situation into an intra-agency situation. Second, many of the tasks which have to be performed are not unique to upgrading and sites and services schemes. Therefore, a single agency would either have to duplicate other agencies or become responsible for at least some part of other programmes which require the same tasks to be performed. Third, it is unrealistic to suppose that only one agency will be responsible for all the local needs of low-cost shelter. There may be, as in parts of India, several state agencies providing for the economically weaker sections of the community according to different formulae or with funds from different sources: self-help groups, philanthropic bodies, industrial organizations and private landowners all play some part in the provision of low-cost shelter.

There is, therefore, the need to discover who is active in the field and how best to make their various activities mutually supportive of each other. It is the essential role of government to provide this background of information and a structure within which specific decisions and actions may be taken.

In the first instance it is important that all sites and services and upgrading schemes are placed within the context of the total expected housing provision, for many of the service providers will also be expected to meet the needs of other types of housing and effective co-ordination will depend upon agreement being reached about priorities accorded to all types of demand. However, according priorities within the housing field will not, of itself, resolve the problems of resource provision, for many of the service-providing agencies will also have commitments to other sectors of the economy. The co-ordination of services provision with housing has, therefore, to be handled at the level of resource allocation between sectors, as well as at the level of allocation within the housing sector.

Service requirements for housing need to be assessed at both national and local level, since housing provision is often a highly fragmented operation and total need has to be estimated if an appropriate allocation of services is to be secured. However, an appropriate allocation is not necessarily an *adequate* allocation and the obligation to meet minimum needs may lead to modes of service provision which may not confirm to the standards of practices of the providing agencies. Thus, co-ordination may not be merely concerned with securing and time-tabling resource allocation, but may also be concerned with the way resources are utilized.

A further aspect of co-ordination arises where the recurrent costs of maintenance and supply of services are not fully recoverable from the users. In these cases the costs of maintenance and operation may impose upon an agency a far greater burden than the costs of the initial capital works. Negotiations about programming may, therefore, also have to take into account the ability of agencies to sustain the ongoing service.

The co-ordination of public sector inputs is therefore a complex and difficult task.

It is rendered even more difficult by the fact that, for many agencies, the requirement of sites and services and upgrading are of no special significance for their own operations and co-ordinations represent no more than a further impediment to straightforward operational management. Although no single agency can adequately control all aspects of housing provision, the co-ordinating body should have sufficient authority to be able to assemble relevant data, to convene meetings, and to monitor progress. Many agencies may lay claim to this function in the hope that it will assist them in bringing other programmes into line with their own, though there is a rather stronger case for the function to be placed in a finance, general planning, or general development organization than in one of the single-purpose bodies. These usually have a broader area of concern and a better information base than is found in the latter bodies.

The effectiveness of the co-ordinating body will depend largely upon the power stratum at which co-ordination is managed. The higher the level of decision-making the more easily may the constituent agencies be controlled in playing their appropriate roles, but the more senior the personnel involved, the less time will they have for the work and the less detailed will be the co-ordination. It may, therefore, be necessary to supplement a powerful, high-level co-ordinating committee with lower-level working parties which will deal with more detailed issues. However, in some administrations, sectoral traditions and practices may be too strong to countenance high-level co-ordination. In these circumstances it may be possible to achieve a well co-ordinated programme by making funds available to the co-ordinating agency so that it may purchase services from other agencies without prejudice to their own budgetary programme.

Co-ordination between agencies is also critical when completed projects are transferred to the local authority or other agency which will assume responsibility for routine maintenance. This frequently causes disputes about the suitability of the original design, the condition on handover, and the desirability of the asset. Disputes on these matters are often further aggravated by the fact that the local authority's income will not rise in proportion to its additional obligations. Furthermore, there may be differences of status and salary between the staffs of the development authority and the local authority, which may generate additional friction. However, much can be done to make schemes acceptable to a local authority by involving them at the initial design stage of a project. In this way agreement should be reached about the necessity for each element, the level of maintenance and costs involved, and the condition of assets at the time of handover.

Arguments are sometimes advanced that the difficulties involved in co-ordinating many agencies could be overcome by establishing special housing agencies to finance, design, implement, and maintain sites and services and squatter upgrading projects, as is the case in some Indian improvement trusts and Pakistan containment boards. However, if this were to happen on the large scale which is needed for sites and services and upgrading schemes, there would in effect be two authorities operating in parallel, both having to levy taxes or charges, but with one locally controlled and the other directly accountable to central government. In many instances special agencies have been brought into being, either because national government, or international organizations such as the World Bank, believe that the local authorities are not able to effectively operate the programmes in question. Yet the creation of alternative agencies has the effect of further emasculating local authorities, thereby making them less able to perform.

Technical competence

One of the most common obstacles to designing and implementing a realistic programme of upgrading and sites and services provision is the inadequate supply of suitably trained staff. In part this is attributable to the general shortage of skilled personnel but, both in the technical and administrative fields, it is exacerbated by the inappropriateness of much of the training which has been provided.

In the housing sector the greatest difficulties arise from training having been received in, or derived from, educational institutions suited to the needs of affluent, high-technology society. These institutions have developed their curricula on the basis of defined tasks and skills and the assumptions that there will be a highly skilled and experienced labour force and that an ample supply of investment capital is available. In those areas where sites and services and upgrading are required, none of these conditions prevail.

As a consequence, many of the professionally trained national, and indeed some expatriate specialists, find themselves ill-equipped to devise and manage a programme based on intermediate and low-technology solutions. On the one hand they do not know the limits of the technology within which they work; on the other, they sometimes regard low-technology design as sub-professional work which they should not have to undertake. These factors of knowledge and attitude tend to reinforce each other to the point where unnecessarily expensive projects are vigorously advocated as the only realistic technical solutions.

A second effect of the conventional form of training is that professionals are ill-equipped to perform those functions which elsewhere would be undertaken by complementary professions. Here also there is a case for educational reform but, for the present, this means that sites and services and upgrading schemes need to be directed by staff with broad rather than specialized knowledge, and that, where possible, there should be access to scarce low-technology specialists.

In the administrative field the shortcomings are of a rather different nature and often flow from a concept of administration more appropriate to an earlier era. In many countries the nature and style of the administrative system was formed at a time when urban settlements were of modest size, when urban growth rates were low, and when the task of administration was seen to be the maintenance of services. Now, however, settlements are growing rapidly and have generated demands to which the private sector does not respond. In these circumstances the public sector has to be more disposed to intervene and to innovate, and the work of administrative staff has to shift from maintaining the *status quo* to positively instigating change. This change in administrative style reduces the differences between technocratic planners and administrators, and is making demands on civil service colleges for new types of training.

However, the new training will not, of itself, change the administrative style of a whole civil service. Improvement will also depend upon the new modes of team working by technocrats and administrators within the public service. It cannot, of course, be assumed that sites and services and upgrading programmes are, on their own, sufficient to change an administrative style. However, similar pressures are arising from other sources and, in any event, every opportunity should be used to develop this new style to improve the opportunities for success in the upgrading and sites and services field.

A particular manifestation of the scarcity of suitable skills is the general inability to measure needs and to set targets. To some extent this may be attributable to the inherited administrative styles previously referred to, coupled with the inertia of existing systems within any bureaucracy. So far as needs measurement is concerned it is also attributable to a lack of enterprise in the use of existing records, with the result that policies are less well founded than they might be. In setting any operational target three factors have to be taken into account: the estimated need, the available resources, and the standards to be achieved. It is usually the case that the needs at the given standard require more resources than are available and some reconciliation must be made. In these circumstances there is usually a reluctance to lower standards, since this implies some previous failure of the administrator, either in setting standards too high or in failing to achieve them. As a consequence, the target is set by dividing the resources available by the cost of one standard unit and describing the quotient as the target to be achieved. This method has a great appeal in administrative terms because it avoids the embarrassment which would result from showing the resources required by multiplying need by unit cost: furthermore, it offers the prospect of an administrative success since arithmetically, the target should be achievable. Thus, where targets are set at all they are designed to give satisfaction within the system rather than to those who are in need of improved conditions.

A more radical approach would be to divide the resources available by those in need, to arrive at the resources available per household. In the first instance this would present a challenge to the technologists to design down to a cost level affordable by the nation. In the second instance, the new minimum standard which would emerge from this design task would probably be lower than the standard originally defined. Thus fewer households would fall below the new standard and the number of households classified as being in need would be less, leaving more resources per household.

At first sight this process may appear to pay too little regard to what are considered to be basic human necessities, but this is not necessarily so. Firstly, if resources are scarce it is better that all in need should benefit a little rather than that some should benefit a lot and others not at all. Secondly, it is a process which only defines how much the public sector can do in meeting the needs of the worst-housed. If it can only do a little of what is desirable then it makes explicit how much must be done by self-help. This, in itself, can have an important impact upon the fixing of priorities because housing standards may be more effectively improved by the government doing what cannot be achieved through self-help, rather than providing the facility which seems to be most urgently required. Bearing in mind the various examples of self-help illustrated in Part One, it could be argued that available resources should be devoted to the provision of plots, leaving service provision to be made as and when it becomes possible.

It must, however, be made abundantly clear, for both political and operational reasons, that the setting of low targets which are widely achievable is only to be seen as a first step in a long-term strategy of incremental improvement. Failure to make this clear can result in the public dismissal of the targets as being both too low and too easily achieved.

ADMINISTRATIVE COMPETENCE

The rate of urban growth in most countries has now reached such a scale that even a modest programme of sites and services and upgrading will be of a size which will give rise to a series of administrative problems. Furthermore, since operations will be geographically dispersed amongst the affected settlements, there will also be structural problems similar to those referred to in discussing central/local relations.

In relation to scale alone, some subdivision of the operation will be necessary to facilitate the efficient management of staff and resources, but the nature and structure of these subdivisions can be a major factor in determining operational efficiency. A common basis for organizational subdivision is that of function, so that there are divisions for finance, personnel, land survey, highways, water services, etc. In a dispersed housing programme, all of these divisions would need some kind of representation in each operational area. In principle, there is no reason why such a structure should not be suitable for the programmes in question, but in practice there are a number of difficulties. The first of these arises from the shortage of skilled and experienced staff for field operations. As a result, field staff are given and seek only limited powers of discretion and tend to rely upon, or take refuge behind, a multitude of regulations and directives handed down from the distant and higher echelons of their department. This situation makes project management difficult in terms of staff control, progressing work, and on-site modification of the project. It also tends to obstruct performance management, since each division will tend to assess its own performance in terms of its own expertise rather than in terms of output of completed units.

An alternative structure which is very often more suited to the characteristics of sites and services and upgrading programmes is the formation of a number of self-sufficient area teams, as in Lusaka (Chapter 3), each of which has its complete complement of skills and is responsible for all work in a specified area. Operationally this structure has much to commend it, both in terms of project management and in performance control, since each team can be assessed in terms of completed units. However, there is often resistance to this structure from senior staff for a variety of reasons. First, where career progress has been upward through functional departments, some senior staff feel ill-equipped to accept broader managerial responsibilities. Second, the structure requires only a small headquarters exercising only limited strategic authority, so that senior posts will be away from the centre and sometimes in unattractive environments. Third, since output performance is more easily measurable and attributable, the hazards of accountability revelations are more severe.

However, it must not be forgotten that there are serious problems of delegation and accountability to be found in most programmes for upgrading or sites and services. In part these spring from the shortage of skilled and experienced staff, but also from the institutional politics of the organizations concerned. In countries where systems are fragile, where skills are scarce, and where government feels insecure, it must be accepted that career prospects may be substantially influenced by nepotism and sycophancy. Furthermore, where salaries are low and the rewards for departing from strict propriety are high, it must also be accepted that there are likely to be irregularities of administration. Both of these factors induce into the administrative process a degree of secrecy which is an impediment to good management. On the one hand it inhibits delegation down the administrative system because this reduces the delegator's area of manoeuvre. On the other hand it inhibits accountability upwards because this could expose the irregular activities which the offender will wish to conceal. The effect of these two tendencies is to create a system in which staff at each level expect those below them to do whatever they are told without question and, at the same time, try to get those above them to issue instructions in such a way that their own activities will be neither curtailed nor exposed. In the worst cases this can reduce the administrative system to a kind of ritual dance which bears no relationship to what is actually going on.

The organizer of an upgrading and sites and services programme cannot expect either to work outside the institutional culture of the administration or to reform it overnight. One must, therefore, try to construct a workable system which will help agencies improve their capability and which will produce a reasonable number of the required units at reasonable cost and deliver most of them to the intended target group. To some extent this may be achieved by concentrating attention upon the output of completed units rather than upon the activities of individuals or subsections within the organization. However this, of itself, will not ensure that the benefits are enjoyed by the intended target groups. The solution must, therefore, be sought not in the design of a foolproof system, but in a more realistic approach to target setting and in the gradual adaptation of political and administrative institutions to an enlarged and expanding scale of operation.

In conclusion, it must be said again that one of the obstacles to an effective administration system is the political environment within which the administration must operate. So long as government is unsure of the extent of its public influence, and/or the feasibility of its adopted policies, it will continue to act tentatively and will be inclined to vacillate. In this situation, positive, consistent, and constructive administration can only be achieved with great difficulty and through great dedication on the part of senior administrators.

Yet the administrative situation is not as negative as it might appear, for the administrative service has a durability and a stability which extends beyond the life of governments, and good administrators can, therefore, provide government with a degree of confidence and competence that they might otherwise lack. However, the 'Achilles heel' of the senior administrator is the quality of middle management upon which he must depend and which has been referred to in a number of the preceding sections. It is, therefore, an obvious conclusion that a first priority must be the improvement of this grade of management. In this respect, the relative novelty of sites and services and upgrading programmes makes them a convenient vehicle for managerial development. Since the task is new, ignorance implies no loss of status and, since the programmes are mostly expanding, there is both the need and the opportunity for a continuous staff development programme. However, although the training should in one sense be specific to the programme, in another sense the principles involved are applicable to many aspects of administration. Training should, therefore, be built into the general structure of public service development.

Lastly, because of the pressing problem of shelter in urban areas, administrators are likely to be given rather more political and financial support for work in this field than for other fields. Improvement will then depend on the administrators themselves to use this opportunity to improve the quality of their own administrations.

NOTES

1. For the purposes of this chapter the term administration is taken to include those professional and technical services which form part of the general support provided to national and local governments for the proper discharge of their functions.

Low-income Housing in the Developing World
Edited by G. K. Payne
© 1984 John Wiley & Sons Ltd

Chapter 10

The Role of International Agencies:
The World Bank

David G. Williams

SOME ISSUES

What have been the attitudes and activities of international development agencies in relation to urban settlements? How have these agencies affected the programmes described in this book, and what impact on the settlement and housing needs of low-income people has their assistance had? In addition to providing improved physical services, what success have their efforts had in opening opportunities for the poor to increase their earnings, widen choice in their access to the components of shelter, and increase their influence over the allocation of their nations' wealth and resources? These are some of the important questions which the aid agencies should be asking after a decade of study and investment projects in this field. This chapter attempts a brief review and some observations on possible directions in the future. The principal focus will be on the operation of the World Bank which is currently the largest lender in this field.

BACKGROUND

International assistance for shelter is a relative late-comer to the development field, except perhaps for USAID* which, in the 1960s, established a housing guarantee fund to stimulate private US investments in developing countries, mostly in Latin America. This programme, however, tended to assist upper-middle and upper-income households. At the other end of the scale, non-government organizations, especially church and voluntary service groups, were working with small funds in slum and squatter settlements to help local communities in providing some basic services such as better health and child care and small water supplies. During the same period international assistance was being used for other types of urban infrastructure such as major roads, water supply, and electrical distribution systems. Very little of this assistance, however, was directed to the needs of the increasing number of the urban poor.

---

* See list of institutions at end of this chapter.

This was partly due to the philosophy which polarized sectors of activity into those in the modern sector which were termed 'productive', the remainder—including housing—being labelled 'consumptive' and therefore not deserving major investment.

What happened in the early 1970s to modify this view, and led to increasing levels of investment in urban shelter with associated policies directed to institutional changes in related areas including land tenure, financing and community relations? One factor, certainly, was the increasing speed and extent of urban growth and the expansion of slum and squatter settlements which could no longer be ignored or swept under the carpet. A second feature was the increasing disparity between the rich and the poor in developing countries. It became apparent that they were not divided simply between the rich in urban centres and the poor in rural areas, but that there were massive disparities *within* urban areas. It also became clear that conventional growth policies were inadequate to deal with this and were leaving out increasing numbers from the development process. Finally, the 1960s saw significant developments in understanding the social and economic processes of urban settlement and migration and the emergence of a new philosophy of housing, developed by Charles Abrams, John Turner, William Mangin, and others, which documented the enormous success of low-income people in building their own housing and producing basic services in the face of opposition by Government agencies and showed that the poor were the central, rather than a marginal, group in the urban economy.

All these factors had a strong influence on policy-makers in the international aid agencies, especially the World Bank and certain bilateral donors such as the Americans and the Swedes. These, and other UN agencies such as ILO and WHO, reviewed and initiated studies which showed the extensive economic contributions of the poor, and described the positive effects which improved health and legal security could have on productivity and the mobilization of savings for investments in housing.

AID AGENCIES' INVOLVEMENT IN URBAN SETTLEMENT

We noted earlier that considerable investments were made in urban areas, but in one sense this was more by chance than design. The structure of international funding agencies parallels that of government ministries, both being organized along functional sectors, such as industry, water supply, transport, etc.: very little attention was paid to the dynamics or the social and economic effects of urban agglomeration, the distribution of benefits, or the linkages between one sector and the other. The World Bank was, and still is, organized almost exclusively along these sectoral lines. Numerous investments were, therefore, made in urban areas, but not as part of a deliberate strategy related to urbanization. However, in the early 1970s the results of the research and analysis in the process of housing and urban settlement, accompanied by the discovery that rural and urban poverty were not being reduced by projects oriented toward conventional growth economics, began to make the Bank more aware that major changes were required not only in project design but also in associated policy areas of land and finance. Thus the concept emerged, in the jargon of the Bank, of a 'direct attack' on rural and urban poverty. Considerable effort was made to define the 'target population' so that project benefits could be focused on this group. Analysis was made by the country economists on income levels and their distribution, and on the costs of basic necessities such as food, water, shelter, and transport. A level of 'absolute poverty' was then defined, which was the point where the costs of these necessities were not covered by income. The 'poverty' group, plus a further group above them living in 'relative poverty', were the target groups, and in the economic evaluation of projects the 'poverty content', (e.g. the numbers of poor directly benefited by the project), had to be stated in the staff appraisal reports. The approach might be criticized as somewhat theoretical and overly concentrated on measures of income and costs, neglecting other social and cultural variables. Nevertheless, it has been a useful goal to force project designers both in Government and in the Bank to investigate the problems, location, and needs of the poor and to come up with more specific and innovative approaches. However, these efforts tended to be restricted in the Bank to projects considered as belonging to the 'social' or 'informal' sectors. These included urban-related lending to houses, and later water supply and sanitation, health, and population-control projects. These sectors probably account for 30–40% of total Bank and IFC lending. About 40–60% of the Bank's lending has a primary impact in urban areas[1] and perhaps 30–40% of this has been strongly poverty-orientated.

Regional development banks such as ADB and IDB have tended to take a similar approach to urban lending as the World Bank. The UNDP has generally restricted itself to funding studies on urban strategy and master plans, although some attention has been given, together with WHO, to analyzing and developing technical solutions to health problems which has subsequently resulted in changes to design in water supply and sanitation projects. Bilateral aid agencies have tended to fund discreet studies and a limited number of physical projects in urban infrastructure, often tied to the bilateral's supplies and equipment, most noticeably with regard to transport. USAID, however, has undertaken some innovative work in training programmes for city administrators and in assisting smaller towns.

WORLD BANK HOUSING POLICY AND SCOPE OF INVESTMENTS

One result of the evolution in thinking discussed above has been the recognition by the Bank of the following major features related to settlement and housing in the Third World:

(a) The need for changes in government policy on land and tenure and sustained efforts to deliver basic infrastructure on a substantial scale.
(b) Government attempts to eliminate unserviced settlements or to stem migration have been ineffective (except in a few special examples such as Singapore).
(c) The vast majority of the urban population cannot afford completed housing units erected by government, unless they are heavily subsidized.
(d) Third World Governments are generally prepared to spend 2–7% of their budget on housing and urban services. The level of demand implies subsidies for providing completed housing units far in excess of the amounts governments are prepared to spend.
(e) The provision of secure land tenure to occupants, and delivery of infra-structure, stimulates massive investments by individual households to build or improve their shelter. Their costs are typically one-third to one-half less than that which government

would invest to build a similar size and quality of dwelling and the structures are usually substantially completed within 6–24 months.

(f) Low-income groups are normally capable of paying, and prepared to pay, for the cost of land and services, provided they have been involved in decisions affecting them concerning service designs, costs, repayments and tenure status. Willingness to pay for housing and basic services (water supply, electricity, etc.), ranges from 10 to 30% of gross income depending on the extent of the service[2] and on income levels, and the degree of control over the asset obtained. Substantial personal savings and loans are often mobilized by the plot-holders to build their own homes.

(g) For most settlers, employment and incomes are a higher priority than better housing. Efforts to encourage local businesses and cooperatives are important and incomes can be raised by allowing businesses to operate in residential areas and the households to add extra rooms for rental.

The implications of the above features for project design mean that housing programmes have to be designed from the standpoint of effective user demand, and not from preconceived notions of 'adequate' housing. In general, the Bank funds for the urban shelter sector have been intended to encourage reform in policies and institutions and provide technical assistance rather than providing major transfers of financial resource. The following criteria have been developed by the Bank for evaluating project proposals and assisting borrowers to develop policies and programmes in the shelter sector:

(a) *Limitation of public-sector investments.* In general, government should limit itself to providing services which families and communities cannot provide by themselves, such as city-wide planning and construction of infrastructure.

(b) *Target population.* Communities of low and moderate incomes should be the principal group to which policies and assistance are directed. This group can generally be defined as those in absolute or relative poverty, which is frequently from the bottom up to the 50th or even 70th percentile of the city income distribution. Programmes should be designed to assist the beneficiaries in proportion to the numbers in each income group and not result in 'token' assistance to the poorest groups. Complementary programmes to deal with the backlog of services (upgrading) and provide for expansion (new serviced sites) need to be formulated. Improvements to existing settlements should be designed to minimize removal or disturbance of residents. New serviced sites should be used primarily to expand supply, and not as decanting areas for squatter or slum clearance programmes.

(c) *Cost recovery and affordability.* The financial resources available to most governments for housing are limited, yet the numbers needing assistance are vast. It is therefore vital that the majority of investment costs in land and infrastructure are both affordable by, and recoverable from, the beneficiaries. This applies where assets are transferred to private ownership, or are largely recovered from local taxes, such as when public services are provided to which specific private benefits cannot be assigned. This implies that site layouts and design standards should be extremely efficient and low service standards adopted in order to minimize costs.

(d) *Security of tenure.* This is critical to establish the confidence of the household and the community and to encourage the household to build and improve their shelters. The form such security of tenure takes varies considerably between countries.

(e) *Scale and replicability.* Institutional, management, and financial aspects of upgrading and new settlement programmes should be designed so that they can rapidly expand to the scale necessary in a reasonably short space of time. In Jakarta this has largely been achieved for the existing residents within 12 years and in Manila the upgrading programme, if implemented as planned, would achieve the same goal in about 15 years. Projects which cannot be rapidly expanded to scale are generally a waste of time, energy, and money.

(f) *Institutional and management arrangements.* The definition of appropriate responsibilities at central, city, and community levels is important to avoid overcentralization of operations and to maintain flexibility and initiative at the lower levels. Suitable arrangements must be established for regular and open communication between the relevant agencies of government involved in developing and financing the programmes (see Chapter 9).

(g) *Mobilizing finance.* Individual savings and institutional funds need to be encouraged to enter the housing sector to provide liquidity for construction financing, long-term mortgage financing and later a secondary mortgage market.

The programmes developed with World Bank assistance are similar in some ways to the approach to housing advocated by supporters of community power such as Illich and Turner, and exemplified by the squatter invasions of the 1950s and 1960s in Peru and Chile. In the Bank-financed projects, the family usually obtains a serviced plot and has a wide latitude of freedom to construct the type and size of dwelling that it wishes. But there is a fundamental difference in approach. The protagonists for community power see housing as one vehicle for the individual family and community to express some control over their own lives rather than being passive consumers of goods provided by others. They argue that this is an important way to force government to respond to the people's priorities, and to redress political power from bureaucratic structures to smaller user-controlled groups. The Bank, on the other hand, justifies owner-built house construction and involvement of community organization purely on the grounds of economic efficiency, i.e. lower cost and greater speed. Since the Bank is owned by governments, and makes its loans to governments, the degree of devolution of power and control which can be accomplished through any project is heavily dependent on the attitude of the particular government to this issue. Nevertheless, individuals within the Bank do share some of the views of the user-control philosophers and in suitable circumstances have been able to prepare projects which are more heavily user-controlled. The early projects in San Salvador are an example in which Bank funds were on-lent to a non-profit private foundation (FUNDASAL) which developed substantial settlement programmes in conjunction with user groups (see Chapter 2). More recently, the Bank has been paying more attention to housing finance, the construction and building materials industries, small-scale and community-operated businesses, and mechanisms to encourage release of land on to the market. These are areas where improvements are required to allow individuals and local groups greater freedom and opportunity to develop their own initiatives in housing.

Since 1972, when the Bank made its first loan for an urban shelter project and 1981, about 50 Bank loans and IDA credits have been made for shelter covering 35 countries. The total amount lent for shelter[3] over the period is about US$1200 million in loans and US$360 million in IDA credits with an average loan amount of about US$31 million per project. Since the Bank funds contribute about 45% to the total project cost, the total amount spent for shelter under Bank-assisted projects through 1982 is about US$3500 million. The average of 25,000 households benefited per project between 1972–81 has grown to 62,000 for the year 1981/82. The breakdown of expenditures among project subcomponents was distributed, on average, as follows: (a) *shelter*[4] sites and services 33%, upgrading 27%, other off-site works 3%, (b) *economic generation*, small scale infrastructure 5%, (c) *community services*[5] schools 5%, health centres and business and markets 7%, commercial and industrial sites 9%, (d) *technical assistance*[6], project management and monitoring and evaluation 4%, design and engineering supervision and training 5%, studies and forward planning 2%.

EVALUATION

What benefits were derived from this expenditure? Under the new settlement components about 370,000 plots were prepared, benefiting about 2 million people, and through the upgrading components about 7 million people have been assisted (generally at lesser levels of service than for the new serviced sites). In most cases, the land tenure status was regularized, offering freehold or leasehold to the occupants[7], or a long-term right of occupancy. The cost per person has varied considerably, ranging from $500 per capita down to $30 per capita, depending on beneficiary affordability and the nature of the scheme. The average shelter unit in Bank-financed projects has frequently cost less than 20% of the cost of units built earlier by the Government (in one case only 4% of the cost!), and among some governments these low-cost solutions have now become the 'new orthodoxy'. About 60% of all costs in shelter projects directly benefited the poverty group, who also represented about 60% of all the beneficiaries of the project. The economic rates of return at appraisal of the projects averaged well over 20%, although this would drop where cost increases were incurred during implementation.

As regards project management, indicators show that costs have generally kept close to estimates at appraisal, but projects have taken much longer to implement than expected. As with other sectors in the Bank, appraisal estimates of the speed of implementation are sometimes overly optimistic. Project development periods have typically been scheduled over 3–4 years but have taken 5–7 years to complete. Nevertheless, urban projects show a disbursement profile very close to the Bank average, despite the greater institutional complexity of many of the projects. There do not appear to be significant differences in implementation time between 'complex' and 'simple' urban projects. Greater differences exist between countries. A continuing problem has been adequate and timely land acquisition. One reason for the speed and scale of upgrading in Indonesia (see Chapter 4) is the absence of land acquisition. Other means of achieving project objectives without large-scale land acquisition by government are now being tried in some new projects. For open land, these include land readjustment schemes in Korea, and in the Philippines loans to private developers who arrange joint ventures with local landowners. In Jakarta initial experiments are being tried with 'guided land development', a simplified form of land readjustment, whereby low-cost roads and unsurfaced rights of way are laid out by government on private land with the agreement of landowners, whose land value rises because of the improvements. The rises are modest due to the low standards, and costs are recouped through a betterment tax.

The effect of the Bank's involvement on government policy and housing investments has been mixed. In some countries in East Africa, and individual states in India, dialogue with the Bank has resulted in significant shifts in policy and funding towards low-cost solutions. In other countries such as Indonesia, where government has been committed to broad-coverage, low-cost programmes, the Bank's aims were already similar, and its funds helped to rapidly expand the scale of the national kampung improvement programme. In a third group, there is either a continuing conflict within the government or changes of policies with changes of government, and projects tend to be accepted for the foreign exchange they bring, without a broad-scale commitment. The major recurring problems seem to be on arguments about standards (fear of 'building slums'), and subsidies. Weak executing agencies are also a problem in some countries.

As in-depth evaluation of the socioeconomic impact of four World Bank-financed upgrading and sites and services projects which have been built and occupied has recently been completed[8], and gives some indication of their successes and failures. They were compared with unimproved 'control' communities of a similar type in order to measure changes. It must be kept in mind that these were the earliest projects assisted by the Bank and modifications in technical and institutional design have been made in the subsequent ones now under implementation. The key findings are:

(a) The projects in Senegal, El Salvador, and Zambia have had a significant impact on the urban housing stocks, and met total supply requirements for the target population of between 20% and 50% in their respective cities.
(b) The quality of houses constructed by the residents was much higher than expected and they were paid for by the residents.
(c) The projects were occupied by beneficiaries whose incomes ranged from the 70th down to the 20th percentile of income in the sites and services projects and down to the 10th percentile in upgrading projects. Subsequent checks indicated that higher-income groups were not buying out the original lower-income beneficiaries. Rents had also remained fairly stable, due probably to the low standards of infrastructure and minimal road widths.
(d) Unexpectedly, the sites and services schemes turned out to have similar income distributions as for the slum and squatter settlements.
(e) House-building costs by residents through self-build and self-contract were estimated as 30% lower than similar units built by private developers, and over 60% lower than those built by government agencies. In the Philippines, about 70% of families upgraded to a level equivalent with government housing within a period of 12–18 months.
(f) The construction activities produced a significant effect on incomes and on employment for residents working for contractors. There was also a dramatic expansion of rental rooms in upgrading areas.
(g) The picture on cost recovery was mixed. It was a major problem in some of the projects where up to 50% of the payments were in arrears. This was attributed not to affordability problems, but to poor management by the agency, uncompleted services, lack of involvement and accountability of the community, and in one case political pressure from the community for a lax attitude to collection. Nevertheless, the overall cost recovery picture across all sites and services projects is better, ranging from 63% collection rate in Africa to over 95% in India and Indonesia, and 98% in El Salvador (see Chapter 2).

(h) There were weaknesses in the administration of building materials loans where the materials themselves were provided.
(i)   Specific employment-creating components were less than successful, partly due to collateral restrictions by the local banks and cumbersome administration.

The general conclusions confirmed the validity of the progressive housing model, but suggested the need for more flexible credit arrangements for building material loans, and clearer arrangements for cost recovery discussed with the community earlier on would reduce repayment problems. At the design stage the project should be consciously designed to be competitive with the attractions offered by the informal housing market. On-plot development should be reduced further, and a bigger variety of plot sizes offered with a greater variety of service standards.

There are, in addition, some further issues which emerge from the experience of sites and services projects which were not fully covered by the above study. One set concerns institutional relations. Problems have occurred through the establishment of special-project units, and it is more desirable to use existing agencies whenever possible. Coordination and cooperation between agencies and different levels of government has been weak in a number of cases and has been much improved where the project has been fully discussed first by all concerned agencies and their interests represented on some kind of coordination Board as discussed in Chapter 9. A frequent difficulty has been the relationships between the development agency and local governments which are not always included as full partners and consequently feel that projects are dumped on them.

A second set relates to physical design and appearance. There is often a tendency for the physical designer in the agency to increase standards during design so that the project becomes unaffordable. This is motivated by a fear that government does not want to be seen building slums, although the very provision of tenure and infrastructure, and the demonstrated response of the occupants in rapidly constructing solid houses, belies this fear. An associated problem is the danger of encouraging large-scale suppliers of standardized building materials which the new residents in the sites and services projects are required to buy for their on-plot development. While this may offer the chance of a more rapid completion of the project with a more standardized appearance, it may also mean that the materials are not suitable for the incremental nature of house construction by the residents. Encouraging large-scale suppliers may also reduce employment and displace the existing and budding small entrepreneurs who produce and distribute the more traditional labour-intensive building materials.

The third set of issues relates to the 'fit' of the project design with the social and economic circumstances of the urban poor. Many of the poor are not regularly employed and more variety in payment times and systems than the standard monthly payment should be devised. A number of the sites and services projects have been located beyond the city perimeter in order to obtain cheaper land. Although the locations are selected so that public transport is affordable to fixed-employment locations, this makes the schemes attractive mainly to the regularly employed. Those who are not regularly employed depend on proximity to higher-income neighbourhoods, markets, and dense urban areas to pick up jobs on a day-to-day basis. The sites and services projects are designed to attract relatively few upper-income group residents and thus do not provide much opportunity for this informal employment. For this reason, and because of their large size, they run the danger of becoming factory-worker and low-grade civil servant ghettos. There may be a number of solutions to this problem. One could be to expand the project scope to cover a wider range of income categories while keeping a major emphasis on low-income groups. Another could be to facilitate the existing informal settlement systems but add some guidance on house location, with services to follow later. This approach, using community-based government officials, is being considered in Jakarta. Another could be to incorporate smaller sites and services sites as infil and perimeter expansion as part of upgrading programmes. In any event, it is important for settlement policies to move from developing large, uniform-income isolated 'project' sites towards intervening more strategically in the land market and to encourage the existing low-level government administrators, non-government organizations, and area community groups to assist the formation of area housing associations. This could guide the settlement process in their communities, with the government offering a range of infrastructure services packages which the housing associations could buy. This approach of incremental upgrading and more active use of area housing associations is in the early stages of consideration in the Philippines, and variants on it have been established for some time in Latin America.

A fourth area which is now receiving more attention by the Bank is to separate financing from implementation agencies. A mortgage bank which can lend or guarantee long-term finance to beneficiaries and can also appraise projects and lend construction finance, can play a key role. It can lend to private developers and housing associations as well as government agencies; it can place government housing agencies in competition with the private sector and thereby improve their efficiency; it can also get national housing agencies out of the business of long-term finance and cost recovery, at which they do not have a good record, and place collection in the hands of private agencies. It can move to raise funds on the private capital markets without relying entirely on the budget as a sole source. Finally, such a financial institution can become an intermediary for foreign funding, thereby relieving agencies such as the Bank from the details of project appraisal. These intermediaries are well established in parts of Latin America and are emerging elsewhere, but will take time to develop their capabilities.

Some of these issues are being tackled in the more recent group of projects financed by the Bank. However, much still remains to be done to transform the standard 'project' into a more sensitive process which can be adapted and manipulated by the end users and expand the scale at which upgrading and new serviced land is provided. At the present time the impact of upgrading projects is beginning to be substantial in some of the world's major cities. For example, most of the kampung areas in Jakarta have already been upgraded over the last 10–15 years and it appears that this is roughly the time-span for an energetic improvement programme to deal with the backlog of improvement and concurrent growth in a major city. The impact of sites and services to substantially expand supply of residential land has, however, been much less successful in the large cities and densely populated countries. The output has generally fallen well behind the yearly increase in low-income families, partly due to the sheer scale of increase and partly to difficulties of land acquisition. There is a need to expand the number of actors in the business of implementation, and to try more innovative solutions. In Manila, private developers are proposing sites and services schemes which are covering the 25th to 70th percentile income groups. Their profits appear to be covered in their lower costs of development (for the same standards) compared to government-developed schemes. The main barriers to them entering the market earlier were the lack of long-term mortgages to their buyers, construction finance and rigid building regulations. The concept of 'guided land development' noted earlier is another effort at innovation.

FUTURE DIRECTIONS

Today's political and economic climate is bringing significant changes to the Bank's outlook and operations which will also influence the urban and housing sectors. High interest rates worldwide are increasing the cost of Bank money to its borrowers. The effect of this is likely to make the developing countries more cautious, probably reducing the rate of growth of their borrowing and selecting those projects which are technically complex and have a high foreign exchange percentage, or a high economic rate of return, for international financing. This does not bode well for the social sectors including housing, although housing can point to direct cost recovery which reduces financial requirements over the long term as a factor in its favour and also a good economic rate of return (ranging between 16% and 46% IRR for Bank shelter projects). The urban shelter programmes of the Bank for 1982–86 have roughly doubled the number of projects in the pipeline compared to the previous 4 years.

High interest rates, together with anti-aid sentiment in the United States and parts of Europe, have resulted in a drastic reduction in IDA (soft loan window) funds. They have also reduced the total funds available to the Bank, with the heaviest impact on its poorest borrowers. China's recent membership will have the effect of spreading available funds even thinner. Concurrently, emphasis is being placed by Bank management on energy development and on greater involvement and co-financing with the private sector. While this will expand funds for industry and mining, it may reduce those available for the social sectors.

Within the Bank, contradictory pressures are emerging. While, on the one hand, reduced lending should allow greater time for improved preparation and supervision of projects, the management has felt the need to demonstrate that the Bank is reducing its administrative costs, although these only run at between 0.5 and 1% of funds committed. The effect of reducing staff time coefficients per project means that those sectors such as urban and rural development which deal with numerous government agencies, and where projects are by their nature more complex and require more staff time, are the most affected by cuts in administrative costs. Two approaches to adjust to these conditions are emerging. One approach is to simplify the projects by reducing the number of components and agencies involved. In some cases, this can be pursued without loss in quality and relevance, but in others it may result in an unresponsive solution to the needs of the country and communities concerned, and hold back progress in institutional and organizational reform. Another dimension relevant to housing and municipal services is to focus on 'programme' lending, whereby less attention is paid to the details of project design and larger slices of ongoing programmes are funded. But a necessary precondition is a suitable agency available in the field to undertake the appraisal and supervision functions for the Bank. This, of course, is a major objective of most bank projects, but in a relatively new sector such as housing and urban development, where numerous agencies and levels of government and financial markets are involved, and the organizational relationships are still fluid, it will still take a few years before programme lending can be established beyond some countries such as Korea and Brazil, which already have capable institutions in this area. Another way to obtain simpler projects in urban services, yet to maintain the coherence in priorities and timing, is to improve local capability in planning and budgeting while funding projects in separate sectors which are consistent with the overall plan and programme. This, of course, should have been a concern of the Bank and other funding agencies from the beginning, but is emerging only now as pressure to use public funds more carefully is growing due to constraints on public borrowing. But the efforts required to estabish effective planning and budgeting take considerable time, and their success is uncertain.

One means for the Bank to influence government spending towards more efficient use of funds and towards programmes which improve the incomes and efficiency of the poor would be to incorporate these concerns as key issues in structural adjustment loans which have been recently introduced by the Bank. These are usually large, and lent not for specific projects, but to the Government Treasury to assist national liquidity. The loan is conditional on the government implementing policy reforms in designated areas such as trade tariffs, industry credit policies, or power prices. There is no reason why such a loan should not focus on government policies of budgeting and standards for sectors which could improve their assistance to poverty groups, and on associated improvements in administrative efficiency.

Although within the Bank more constraints are emerging, opportunities for expanding basic urban service programmes in developing countries are increasing. Many governments have found that their sites and services and slum upgrading programmes are feasible and very popular. A base of popular support has been established, and in some countries has exerted pressure on the government to continue and expand these programmes. This could be achieved by helping communities and interest groups to form urban development and housing associations and encouraging both private and public agencies to address basic needs. Greater emphasis also needs to be placed on policy changes regarding the land market, planning and building standards, and finance, to allow low-income groups easier access.

Releasing sufficient land for low-income settlement at an affordable price is still a major problem and land acquisition by government agencies is very slow. Although a capital gains tax on transfer might reduce prices it is unlikely to be implemented quickly in many countries due to the influence which landowners wield in government. Another option is to provide low-standard infrastructure in selected areas together with betterment charges or a tax on idle land. Mobilizing long-term mortgage finance, reducing subdivision standards, and assisting private developers with information on available land, construction finance, and off-site infrastructure, are other ways in which government can improve the land and housing markets without entering directly into land acquisition and development itself. The Bank is assisting several projects which contain these elements, and expects to do more on these lines in the future.

Slum improvement and sites and services programmes have normally been introduced first in the capital or largest city in a country, where they are easier to administer and where the service backlog is worst. Now that these are well established, projects are being introduced to a wide range of secondary and smaller cities. This raises a major issue concerning their management and relationships with municipal governments. The programmes have usually been started by a central Ministry of housing or public works but as they expand to other cities the organizational problems of central control have become severe. It is essential for municipal governments to take the lead, especially in the case of slum improvement, which is meshed into local politics and services. The central agency role then changes to that of establishing the main policy framework, allocating funds, and providing technical assistance and guidance on standards and procedures. Concurrently, central financing mechanisms such as a municipal works fund, and appropriate links between development agencies such as Public Works and the Ministry of Local Government, will need to be considered. Adjustments in responsibilities for local services and taxes between central and local levels may be needed. At the municipal level, reforms are often necessary to raise local revenues, and in staffing and administration. Many slum improvement programmes funded by the Bank are now in this stage of devolution and expansion, and these concerns will need time, skill, and sensitivity on the part of Bank staff and consultants over the next few years. As these arrangements are established and become operational, true 'programme' lending will become possible.

SUMMARY

Compared to the scale and speed of urbanization in developing countries, the efforts of international agencies have been on a relatively modest scale. Yet while the need for investment in urban settlements is growing, the international financial climate and pressures on development assistance are combining to reduce or reverse the rapid growth of investments which the World Bank made during the 1970s in low-income settlement programmes. These programmes are at a stage where, in the medium term, they could become more self-sustaining without external assistance and reach a scale where they have a significant impact. However, the gains now made are likely to be eroded unless a major effort is made over the next few years, both by governments and the Bank, in firmly establishing the policies and organizational arrangements to encourage government agencies, municipalities, private developers, communities, and families to participate in a complementary way in improving and developing their living and working environments.

ACRONYMS AND TERMS USED
IN THIS CHAPTER

ADB   Asian Development Bank. A similar organization to the World Bank but lending exclusively in Asia.

Bilateral aid Aid arrangements between two nation states.

IDA   International Development Association. An affiliate of the World Bank which finances development projects in the poorest countries at concessional terms.

IDB   Inter-American Development Bank. A similar organization to the World Bank but lending exclusively in Latin America.

IFC   International Finance Corporation. An affiliate of the World Bank which promotes private enterprises in developing countries through equity participation and loans.

ILO   International Labour Organization. A member agency of the UN.

IRR   International rate of return.

LDC	Less developed country.
UN	United Nations.
UNDP	United Nations Development Programme. A department of the UN concerned exclusively with development planning and programmes.
USAID	United States Agency for International Development.
WHO	World Health Organization. One agency of the United Nations.
World Bank	Official name — International Bank for Reconstruction and Development. Lends money to priority development projects in developing countries. Its 142 member governments have contributed to its capital, but the major part of funds for lending is raised in international capital markets.

NOTES AND REFERENCES

1. These estimates are necessarily approximate since the Bank does not analyse its lending along these lines.
2. For a minimally serviced plot, the lowest income groups are usually prepared to pay 10% of income.
3. For sites and services and upgrading projects, including infrastructure, social services, housing finance, and small-business components, but excluding major city water supply and urban transport components in loans.
4. Also includes loans for building materials to project beneficiaries.
5. Also includes software such as community health works and programmes.
6. Mostly for consultants. Local staff costs would amount to a further 4% to 10% to total project costs.
7. Except the upgrading programme in Indonesia, where existing land rights are complex and the traditional right of occupancy is generally respected by both private and public landowners.
8. Prepared by the Urban and Regional Economic Division of the Bank, in association with IDRC (Canada), it will probably be published in the Bank's 'Working Paper' series. The projects are located in Senegal, El Salvador, and Zambia (constructed between 1973 and 1977), and in the Philippines (1978–81). They were evaluated by local professionals independent of the implementing agency, but using the Bank's advice on analytic techniques and methods.

Low-income Housing in the Developing World
Edited by G. K. Payne

Chapter 11

The Role of International Consultants

David S. Walton

INTRODUCTION

International consultants have played a significant role in the initial feasibility studies which established sites and services and upgrading projects in a whole range of countries and supported locally generated initiatives in even more. They have also undertaken sustained technical assistance programmes.

I cannot pretend that this chapter is in any way a comprehensive review of this experience, which has involved numerous consultants and consultancy firms from a number of countries[1]. However, through connections in consultancy, related academic institutions, and the World Bank, a general picture of this experience can be established. Thus, whilst the attitudes expressed here are largely based upon the experience of Halcrow Fox, they are also corroborated by the experience of many colleagues in different companies.

One would expect the consultancy role, particularly that of international consultants, to diminish in the future, as the process becomes understood and properly managed by local professionals and as the number of places for new programmes declines. This chapter may thus be a swansong of an interesting period of work, and there are signs that commissions in the area will diminish rapidly. However, there is room for doubt about the total end of consultancy involvement. Despite the expense of hiring top-grade foreign specialists, they do, at least, generally perform. Unfortunately, in many countries it may be a long time before an adequately large, committed and stable cadre of local expertise is available. However, sites and services are a difficult business for the consultant. I hope in explaining the nature of the difficulties as we have found them, that some improvements may emerge—both regarding the performance of consultants and, more importantly, the effectiveness of programmes on which they are engaged.

THE CONSULTANT IN RELATION
TO THE CLIENT

Someone said recently that a client's most frustrating characteristic is the inability to recognize his own enlightened self-interest. This, from my experience, is at the core of the problems faced by consultants when they enter the very low-cost housing field.

In any single job, there is effectively a series of clients:

(a) a variety of central and local government bodies, probably only one of which is responsible for contracting the consultants, but which may be neither responsible for day-to-day project administration nor the executing agency;
(b) a funding agency, such as the World Bank, which will have its own expectations of the project; and, perhaps above all
(c) the community or communities within which settlement upgrading, or sites and services, are to be applied.

Both within each of these groups and between them there are generally wide, even violent, divergencies of views on which approaches are relevant. In particular there are often powerful people in government who do not believe in the general approach described in this book, and thus project preparation and implementation take place against strong and influential opposition; conflict between the progressives and reactionaries in government is the usual context of the consultant's work in this field.

The consultant is an additional occasional player in this game. He is the least needed and, unlike the other parties, has no obvious long-term stake. It is often unclear from the reactions of the others to him whether he is a player, the referee, or the football. As he sets about his various tasks the reactions of three different parties, and the sub-sets within them, are such that one can despair of the inability of each to recognize the changes and trade-offs in their stances which are required if an effective programme is to be developed.

THE ROLES AND PARAMETERS OF CONSULTANCY

The roles

There are four main functional roles the international planning consultant plays in the field of low-cost housing:

(a) feasibility studies;
(b) detailed design;
(c) technical assistance;
(d) assistance to funding agencies.

The first three of these are the most important.

Feasibility studies involve the preparation of specific projects which are often pilot schemes for a longer-term programme. The work includes project identification, the preliminary design of technical and institutional alternatives and evaluation of the costs and benefits of each, and the definition of a project and programme for financing. The subsequent detailed design of physical and institutional project components may be undertaken either by a consultant team, in a similar fashion to the feasibility study, or as part of an ongoing technical assistance role.

Technical assistance involves the provision of staff to help municipalities and line agencies, such as National Housing Authorities, to develop appropriate programmes of action, get them under way and coordinate the investment. The consultant becomes a coordinator/manager—a working executive within an agency of government, working alongside, assisting, and training local staff.

Assistance of funding agencies usually takes the form of an individual consultant acting virtually as a member of the funding agency staff. Most commonly this is for a short period, either at the initial project identification stage or for the purposes of project appraisal during and after the feasibility study.

Nature of commissions

Invariably, the explicit attitudes and policies of different agencies are in conflict, the guidelines of the funding agencies are unwelcome to government, and the communities have different priorities from either the government or the funding agencies.

The consultant is employed in order to produce a positive and generally supported programme of action in such a situation; a programme acceptable to all three client bodies which is also practical. A consensus of acceptability is desperately difficult to find and practicality is frequently in conflict with what is acceptable. For example, many programmes have been designed and adopted, but remain very delayed or unrealized because of inadequate implementation capacity of one sort or another. To get the various clients to face up to hard realities is the most difficult, but perhaps the most important, of the consultant's tasks.

The work is by nature multidisciplinary. Project design will include physical, economic, social, and institutional plans. The team will include planners, architects, engineers, economists, sociologists, and specialists in disciplines ranging from low-cost construction technology to municipal finance.

Reasons for appointment

In obtaining a job, the planning consultant is almost invariably bidding in conjunction both with other international consultants in complementary disciplines, and increasingly with local consultants. A typical World Bank housing feasibility study may, for example, have a manpower input of some 50–60 man-months. Half of this will go to local consultants (of varying ability and interest), for junior engineers, architects, various local academics, draughtsmen, and support staff. Of the remainder, perhaps 15 man-months may go to planning (including project management), 5 to economics, 5 to engineering, and 5 to specialist support.

The consultant generally gets appointed because of:

(a) the experience and qualifications of his staff;
(b) the firm's record on similar projects;
(c) the adequacy of the proposed work plan;
(d) the repute and connections of his local partner or agent;
(e) above all—he gets the price right.

On all evaluation systems the quality of the team is all-important, particularly the project manager. All staff would be expected to have extensive practical experience abroad and generally be over 30 (often 35–40 or more for senior positions).

Sites and services as consultancy business

In the final analysis, planning consultancy is a business, in that income has to exceed expenditure. The total fees inevitably look large— say US$330,000 for a typical site and service feasibility study— but by the time expenses such as accommodation and air fares have been paid and the local consultant has had his share, there will be US$150,000 left, of which the planning consultant may get US$75,000 and engineers, economists, and so on, the remainder.

The planning consultant has to invest US$8000–16,000 on a significant new job, pay salaries and expenses well ahead of being paid by the client, and meet the financing of these gaps. If there are any overruns (which are frequently beyond his control, arising, for example, from the government not providing promised maps or data), he is very fortunate to be paid any extra and he may have a great deal of difficulty collecting his fees.

In addition, the consultant has to keep a base load of work coming in constantly. Many jobs are only 3–8 months in length. There tend to be long gaps between one commission for feasibility and another for execution, which means extensive unremunerative time and expenses and the risk of losing one's team and its knowledge of the situation. Only the longer technical assistance contracts permit any reasonable length of confidence of surety of income, and thus reliable quality of staffing and commitment to the task.

The structure of consultancy also poses problems. The consultancy profession has developed with a series of relatively specialized and separate sectors— engineering, architecture, management, economics, and planning, for example. However, the range of skills required in sites and services covers all these areas: thus hybrid teams often result, with the lead firm perhaps having only a low share of the input and other firms or individual experts taking the remainder. This adds difficulties in making an effective business out of consultancy in this sector, especially if one is the lead rather than sub-consultant. Moreover, questions of responsibility and professional liability can emerge which become more complicated in a grouping which includes both foreign and local consultants.

It is worth noting the importance of individual specialists in certain fields— sociology, finance, economics, land administration, and institutional planning in particular. The most suitable advisers are frequently individuals, consultants, or part-time consultants from academic institutions. These may be found at home, or more often in the country of the project, where there are frequently extremely highly qualified and appropriately orientated individuals, who can be available on a part-time rather than a full-time basis and whose advice is invaluable. However, the costs are likely to be an unmet expense for the main consultant, programming problems are frequent, and there is often jealousy from within the client agency of the local 'expert'.

Despite these difficulties, it is a type of work which is professionally fascinating, as well as important, and most consultants have just about learnt how to make an operable business out of it.

THE MAIN ACTORS

The international consultant can easily get the impression that he— or she— is in the unenviable position of being criticized by all the actors involved in a project. Thus, government officials may regard consultants as agents of the funding agency, whilst agencies such as the World Bank may consider that they have sold out to the pressures imposed by a client government. Probably the best indication of a successful and appropriate role is when the consultant *is* criticized equally from all sides! Nevertheless, each actor in the field has distinct interests which have to be recognized.

The funding agency

The World Bank has, of course, been the main force in this area since its urban poverty initiatives, following the Nairobi Declaration in the early 1970s. The majority of the remarks here may appear critical of the approaches and staff of the Bank's Urban Projects Department. However, the opposite is true. They are made in the hope of assisting a little in the further development of a most important progressive initiative which has gone far and must go further.

Despite some major successes, there have been too many delays and failures in certain places. While the reasons vary from project to project, the Bank sometimes appears to be its own enemy. A whole litany of principles—affordability, no subsidy, targeting upon the lowest income groups, minimum cost, lower standards of plot size and infrastructure, full cost recovery, replicability, market value of land, and so on have necessarily had to be formulated and applied. As the principles are applied in the design of a project, resistance of one form or another arises. For example, the poorest housing conditions—the most apparently necessary areas for upgrading—will probably include substantial proportions of people outside the target income group. It may be socially impractical to consider a re-blocking exercise that articulates plot size relative to income, and financially and practically unwise because of the structure of the area or the dwellings. The principles thus come into conflict with each other and with practicalities. A whole series of compromises and trade-offs become involved in arriving at a practical and acceptable response, and an over-fierce advocacy of principles tends to increase resistance.

Similarly, at the project design stage much is unknown, particularly about real community reaction as one moves into implementation, and certain issues may be best left reasonably open and flexible for later resolution. The natural desire to batten down project components as accurately as possible may on occasion be counterproductive.

Part of the difficulty appears to be that the need to comply with guidelines and timetables for the Bank's internal procedures is often very constraining on handling the local situation, and it is often very difficult for the Bank's staff to exercise the order of flexibility required. Frustration in Government is often heightened by the mission approach—with intense periods of interrogation and debate on changes at regular intervals.

On occasion it is also possible that schemes and procedures have been over-designed. In poorer African countries in particular, a sort of organized squatting approach with later registration and cost recovery arrangements would often appear a more implementable response than the setting up of a whole range of systems for site development, survey, registration, beneficiary selection, resettlement, banking, and so on. Often systems in these areas are handed down from colonial practice designed for middle-class expatriates, which are impractical to adapt to the real situation. If I remember correctly, there were 21 steps in formally obtaining a building loan in Tanzania, which was too much for either the applicants or the administration to cope with (see Chapter 6). While it is difficult for an agency as essentially formal and legal as the Bank to encourage governments to reduce formality and waive legalities, it often appears desirable.

The same considerations apply to plot surveys and registration. Colonial land title procedures which require individual grants and surveys, and were designed for agricultural holdings, can become the necessary procedures for plot allocation in sites and services programmes. Usually there are not enough surveyors to do the job, and the cost and delays are too great. The alternative of granting title according to layout plan is illegal yet desirable.

The push towards urban land reform, or at least government using the powers available, but not exercised, is another area where, despite the complexities and political sensitivities, the Bank has, I consider, been too reticent on occasion. The search for suitable sites gets progressively more difficult where 'hope' values (often themselves stimulated by project preparation initiatives) exceed affordability, the real market, or opportunity cost. Land prices may cause the production of schemes too far from centres of employment and convenient affordable transport. Sites can be taken up far too slowly and bring the programme and approach into disrepute.

In the future, a movement to more varied schemes would offer several advantages. Potential internal cross-subsidy and thus affordability are limited if the components are solely related to poverty group needs. The wider benefits of infrastructure provision can create values lost to the schemes if it is too restricted in scope and a monotonous 'ghetto' type character of large schemes with too many repetitive low-cost elements can result. This could be overcome if schemes had larger land takes, a variety of open market commercial, industrial and residential uses, and with say 50–70% of the scheme orientated to the poverty group components. This would add to the quality and reputation of the approach in government, and a stronger social, economic, and environmental character would result.

Most schemes would also benefit from more 'non-recoverable' items in amenity terms, particularly in public open space, landscape and recreational facilities, that allow the residents of the 'poor areas' to feel they are being treated equitably when compared with other areas of town. On occasion, the differences in standards of public goods can be extremely provocative in community and political terms, and make adoption and continuous support of the concepts even more difficult.

On the institutional front, I consider there are two useful lessons. A typical steering group of a new project may involve the government's Mortgage Bank, its prime housing agency, its economic planning agency, the departments concerned with lands and public works, and the mayors and senior engineers of the main cities involved. As the project becomes defined, it becomes necessary to allocate responsibilities. Horrible hybrids of split responsibility and accountability often result—with almost everyone having some involvement and no-one in clear central authority with the necessary powers and position to secure implementation. This is another easy problem to see, yet far more difficult to overcome, especially as each situation has to be examined on its own merits. However, a plea must be entered for vesting responsibility for a particular scheme in one agency and, if possible, with one person in a central position of authority.

The second point is that I feel this should be linked with increasing decentralization of scheme responsibility and authority to local governments or agencies away from central government. This is a particular problem because the central government agency is automatically located in the capital city which is usually where the worst or largest problems are to be faced. There is thus an automatic tendency to confuse general policy with execution and to over-centralize. Ideally, there should be an increased separation between policy formulation at national level and executive responsibility for scheme development and administration. This has been done progressively in the Philippines and Indonesia with regard to regional cities. There are also some pointers in Kenya and Tanzania. Whatever the situation, it is essential to stimulate local agencies and give project teams full authority to execute the schemes in their areas.

The project preparation approach of a 6–9-month study commission followed by appraisal, loan negotiations, and then later implementation, can also have some unsatisfactory side-effects. At the end of the job the team disperses, there is no-one left to help government follow through, and the consultants' staff are on down-time waiting to start again and losing money. A lower input 6–12-month 'holding presence' should be part of such commissions in order to maintain momentum. In addition, the staffing of implementation-phase design and site supervision is frequently, for cost minimization reasons, extremely weighted in favour of the local consultant, while the expatriate consultant is expected to be contractually responsible. Thus, responsiblity is unfairly distributed in relation to the inputs required to ensure the job is done properly. The principle should be adopted that whoever has the majority share of the inputs is the prime consultant and contracting party.

Two other reflections occur. It is very frustrating, if not unprofessional, to find a direct competitor from the same country as a consultant on a Bank mission with access to the consultant's client and work. Secondly, time for appraisals and missions should be allowed for in the work programme and not take place over the final period of report preparation.

The government

The problems of re-orientating institutions or creating new ones, of changing standards and procedures, and of obtaining land are difficult, cross many departmental boundaries, run into entrenched attitudes, and even create constitutional problems. A real will and powerful support in government are often lacking but are nevertheless indispensable. There is usually a battle between the progressives and reactionaries in government, and too often the progressives are the young professionals whose career prospects are dependent on the goodwill of their reactionary bosses. Perhaps one of the most important roles of the international consultant is to represent the former and give their ideas credibility and authority, especially as the consultant can perhaps gain access to political levels not possible to those working within the government hierarchy.

The weaknesses of conventional housing development approaches in both economic and practical terms are often only dimly perceived by those whose support of new initiatives is most crucial. As a consultant, I have often found it necessary to establish informal lines of communication and dialogue with the higher personalities in government, so that they can realize the nature of problems and then lend their weight and leadership to the support of the new approach.

In my experience, government likes to proceed by consensus, and as the project proceeds it is necessary to build up general support, and avoid major departmental heads either losing face, or becoming entrenched opposition. The danger in this is that the end-result may be the 'lowest common denominator', and as such not an effective or a robust response to real needs. Two principles are useful here. First, while forcing the tabling of issues one should not attempt to force their resolution if it is not achievable, since this can produce a counter-productive over-reaction. Second, if the issues appear intractable, the consultant can use time both to allow the opposition to reconsider and amend its stance and for the team to decide on alternative 'sales' approaches, or variations on the principles.

The higher levels of government often have the political awareness of the need for new responses to providing shelter, while departmental heads frequently regard themselves as the custodians of past approaches and standards, too many of which are out of date and irrelevant hand-downs from colonial administration. These reactionary attitudes are usually best overcome by manoeuvring over time, rather than through direct and continuing conflict. In the areas of institutional and procedural change 'the vested interests' are strong, and similar attitudes exist and are often more entrenched over such issues as urban land reform.

The community

Almost invariably consultants find that they try to interpret the needs of the project communities, and tend to find themselves championing their interests.

First, there is the problem of finding out what people really want. The individual's perception is constrained by what he has already experienced and it is difficult for him to make useful comments on squatter upgrading, or sites and services housing, which may be totally outside his experience. In any case, the Third World citizen is often unaccustomed to expressing himself on public matters, and snap reactions to unexpected questions in a formal social survey may be of little value. Responses are often coloured by what the respondent either thinks the interviewer wishes to hear— what is fashionable, 'modern' or 'civilized'—or should hear, because of the fear of authority, for example. The 'head of family' view may also be very different to the total family view, especially in societies where women are not expected to speak their minds.

Interpreters are usually needed to make contact with local residents, but even with excellent translation facilities there can be many problems in collecting and then understanding information. First, people have powerful incentives to mislead when they perceive that the nature of their replies may affect their benefits under any future project. Potential beneficiaries have been known to tell the most dreadful lies when access to scarce housing is at stake. Even when the respondent is eager to cooperate fully, he may have difficulty in understanding what is intended. Gaining the truth is like trying to reach the centre of the proverbial onion—you peel off layer after layer, and it takes a long time.

On most projects, household surveys are carried out to get as reliable an overall picture as possible on matters such as demographic structure, dwelling conditions, income and expenditure, values, and attitudes. In addition, drawings and notes are made of dwellings, their structure, services, condition, and use, in order to understand lifestyles. Formal and informal meetings are held in order to talk in depth to local leaders and other key personalities. Needless to say, many leaders who present themselves as responsible to the 'whole community' often turn out to be firmly tied to one particular faction or kin group and may put forward views and solutions which are quite contrary to those of their neighbours. Under such conditions it is difficult to get the right balance between the flavour of in-depth interviews and the cross-sectional picture of a formal survey. All this is not just a role for the team member who specializes in social matters: the whole team needs to get the right orientation from immersion in the community. An intensive series of house-to-house visits is always a good start to a project, followed by regular contacts as the project proceeds.

Going beyond the collection of information, it is usually felt to be a desirable goal to enlist the active participation of local people in a project. But communities vary in the extent to which they are ready for this. Some squatter settlements are bursting with self-help and self-confidence while elsewhere, in many parts of the Middle East for instance, there is little tradition of voluntary association and in some places government has been so aggressive in suppressing alternative sources of power that residents are too frightened to take part in any kind of civic activity.

How can we understand the problems and aspirations of people with totally different lifestyles and value systems? Consultants are rich, educated, and Western; but then so are most politicians and professionals in the client body (if not more so). Sadly, they and other members of the local middle class are often unaware of the conditions poor people actually live in; or, if they are aware, they may refuse to acknowledge it. This can evolve into the consultant trying to educate or contradict his client on the situation of his poorer compatriots, which is not an easy task politically. However, the critical need is to make people in government — politicians and senior officials in particular — realize the nature of their housing problems and the need for very committed support to the philosophy of sites and services and settlement upgrading.

In principle, one would think that the international consultant should move out of this area quickly, leaving the field to local professionals who have the language and other understanding to relate more accurately to the community. But I am not too sure about this generalization. The 'foreigner' can be seen as a sort of symbol of the new initiative, and not necessarily a total servant of the authorities of whom the people are so often suspicious. A sense of both access to real support and innocence from local patronage can also be conveyed by the right staff.

SUPPORT CAST

Local associates and counterparts

There is a dogma widespread amongst governments and funding agencies that local expertise should be developed and knowledge and skills transferred through the international consultant working with local firms. The reality is often somewhat different, and the involvement of the local firm is, on occasion, dominated by pecuniary considerations rather than concern about the quality of the project. In many countries, of course, there are committed and talented professionals in the various technical areas involved. In Kenya, for example, local expertise in all areas is very high whether at a company or an individual level, or in the academic institutions. There is thus a very limited need for external consultants there or in most of Latin America and large parts of South-East Asia. The competent local consultant is more cost-effective and thus to be preferred, providing the best people are not too busy to play their role in project preparation. Similarly, within government agencies there are numerous examples of very highly motivated and skilled professionals who have little need of foreign assistance.

An 'in-house' or local consultant project is thus to be preferred when the skills and motivation are available on an adequate scale. However, this is not always the case, and there are situations within which foreign consultants may be able to offer a useful service. Where this is the case it is often advisable for the foreign consultancy to have a single local associate in any country where it operates. Clients tend to expect this, and to associate one local consultant with one expatriate. The regular association benefits both sides through the thorough understanding which the key personnel acquire of each other and of the other firm's characteristics.

Where possible, it is best for the consultant to develop associations with professional companies rather than agents. This helps get the price right as the professional firm can, at least in theory, make a substantive contribution to the work in return for their share of the fees. It also commands more respect from client and funding agency. However, we have on occasion been severely let down over the poor performance of the other party, with penalties in cost overruns and quality of the job. It is best to take little on trust and, at an early stage, reach a formal agreement between the parties specifying the roles and responsibilities of each very clearly.

Looking to the future, I would like to think that funding agencies and clients would try both to take a more realistic attitude regarding the professional capabilities of local consultants and be more rigorous in their examination of them. In addition, price competition is a major problem resulting in the job frequently being squeezed too tight; and a strict use of the two-envelope system is to be preferred. In general, either the local or foreign firm should be clearly in the lead, with the other as subconsultants. Job-specific joint ventures are in practice very difficult to operate in this particular area, and should not be encouraged.

Educational institutions

The exercise of taking people from a variety of different cultures appears a sort of comparative modern urban geography, and it is difficult to see how improved technical responses to particular local circumstances will necessarily result. However, the philosophic 'orientation' and the confidence gained in tackling problems to be found throughout the developing world probably makes international education worthwhile. Local professionals working alongside technical assistance staff and consultants is as effective as any other approach I have seen, especially where a teaching component is built into the work programme. Good examples of this can be found in the work of NHA in the Philippines, Perumnas in Indonesia, Ardhi in Tanzania, and UDD in Jordan, all of which combine research, training, and consultancy services for central and local government in their respective countries.

However, training is a real problem. Those given courses rapidly get promoted or transferred and staff turnover is high. The key engineering staff, in particular, are often either too set in their ways, have better prospects doing different work, are too inexperienced for real authority or, when given early authority, move on rapidly to other things.

For the future, higher government salaries and status appear essential to obtain and keep a core of good-quality staff in any project agency. However, this is frequently impossible, and devices such as special allowances have to be invented to try to maintain staff loyalties.

Planning education oriented to the provision of shelter in the Third World is offered at such institutes as the Developing Planning Unit, INLOGOV, Oxford Polytechnic, and the Institute of Housing Studies. However, engineering — the key to implementation — has virtually no comparable institutions or courses in universities or polytechnics to orientate engineers to the type of low-cost municipal and constructional engineering involved. This seems a matter for the attention of the engineering professional institutes and educationalists.

Training

One of the problems for the consultant is that somehow he appears to be expected to help in the development of local expertise either in government or in consultancy without being paid for it, and without the local staff to receive the training. Occasionally, training requirements are specifically planned and costed in, and when this is done there are fewer problems. Unfortunately, budgets are so tight that generally this element is squeezed out, even if it is included in the first place. In addition, salary and other conditions embedded in the government system may virtually preclude suitable staff being attracted to the programme.

It is always frustrating for consultants to be asked if they have given adequate attention to training local staff, or helped or hindered the development of local capability. Generally, consultants are there simply because there is not an available local capability and the need is first and foremost for better shelter and services for the needy and not for training staff which the client body probably does not, or cannot, produce in any event. Thus, for the future, adequate training budgets and financial conditions to attract and retain suitable local staff are prerequisites for building up a qualified cadre of local expertise.

CONCLUSIONS

Much of what is in this chapter may appear critical of the sites and services approach — because of the many difficulties and failures involved. However, I must declare my colours and say that in principle I am a very firm believer in the overall philosophy of this type of response to the huge need for access to shelter and basic services, and see no realistic major alternative.

However, whether the approach is based, for example, upon the sort of structured principles the World Bank has promoted, or more informal community action, success appears to depend a great deal on the structure of the particular society. Appropriate and effective responses therefore vary enormously, and generalizations are difficult, but I will make an attempt. Where there have been failures, it appears to me they are failures of.

(a) inappropriate institutional and land tenure systems;
(b) lack of support at governmental level (lack of political will);
(c) lack of local, i.e. community participation;
(d) over-imposed dogma of full cost recovery/target population/minimum costs and

standards (the principles are correct perhaps, but in practice they are frequently impractical and unacceptable, and a more flexible approach is necessary);

(e) lack of implementation capacity in government and unrealistic expectations of the rise in that capacity;

(f) the structure of professional assistance which is too often temporary, uncoordinated, partial, and uncommitted;

(g) failure to remove inhibiting over-formal and complicated procedures, such as plot surveys and mortgage loan systems;

(h) an over-dependence upon municipal or governmental intervention. Experience suggests that the private sector generally provides far better value for money than government agencies can achieve direct. Opportunities should therefore be sought to harness the skills of the private sector in housing for low-income groups.

In the future, I believe the following matters also deserve greater attention:

(a) *Urban land.* In most countries there needs to be a fundamental examination of land prices, land availability, procedures of survey, acquisition, disposal, and registration. One way or another this seems a major stumbling block to effective policy execution. Even in Tanzania, where the government has total land control and a nationally adopted philosophy of 'sites and services' as a main strand of its national housing policy, the 'colonial' survey and registration procedures have proved a major inhibition to effective execution (see chapter 6).

Elsewhere the land market in areas of rapid urban growth pushes prices (and opportunity costs) to levels where, without policy intervention, there is little hope of the lowest income groups obtaining residential plots which they regard as acceptable and reasonable (see Chapter 5).

(b) *Institutional procedures.* Development is bedevilled by excessive controls and inhibitions: building regulations aim at impossibly high standards, and plot registration or mortgage procedures are far too complicated. In most places there is a whole panoply of formal controls—often inherited from colonial regimes—deployed by a series of inaccessible and unrepresentative bodies. Procedures should be simpler, quicker, and more readily understandable.

(c) *Role of technical assistance and advisors.* The present system of 6–8-month project preparation studies by consultants is unsatisfactory. There needs to be a longer-term consultancy involvement for this activity to be fully effective, perhaps in the form of 'in-house' assistance, where the consultant's role is not just tied to a particular project, but involves advice to government on a range of policies and programmes.

NOTE

1. These firms include Shankland Cox, Llewelyn-Davies, Roger Tym, Clifford Culpin, Buchanan's, Gilmore Hankey Kirke, Huszar Brammah, Alan Turner, Dar al Handasah and Halcrow Fox from the United Kingdom; SCET, Group Huite, BCEOM from France, PADCO from the USA, and Pak Pow and Kinhill from Australia.

Low-income Housing in the Developing World
Edited by G. K. Payne
© 1984 John Wiley & Sons Ltd

Chapter 12

People's Participation in Housing Action: Meaning, Scope and Strategy

Kirtee Shah

MEANING

To discuss the meaning and scope of people's participation in housing action purposefully, it is first necessary to question the commonly held view of housing and the housing problem. This view normally accepts as legitimate only those dwellings which have formal tenure status and are built in accordance with municipal bye-laws by formal public or private housing agencies. It overlooks the reality of other forms of shelter built without professional control or legal tenure and in violation of government bye-laws, using cheap and unattractive materials, no matter how many there are or how closely they match needs and resources.

Even an elementary analysis of the situation in most developing countries, however, would reveal that as a result of this view of housing:

(a) the gap between demand and supply is enormous and widening rapidly;
(b) the present level of public investment in the housing sector seems quite inadequate in relation to this level of demand;
(c) formal housing agencies in both the public and private sectors are neither building fast enough to meet demands nor cheap enough to reach the poor;
(d) faith in the ability of such agencies to meet total demand appears exaggerated, if not misplaced[1].

In Bombay, over 4 million people already live in slums and around 300 new migrant families enter the metropolis every day, yet the cumulative effort of all conventional housing agencies seldom produces more than 25,000 housing units in a year. A World Bank Study[2] has also shown that 55% of the households in Mexico City, 35% in Bangkok, 68% in Nairobi, 47% in Bogota, 64% in Ahmedabad, and 63% in Madras are unable to afford the cheapest dwellings available in the open markets of those cities.

SCOPE

The net outcome of this situation is a widening demand–supply gap, insufficient investment, high costs and a slow production rate of new housing, coupled with relatively high rates of urban growth, widespread poverty, unrealistic policies, and neglect of the housing stock informally generated by people. This combination has generated a housing crisis in most developing countries, in which the worst sufferers are the poor. Much of the reason for this is due to official hostility to housing actions promoted by the poor themselves. One is tempted to conclude that at the root of the housing crisis lies a lack of desire on the part of the authorities to recognize, understand, and imaginatively exploit informal housing processes. Yet failure to acknowledge this sector of housing supply means being blind to a staggering reality, because in many cities the populations living in slums or squatter settlements are increasing at twice the rate of total urban populations.[3] It also results in the loss of a formidable resource—people's ingenuity and energy—which, as international experience and the case studies in Part One have demonstrated, has the potential to contribute substantially to the solution of housing problems.

The first step to stimulating people's participation in housing action, therefore, is understanding people's actions. The second is to facilitate these actions and processes. Mobilizing the creative energy of people through formal agency mechanism to achieve the societal objectives comes third. This does not mean that participatory concepts are easy to incorporate in any type of scheme or that users can meaningfully participate in a conventional agency-managed traditional house-building effort. (If users are to be seriously involved, major changes must take place along the line—in design, planning, construction, and management practices.) It is often also found that in an agency-promoted self-help housing scheme the organizational cost of promotional effort and opportunity cost to people combined together exceed the direct savings effected through so-called self-help!

Faced with the problems of low income and massive demand, the traditional construction agencies are inadequate when building conventional houses and, in their existing form and working style even less adequate when attempting non-conventional, participatory solutions.

STRATEGY

The concepts of self-help and people's participation caught the fancy of authorities during the 1970s not so much because of their intrinsic worth as their practical value and the manifest failure of conventional approaches. Alternatives simply *had* to be found.

This search led to the now familiar concepts of sites and services, squatter upgrading, and environmental improvement. Though in practice they looked quite simple, (so simple that one wonders why they weren't in vogue earlier), the underlying principles necessitated a significant departure from existing practices, a notable change in perspective, and the adoption of a new set of values—both for the housing client and those who made decisions on their behalf. These changes included:

(a) a major shift in attitude towards the role of people as users (not an idle burden but a productive resource);

(b) a new interpretation of, and approach to, user's self-initiated housing actions (in that they represented solutions as well as problems);
(c) a new definition of a house (a shelter sufficient for long-term occupation);
(d) a redefinition of the housing task (not necessarily permanent buildings but an adequate environment);
(e) a new role for the traditional housing agencies (not controllers but facilitators);
(f) a new relationship between agencies and housing clients (not givers and receivers but partners);
(g) a new economics (not charity but investment);
(h) a new definition of scale (not symbolic gestures but total coverage); and
(i) for some, a new vision (not houses alone but overall development).

The most important aspect of this change was the recognition of the role people played in the housing process and acceptance, as legitimate form of shelter, of their own creations and building standards, irrespective of their quality or legal status. Projects such as sites and services and settlement upgrading started with an assumption that the building of a shelter was something that people were perfectly capable of organizing for themselves.

As the case studies in Part One of this book have shown, many upgrading projects started from the point at which the users stopped. First, the authorities accepted whatever was worthy of preservation and improvement. Second, the external involvement was confined to the provision and maintenance of environmental services such as drinking water, sewerage, drainage, pathways, access roads, electricity, transport and community facilities such as schools, health clinics, and shops, for which individual action was not feasible. Third, costs were kept to a minimum so that a larger coverage was possible. The upgrading approach, in some ways, is therefore a reversal of the normal definition of people's participation, in that external agencies participate in people's programmes rather than making people participate in theirs.

The acceptance of slums and squatter settlements as a proper starting point for external intervention has given a head start to upgrading schemes. Compared to the sluggish pace, high cost, and limited coverage of conventional housing projects, upgrading can reach the poorest at less cost than new development, cover large settlements, and take less time to execute. For example, in Calcutta the slum population is about 2.5 million people, scattered over 3000 locations, and over a period of about 30 years not even 2% of these were rehoused under the Slum Clearance Scheme. The Bustee Improvement Programme, however, has benefited more than 1.6 million people living in 1500 locations over a period of about 9 years (1971–79), at a cost of about Rs.150 (US$17) per capita. By 1982, the total coverage is expected to pass the 2 million mark at a total cost of Rs.450 million (US$50 million) since commencement.[4] Similarly, as Jere shows in the case of Lusaka (see Chapter 3), the projects have prepared or upgraded 17,000 dwellings in four large squatter settlements, 7600 plots in overspill areas, and 4400 fully serviced plots on six different new sites.

Although they work on more or less the same principle, the Calcutta and Lusaka projects differ significantly in one major respect — people's participation. Whereas in Calcutta participation is neither sought nor obtained, a planned effort is made in Lusaka to involve people and facilitate that involvement. In Calcutta, planning, resource-raising, decision-making, and execution are all done by the Calcutta Metropolitan Development Authority and residents are mostly passive onlookers. During the first decade of CMDA's s no serious effort was made to build a Community Development Cell as both and the Madras Urban Development Authority had done in the early stages of Urban Development Projects. Neither were any arrangements made in Calcutta any other public or private institutions to train community workers who could i... .orm, educate, and involve residents in some aspects of the work. In Calcutta, therefore, although the concept is innovative, implementation has been conventional.

In a massive and complex programme like that of Calcutta, it is difficult to pinpoint the effects which this absence of participation has had. Some indicators, however, are discernible. First, the degree of client satisfaction in Calcutta's improved bustees is relatively low. Any fault in quality or performance of services is blamed upon CMDA and charges of corruption in contracting and execution are frequently made. Second, maintenance of the improved services is poor. CMDA take it upon themselves to clean every blocked sewer line, replace stolen water taps or broken street lamps, conduct minor repairs in overflowing toilets, replace or repair garbage pits, or fill up small potholes on the paved streets whilst people blame it for faulty installation and tardy maintenance. Maintenance is becoming a serious burden both on the CMDA and Calcutta Municipal Corporation. It is difficult to say of people's active involvement in planning or implementation would have made any difference to maintenance performance, but CMDA admits that for effective maintenance of services some community-based organization or structure is unavoidable. Third, despite a heavy public investment in improving services and facilities, the overall environmental picture is not particularly different, though it has reduced deficiencies in basic services. Fourth, a matching response from the community, in the form of indigenous investments in upgrading shelter and other works, does not seem to be readily forthcoming, though it would normally be expected. Fifth, CMDA itself seems to acknowledge the problems, since it is currently searching for an appropriate organizational model to stimulate participation in future schemes. The next phase of the Calcutta Urban Development Project III apparently includes measures to involve local communities.

The value of participatory development is just beginning to be felt in Calcutta, whereas the Lusaka projects have achieved a definite strategy and method for doing so. In fact, community participation in Lusaka is seen as

(a) an integral part of project design (not something to be added on as an after-thought);
(b) necessary for successful implementation ('to secure trust, approval, and cooperation of the affected residents');
(c) a way of dividing responsibility between the community and authorities;
(d) part of a carefully planned and systematically managed organizational framework involving trained community workers, a separate Housing Project Unit within the City Council, and the formation of road planning groups;
(e) an active collaboration with the concerned political party organization (neither necessary nor possible in other situations and countries—however the relationship with the local political system is an important ingredient of any strategy seeking people's participation);
(f) sympathetic to local traditions and ways of working;
(g) managed imaginatively by creating necessary supporting arrangements (for instance, material loans for shelter improvement).

It must be self-evident that a well-conceived and properly organized effort like that of Lusaka's would encourage particiation and stand a good chance of achieving its objectives. Two special aspects of the Lusaka projects, however, merit special attention. The first concerns the support created to help people help themselves. A breakdown of project costs shows that 22% of total expenditure (the largest single item), is allocated for building materials loans to be spent by users themselves in improving their shelters, yet no such provision is made in the Calcutta Bustee Improvement or Kampung Improvement Programme and in the Madras Urban Development Project,[5] they are only from local sources like banks. It is arrangements like this, however, which help people play their role effectively.

The second aspect refers to cost recovery performance which, according to Jere, is not very satisfactory in Lusaka. He ascribes the failure to high instalments, inadequate debt collection machinery, poverty, incomplete installation and poor maintenance of services, lack of continuous community education, and ineffectiveness of legal machinery to penalize defaulters. Whereas this analysis may be correct, it remains to be shown whether the participatory way of working has influenced cost recovery rates, and not much dependable evidence for or against is available. However, this writer knows a few cases of non-housing projects — loans to poor tribals for buying buffaloes in South Gujarat, India, for instance, where the involvement of beneficiaries has positively influenced loan repayment performance. Though general conclusions are difficult to draw, at Dholka, Ahmedabad, the Ahmedabad Study Action Group (ASAG) has estabished a direct relationship between participatory method of working and an improved loan recovery performance.

THE WORK OF NGO'S

Although many local authorities throughout the developing world are experimenting with participatory forms of housing development, non-governmental organizations are among the strongest advocates of participatory practice. In recent years, a wide range of such organizations have become involved in various experimental projects throughout the developing world. Though small in number compared to the task, they are growing fast, as the Habitat Conference in Vancouver showed, they are beginning to make an impact.

To most NGOs, people's participation involves much more than the provision of unskilled labour in constructing low cost houses. For most of them it is a means of building communities as well as houses. Though it may sound romantic, and look slightly uncharitable to external agencies, a prescription suggested by a community worker summed up the sentiment eloquently when he said

> if we want to build houses faster and cheaper, instead of depending on centrally organised and professionally managed housing agencies, we should create and activate local organisations. For building materials, instead of searching formal markets and research laboratories, we should activate and tap those innumerable channels through which slum dwellers and poor villagers obtain materials. For the skills, instead of running after professionals, we should put to use the innate building skills of people. And for the financial resources, public funds should be augmented by people's

informal resources. The essence of the whole thing is to release the energies
of the people and to put to creative use their natural skills and talents. Once
this is done, a multitude of options would emerge and the problem would
begin to appear solveable. This process of releasing and creatively using
people's energy is the sum and substance of people's participation.

Though there is a common thread binding them all—faith in people and participation
as a means of change—the NGOs differ vastly from each other in philosophy, approach,
and method of work. A number of examples already exist, however, which may point
the way for the future and some of these deserve mention.

VM El Salvador

As Deneke and Bamberger have shown in Chapter 2, FUNDASAL is one of the largest
non-governmental housing agencies in the developing world and has the distinction of
being the only NGO running a World Bank-aided sites and services and upgrading
project. It has a strong bias towards community development and considers housing
as a means of mobilizing people for that objective. It has one qualified, trained, motivated
and well-paid Community Organizer for every 150 families, and lays great emphasis
on community contact, education, reflection, and group action. Though it views housing
of the poor in the broader societal and structural context, the Foundation does not permit
this larger perspective to adversely influence its performance on the ground. A team
of qualified professionals—architects, engineers, managers, and others, work in close
collaboration with community organizers to ensure that projects are completed within
cost and time limits and ensure that supervision and materials are of reasonable quality.
It has therefore achieved considerable success despite the formidable political problems
facing the country.

Freedom to Build

'Freedom to Build', a non-governmental group operating in Manila, prefers user-
controlled housing action to what it regards as alienating and expensive professional
control. 'The greatest untapped resource for housing', it suggests, 'is the capacity of
the poor to provide their own housing—a capacity that has been stifled by professional
control, high standards, legalisation processes and the demanding requirements of
financial institutions.'[6] In its work, Freedom to Build refuses to play a leadership role
and takes no responsibility for construction or organizing people. Instead, it organizes
itself so that people involved in building their houses can utilize its services; in short,
it believes in facilitating, not doing.

The group's activities started in the mid-1970s with the Dusmarinas Resettlement
Project, a 234 ha site 34 km outside Manila, where about 4000 evicted squatters have
been relocated since 1974. Each household is given a serviced plot on which to build
its own house, helped by a unique form of building supply store which provides a variety
of cheap reject or recycled materials. The store is the most substantial assistance to the
resettled families but Freedom to Build has several other strategies to make house-building
easier. For example, it runs a small centre which manufactures and sells, at a reasonable
rate, windows, doors, stairs, and other building components.

It also provides technical assistance such as trained carpenters, supplies vehicles to transport materials, and helps people organize themselves into saving clubs called 'Paluwagans'. Freedom to Build's success is that with limited staff, small overheads, and little political risk, it is able to aid and reinforce people's own housing actions.

Building Together Company

The Building Together Company was promoted in Bangkok in 1978 by the members of academic organizations, non-government voluntary agencies, and government agencies united by their desire to 'explore ways and means of assisting low-income people to gain access to secure housing arrangements are part of a process of community building'.[7] It believes that for people's participation to be a success it is necessary to create structures in which people's efforts can be channelled and coordinated.

The Building Together Company is at present completing a project of 220 houses in Bangkok city. In this systematically planned project (some think it is over-planned) land is purchased on the open market, unlike most government projects which subsidize land. The carefully selected participants were divided by lottery into cluster groups of 16–20 families to form the basic organizational unit of the project. Participation was then sought in three main stages. The first involved compulsory attendance at an educational course divided into ten week-end sessions to help build an initial bond among members. The second followed the procedures developed by FUNDASAL in El Salvador and concerned site development by outside contractors, mutual aid construction of basic houses, and self-help completion of houses and various community works. People were not involved in site development but participated in mutual aid construction of their clusters and the houses. In the third stage they gradually completed and improved their houses and undertook community projects. This process was designed to save time by employing outside contractors, but limited participation to house-building.

The availability of professional skills in design and planning, a complex organization for community participation, simple but relatively advanced construction techniques and a pragmatic approach, distinguish this project which, though building relatively expensive and high-specification houses, produced them at a much lower cost than similar units on the private market. Though the scale is small it is a pioneering approach in a country where few others existed before, and in that sense it holds some promise for Thailand's poor.

ASAG

The Ahmedabad Study Action Group is a multidisciplinary, non-profit organization. It is run by professionals and started its activities in the early 1970s, since when it has undertaken some relatively large housing projects for urban settlers and poor villagers in Gujarat, India. It also subscribes to a participatory way of working which believes that housing can be an effective means of initiating overall development processes as well as producing better quality houses. ASAG considers that housing should not be seen in isolation and most of its projects are multi-sectoral, involving housing, community development, income supplementation, delivery of basic social services, etc. The projects are mostly managed by a multi-disciplinary team of professionals in active collaboration with local communities.

In the housing component of a socioeconomic development project, ASAG tries to involve clients in different stages of project planning and implementation—site selection, design, material management, construction, site supervision, allotment, loan recovery, etc. In the socioeconomic development part of the project, which usually follows the housing part, the individual motivation and collective strength resulting from a participatory method of obtaining houses becomes a useful starting point for addressing other problems of the community.

In a recently completed rural housing project[8] under which over 2000 poor families built inexpensive houses for themselves with ASAG's active involvement, the participatory method of work yielded some positive results. The families played an active role at all stages of development and subsequently organized themselves into a Milk Producers' Cooperative and a Women's Handicraft Society. They then planned steps to solve other long-standing problems, such as a defective water-supply system and inadequate space for the village primary school. In one case some members of the oppressed Harijan caste developed sufficient self-confidence to involve themselves in village politics—an act which undoubtedly resulted from their experience of the participatory housing project.

An essential element of ASAG's work is a belief that intermediate agencies should extend beyond advocacy on behalf of the poor, to negotiating between people and authorities, organizing people, and mobilizing resources. It should include information and experience sharing (with other organizations of a similar nature and particularly with those who make policies and design programmes), education (of communities, leaders, and administrators), and effective action to bring about necessary changes (alternative policies, relevant programmes, sensitive organizations).

Bogum Jahri: Korea

There are many other NGOs of quality and commitment doing pioneering work in this field which it has not been possible to discuss due to lack of knowledge and space. However, it is necessary to make a passing reference to one case which is rather unique. In the Bogum Jahri area of Seoul, Korea,[9] under a harsh political climate, about 170 conventional-looking houses have come up which are built by evicted squatters. There is nothing unusual about the houses. What is unusual, however, is the manner in which the people are motivated and strengthened in their resolve, to initiate action for community development and improvement. The leadership in the Bogum Jahri Community Building Project came from two individuals, a priest and a university student who lived in Seoul's largest slum for more than 2 years when eviction notices were serviced and their shack was among those to be torn down. The entire process of group motivation, organization, and action revolved round this unique gesture of sharing and sacrifice. In a special kind of way it created a positive climate for self-help and the emergence of a new community life. It also illustrates the value of personal relationships in developing both settlements and communities.

Other agencies

Any discussion of people's participation in sites and services and settlement upgrading would be incomplete without a mention of those agencies which, though not directly involved in grassroots work, have significantly influenced and aided the practice of people's participation. The World Bank, perhaps the most unlikely institution to adopt such a concept given its essentially conservative banking role, should top the list on account of its vigorous promotion and heavy financial commitment. It has invested considerable funds and expertise in research, advocacy, education, and arm-twisting to spread the message and change the attitudes of governments, planners, and bureaucrats. Whatever arguments may be raised against its role, it cannot be denied that, but for the Bank, such large-scale investments would have been difficult, if not impossible, even with sympathetic local support. In particular, the World Bank deserves credit for three things

(a) its research effort, both at pre-project and post-action stages, in showing the problem in its overall economic and organizational perspective (this analysis had been missing and probably still is in most developing countries);
(b) converting an area of charity and social welfare into one of economic investment (in Madras, the Bank was instrumental in replacing policies of heavily subsidized slum-clearance tenements with a programme of sites and services and upgrading run by the MMDA, which achieved a 100% cost-recovery record;
(c) making available major investments which are permitting action on a suffciently large scale to effect improvements at both city and regional levels.

Other international development aid agencies prefer to operate exclusively through non-government organizations. They are helping the NGOs in their participatory work by providing the staff salaries of community workers, training support, matching contributions, working capital and various other kinds of assistance. Misereor, Germany in the case of FUNDASAL; American Friends Service Committee and UNICEF in the case of Lusaka; UNICEF in the case of the Hyderabad and Visakhapatnam Urban Community Development Projects; Bread for the World, Germany and Selavip International in the case of the Building Together Company; EZE, CEBEMO, Oxfam, Swiss Aid and other agencies in the case of many small and big non-government voluntary organizations. They also assist in undertaking small or large demonstration projects and evolving ways of usefully involving people in the housing process. Agencies such as Selavip International, besides helping specific projects, are actively promoting networks among the non-government housing agencies. Many view this dependency as detrimental to the freedom and effectiveness of voluntary agencies and positively harmful to the ultimate objective of making the poor self-reliant, but it is a fact that such assistance is playing an important role in helping the non-government agencies — and occasionally even government agencies — to experiment with participatory methods of working.

CONCLUSIONS

This discussion still leaves some of the conceptual, organizational, and operational issues relating to the practice of people's participation unresolved. Faced with enormous housing deficits and widespread poverty, are sites and services and upgrading projects the real answer? Or are they, as Madhu Sarin[10] pointly asks, an excuse to withhold investment and delay a push for real change? Do they legitimize and sanction illegal encroachments? Would they accelerate migration to big cities? Would they permanently blot the urban landscape and institutionalize urban decay? Is there a sufficient commitment on the part of the authorities and, if so, are the existing institutions and organizations in their present form, attitude, and organizational structure, adequately equipped to involve people?

Some questions are even more fundamental. In an unequal, unjust, and exploitative social structure, can an establishment promote a genuine participatory practice which may bring more power to local residents and subsequently disturb the power balance? Wouldn't it be tempted to manoeuvre the situation for its own benefit?

It would be pretentious to claim to know all the answers to these questions, though a few have been discussed briefly above. There can be little doubt that as long as the socioeconomic structures which cause poverty remain, slums and squatter settlements will remain an integral part of the urban landscape. Participation as discussed here cannot change that, and its role in the housing context is largely limited to helping people house themselves and changing both attitudes and institutions to make that possible. Even that task is a daunting one, however, and will tax the skills and commitment of all those professionals who consider it worth pursuing.

NOTES AND REFERENCES

1. In 1978 a working group on the role of the banking system in India estimated that by 1983 there would be a 'deficit' of 12.8 million houses in India's cities, which was at least seven times more than either the public or private sectors could supply. It also concluded that using existing building standards and costs, capital investment would have to be five times higher than present levels—a hopeless prospect.
2. World Bank, 'Housing', sector policy paper. IBRD, May 1975.
3. Orville F. Grimes (Jr.), *Housing for Low Income Urban Families: Economics and Policy in the Developing World*. IBRD.
4. UNICEF, 'Integrated Bustees Development Programme—Calcutta Overall Plan of Action'. Internal Document, Mimeo.
5. Louis Menzes, 'Sites and Services and Slum Improvement: An Approach to the Shelter Problems of the Urban Poor: Preliminary Conclusions from the Madras Experience'. New Delhi: Ministry of Works and Housing, Mimeo.
6. William Keyes, 'The Freedom to Build project in the Philippines: bringing resettled squatters into the orbit of development'. In *The Practice of People's Participation: Seven Asian Experiences in Housing the Poor*. Edited by P. J. Swan. Bangkok: AIT, 1982.
7. Schlomo Angel, and Paul Chamniern, *The Building Together Project in Bangkok: Erecting a New Neighbourhood on the Principle of Mutual Aid*. Bangkok: Vorratnchapihan AIT.
8. ASAG, 'Rural Housing and Development Programme: Ahmedabad District—An Assessment', Mimeo.
9. S. J. Daly, 'Community building in Bogum Jahri: Korea: starting a new life with evicted squatters. In *The Practice of People's Participation: Seven Asian Experiences in Housing the Poor*. Bangkok: AIT, 1982.
10. Madhu Sarin, 'A Critique of "Sites & Services and Slum Improvement": are they an excuse to further withhold investment on the real needy? Are they delaying a push for real change?' A paper written for the Seminar on Non-conventional and Alternative Approaches to Shelter the Urban Poor: Local and International Experience: Bombay, Delhi, Calcutta, Hyderabad and Ahmadabad. ASAG, January, 1981.

Chapter 13

Finance and Affordability

Roger Tym

INTRODUCTION

The last 20 years have seen enormous strides made in the understanding of the relationship between standards of shelter provision, the volume of production that can be achieved, and the need to ensure that what is provided is within reach of the financial resources of the poor. The new movement has also brought with it a realization that huge gains can be achieved in housing provision by carefully nurturing and improving the shelter that the poor have built for themselves—without reference to building or planning regulations or any articulated concept of public health and safety in densely packed housing areas.

Efforts to institutionalize this approach through the medium of a sites and services programme have frequently been frustrated. Land has more often than not proved the most difficult element to plan for and control; costs are very often too high for land in the locations where the poor need to live, closely associated with the source of their incomes, and the acceptably priced land is often too far away to be really attractive.

In parallel, unless equal efforts are made to improve the means whereby the poor can earn a living, attempts to improve their housing alone will always be frustrated. For many in the developing world, housing is not always their principle concern; the education of children to lift them from the poverty of their parents is frequently the main aspiration, and the need to maintain an adequate income from whatever source may often predetermine an attitude to housing, especially where it is located, that might otherwise be difficult to explain.

There is no other way of understanding and quantifying these priority listings than by asking those for whom the improvements are designed; the poor are articulate about their poverty and how to improve it. All of the expressed needs become evident in the financing characteristics of particular programmes and projects. To strike the right level of cost is of immense importance if the programmes are to be regarded as ones that could be repeated on a large scale, for if the resources of the poor are inadequate to meet the costs of a shelter programme, then the programme will have failed (see Chapter 8 for an example of a more sensitive approach). In the poorer developing countries where as many as 85% of the population cannot afford to purchase housing on the open market, any efforts to subsidize housing programmes from national resources will result in programmes that simply cannot reach out to the poor in any significant numbers at all. Subsidization on anything but the most insignificant scale can have no place in mass housing or shelter programmes. These ground rules are by now well established as illustrated on the Ismailia case study (see Chapter 7). They do, however, dictate the shape and form of the kind of financing arrangements that have to be considered in the search for successful programmes.

This chapter on financing urban development concentrates on three basic areas: policy issues, technical issues, and some practical problems that transcend any boundaries of particular professional involvement. It is about the role not only of the financial and economic specialist, but equally also about the vital contributions all other specialists make to the financial and economic dimensions of urban development issues. For the financing of urban development, and particularly shelter, is without question an issue of considerable political significance. It is the stuff of electioneering and elevation to high political or administrative office: it is about policy and only secondly about techniques. The role that the adviser has to play, whether he be a consultant or government officer, is very often that of policy changes in the redistributional system of the wider economy, an advocate of a lowering of standards of provision to achieve a much wider and extensive 'clientele'. The purpose of this chapter is to explore some of the principal areas where policy issues may arise and to examine the technical as well as the philosophic responses to them.

DEFINING THE TARGET POPULATION

The first issue in the definition of a policy for financing urban development is the question of who are to be the beneficiaries — the 'target group'. Generalized definitions are always prone to difficulties, but the 'target group' is usually that element of society which finds itself incapable of entering the formal housing market because of a basic lack of economic resources. The formal housing market, for rent or for sale, is that market in which housing is available at acceptable space, environmental and health standards; which has full title, and which has an adequate provision of infrastructure. The target group for urban projects is often delineated as the lower 50% of the income-distribution profile, but this definition is an arbitrary rule-of-thumb and should be varied according to local circumstances. A typical household income profile in the poorer nations of the developing world will show a high concentration of income/wealth amongst the wealthiest 5–15%, with a broad incline between the 15th and 85th percentiles.

It is, of course, one matter to define them, but entirely another to make sure that they are the ones whom the benefits of the programme actually reach. There are a number of characteristics of a target group that are important. Some are concerned with lifestyle and with preferences for the physical conditions of their surroundings. Others, of concern here, relate to their economic circumstances. Firstly, it is important to establish what the basic social unit is which occupies the housing unit — is it a single nuclear family, or wider extended family, in which the unit stretches over a number of generations — children, parents, and grandparents. Whatever the particular form the 'household' takes, it needs to be seen as an indivisible unit requiring economic sustenance, and able to provide from its collective financial resources for shelter, food, education, travel, clothing, etc., and the other necessities of life.

ASSESSING AFFORDABILITY

To establish just what level of cost for new or improved shelter could be supported by households requires a considerable understanding and insight into the lifestyle of the target group: their total earnings, security of the principal and secondary sources of income; their savings, and their capacity to save at all; the spending patterns of the group, and the importance, expressed as a proportion of total income, they attach to new or improved shelter provision. The actual amounts affordable are a function firstly of the amount of household or family income. Considerable care has to be taken not only to try to achieve a realistic assessment of incomes, but to make adequate allowance for the fact that, within broad socially defined categories of the 'poor', there are wide differences in actual incomes, resulting in equally wide variations in ability to afford absolute amounts. As a general rule, within the lower income groups the lower the income of the household, the smaller the proportion of income that can conceivably be set aside for housing. A greater proportion has to be allowed for food and other essentials.

Savings cannot be presumed to be available for investment in shelter; they may have been made for entirely different purposes. Savings will normally be the substitute for insurance against sickness and incapacity through old age.

Nevertheless in some countries where climatic conditions require a high level of investment in thermal protection, such as Iran or Turkey, security of adequate housing induces some households to devote more than 50% of total income to rent. In South India, for example, by contrast, it appears to be difficult to induce households to outlay more than about 10% of income for rental payments. Climate is only one, arguably small, element in the formulation of household budgets. Cost of food as a proportion of income, and the dependability and continuity of income, are by far the principal determinants of resources available for shelter (see the Tanzanian case study, Chapter 6). But the comparison of tropical with non-tropical conditions serves to illustrate the point that the proportion of income that can be assumed to be available should be derived from local conditions—economic primarily, but also climatic and cultural. Only as a first, rough approximation should any rule-of-thumb value be used, such as the common assumption that 20% or 25% of income can be assumed to be available. Figures or values such as these need very careful evaluation in the light of prevailing social, cultural, and economic circumstances.

Household incomes are always difficult to measure, and usually impossible to record accurately. This is not of course to say that the world is a universally dishonest place. However, whilst records may be available of the earnings of the principal income-earners in regular employment, they normally will not be available with any degree of accuracy or reliability for the supplementary incomes earned by wives, children, or grandparents, or if the principal earner is self-employed. Often these supplementary incomes are dismissed as being insignificant, but a survey, for example, of Ghanaian itinerant women traders, carrying goods as head loads, showed that the weekly earnings from this source would equate to the weekly repayments that would be required if the household were to take a serviced plot in the proposed sites and services project. Wives, grandparents, and children should not be presumed to be indulging in economic activity for the sheer joy of it—it is usually a vital supplement to an inadequate or insecure principal income.

Very considerable variations in households' economic circumstances can occur within the middle spectrum of incomes, and in preparing estimates of the ability of households to afford to pay for new or improved shelter, these differences should not be overlooked. Recalling that food is a prime essential call on income, the marginal propensity to spend on shelter will vary considerably from one income sub-group to another, and from country to country. There is no universally applicable prescription as to what the appropriate proportion of household income should be; each case must be examined on its merits, against the realization that if too high a proportion is presumed then the shelter provision will either not be fully utilized, or will be taken up by a higher income group than the targeted one.

Standards of provision—of water supply, of land per plot, or road surfacing or whatever—have to be derived from a rigorous examination of the particular economic circumstances of the target group. Whether or not there is to be any subsidization of a shelter programme, it is essential to ascertain from the outset just what level of provision could be afforded by the target group from its own resources and what the package should most beneficially contain. If an 'acceptable' standard cannot thus be achieved for the weakest economic sub-sector, then internal cross-subsidization, or external subsidization, may be deemed appropriate. But subsidies as such should never be presumed. The reduction of standards to an 'affordable' level and the removal of subsidies is an immediate and uncomfortable act; the fact that vastly more people will benefit as a result takes time to manifest itself and is far less perceptible or explicable.

Traditionally, the poor of the developing world do not borrow on long-term commitment either from private sources or from government. Their sources of credit, such as exist, are largely to be found from family savings and from short-term money lenders, charging generally exorbitantly high rates of interest. They do not, either, usually participate in formal savings schemes, and the concept of entering into long-term commitments has to be introduced gradually, with understanding and through close contact with the people or their community organization (see the El Salvador case study, Chapter 2).

The lack of any effective security for loans places the poor at a considerable economic and commercial disadvantage; they have traditionally had no means of access to normal credit facilities. In entering into formal borrowing commitments for new housing or serviced sites projects, land has to be seen as first and foremost the main source of collateral, but often the greatest source of security for a loan for the purchase of a serviced site will be an intangible; namely the fact that for perhaps the first time in a lifetime, the household has a sense of the security of its tenure. Experience has shown that considerable sacrifices will be made to ensure the continuation of payments if the alternative is to lose that security. Another element is important: if the borrowings exceed an affordable amount of repayments, then the loan will be at risk. Repayments must be within affordable limits, and defaulting minimized. Experience in South India and Mexico shows that where care is taken in the screening of participants to match their borrowings to their feasible repayment capacity, defaulting can be reduced to within very acceptable standards.

In the case of improving existing urban settlements, very often savings and loans associations organized on a localized basis can provide a substitute form of collateral. In the kampungs of Java (see Chapter 4), for example, local village heads organize savings schemes to which families make daily contributions. From the generated resources of the fund, pit privies and septic tanks are provided to families selected on a lottery basis.

Very often the monthly repayments of loans for the purchase of a serviced plot will be so small that the revenue costs of preparing a project, administering a loan, and managing the project will approach or exceed the repayments. These projects are unavoidably labour-intensive and every effort has to be made to find substitutes for formal administrative procedures, such as encouraging local community groups to constitute and organize themselves as small local government units, cooperatives, or other forms of mutual association able to undertake some proportion of the project administration.

Once borrowings have been made the general experience seems to be that the poorer the borrower, the less chance there is of his defaulting, providing that care has been taken to ensure that the expected repayments are within the capacity of the borrower to afford. However, many borrowers will not have a regular monthly or weekly income from which to make regular payments, and technical defaulting may occur one week or month if, for example, the principal income-earner in the household has been sick, or if income fluctuates seasonally. If allowances for these fluctuations can be made, then defaulting will be minimized, and lending programmes should have built into them a counselling and care service that would not ordinarily be present.

Finally, the question of affordability has to be seen in the context of the costs of the loan itself. There are two basic determinants: the rate of interest charged and the length of time over which repayments can be made. The simple principles are that the higher the interest rate and the shorter the loan repayment period, the higher will be the actual monthly or recurrent repayments. Conversely, and all other considerations apart, more in terms of shelter provision or equipment for business expansion can be afforded the lower the interest rate and the longer the loan repayment period. But that of course is a counsel of perfection; loan repayment periods, for example, should never exceed the probable life of the investment, or indeed of the length of time over which the borrower may be expected to be either able or inclined to continue his repayments. Where, for example, loans are being made for building materials to extend existing housing, consideration will have to be given as to whether further improvements and therefore borrowings are contemplated, and, if so, whether the length of the present loan should not be made as short as feasible to avoid a situation arising where an attempt is being made to repay more loans than can readily be afforded at any one time.

There are no rules about what interest rates should be in any given set of circumstances. However, any rate below the current cost of commercial borrowing—for example, the rate offered to higher-income groups—will be a form of subsidy, taking the form of subsidizing the cost not of housing or materials, but of the finance to provide those capital goods. Whether to offer such a subsidy or not is a political decision, but the use of scarce financial resources in this way reduces the chances of a programme being self-financing every bit as much as if the cost of land or materials were subsidized below market price.

Finally, however, the effect of inflation has to be introduced. If, for inflationary reasons, the earnings of a household may be expected to rise from one year to the next, the actual year-by-year proportion of income represented by the fixed amounts of the loan repayment will decrease. Other factors, such as increases in other household outgoings, may mean that this effect should be ignored. So long as fixed-interest loans for shelter provision can be made available at commercial rates of interest, the poor should be given every incentive and assistance to indulge in capital formation and saving by these means.

It should not be assumed that if the affordability sums add up, then the product will be marketable; there should first be a market assessment of potential investors' preferences. The proportion of income that would have to be set aside is only one of the determinants; location is probably the most critical, but standards and plot sizes are key issues as well, all of which have to be contrasted with the alternative conditions of informal occupation. What matters most is the perception of these benefits and their alternatives by the would-be applicant, especially with regard to any hidden costs such as the threat to the family unit resulting from large distances between residence and work locations.

ASSESSING COSTS

There are basically five elements in the shelter sector that have to be financed. They are land, on-site infrastructure, the superstructure, design and management costs, and interest payments on capital. To an extent, all must be regarded as variables in the eventual financial composition of a shelter programme. It is axiomatic that land and good title to it are essential, though the determination of its value and price is often a very difficult matter. Suffice it to say here that rarely are the issues explored fully enough to determine even the market value of land in a fair and equitable manner. The aggregated financial resources of the developing world's poor are rarely able to match the expectations of urban landowners, for whom the appearance of squatters on their holdings represents a trespass on their rights. One of the real dilemmas of the new urban poor who cannot afford the costs of travelling any distance to work is that their livelihood is usually derived from the metropolitan core area where land prices are highest.

The cost of land is the first debit from the sum total of what can be afforded. There are no rules as to what proportion of the affordable amount it should be, except that every effort should be made within the bounds of economic and design sense to limit the amount taken in financing land, and this means limiting as far as possible the amount per plot. But if there is any prospect in the future of expansion of the basic shelter unit, which will require extra space, sufficient land must be available from the outset (see the use of the 'spare plot' mechanism in Mexico discussed in Chapter 8).

In cases where illegal occupation is to be legalized or a long-term interest made available instead of mere occupation rights, great care must be taken over the assumptions that are made about what could be afforded by households who previously had paid little if anything for land they occupied. Security of tenure might seem to be of paramount importance to people who hitherto could be dispossessed at a moment's notice; but very often the realities are not as simple as that. Frequently, in reality, there is little immediate prospect of squatters being moved on, though they are in illegal occupation, and the granting of full legal tenure, therefore, cannot be seen as a cost or charge that always would rank highest in household budgets. Frequently the actual occupants may be sub-tenants of a superior tenant to whom tenure is granted, and who may then wish to realize the increased value of his landholding by evicting the former squatters who may now be unable to pay a higher rent. Illegality cannot be condoned, but in these circumstances what is legal and acceptable is often and usually a matter between squatter and legal owner. Where coexistence is practical, and a gradual move to recognition of some form of tenure seems likely, the existing situation can often be allowed to continue, or at the very least, moves to secure full legal tenure for the squatters should be approached with the utmost caution.

In many circumstances landowners will have realized that the value of their land is primarily determined by its current use, and to change the current use would require huge investment. Landlords in these circumstances should be persuaded to grant tenure themselves without government intervention. Governments have a poor record of being able to attribute and fix fair values to urban land, and they should be called upon to do so as rarely as possible.

Nevertheless a sensible approach to land pricing is essential, for if land is underpriced in the calculations of the cost of a project it will amount to a hidden subsidy. But differing political systems adopt different views as to what properly constitutes the true opportunity cost of land in urban conditions. In situations where government has taken upon itself the right to determine for what purposes urban land will be used, the value will be determined accordingly; increased degrees of sophistication in land use control can be introduced by governments to determine in increasing detail the value to be attributed to land. It is a matter of policy and considerable judgement, however, to determine where the dividing line lies, between, on the one hand, a sensible rationalization of market forces such that the scarcest and highest-value potential uses are not allowed to influence the assessment and result in overvaluation of the cost of land, and on the other hand, an artificial suppression of land costs by government such that a hidden subsidy creeps into the equation. In the final analysis, if land has to be bought from private landowners the speculative element of assessing the cost will be removed; the actual price paid will be determined partly by the degree of control over land use and hence market determinants of value; partly by the willingness of governments to hold to these determinants, very often in the face of litigation; and partly by the inclination of the judiciary to acknowledge the validity of this form of government intervention.

Off-site and on-site infrastructure and the minimum of on-plot utilities are second to land in importance as a call on household shelter budgets. These works simply cannot successfully be organized by the individual. They are public as opposed to private goods. How much of this infrastructure should be charged to the project householders is a matter for debate in each case. As a general rule, however, the poorer sections of society are politically less able to ensure that they are provided with expensive infrastructure works out of regular municipal budgets and therefore the more realistically these can be financed by the project participants themselves, the better. This may be a cynical view, but it is usually realistic.

This is not to advocate, of course, that the poor should as a matter of principle pay off-site costs, for that would clearly be inequitable.

The presumption is too frequently made that the poorer sections of the community can make no contributions to municipal revenues and that presumption is sufficient to convince the authorities that, as a result, little can be afforded for the areas where they live. What is required is the political will to break that self-fulfilling argument, and to find out what the poor actually could contribute. At the very least, this will usually be sufficient to provide a regular fund for maintenance, even if no contribution can be made to the original capital costs. On-site infrastructure costs fall into a somewhat different category, and there is a clear case here for the costs to be recovered from the occupants.

What is 'appropriate' will depend upon circumstances. Where no piped water supply is available within a reasonable distance, there is little or no point in providing any washing or sanitary facilities that would require such a supply unless one was to be made available in the near future. But potable water and the harmless disposal of human waste should rank highest in any provision. These are the two elements which a family alone cannot adequately provide, and the capital equipment on the site to enable it to enjoy the benefits of them has to be the subject of rigorously applied minimum standards.

The financing of the superstructure itself ranks last after land and infrastructure works, only because much if not all of the superstructure can be built by the household in an incremental and informal fashion. But even if superstructure works are to be carried out on a self-help basis, the costs of materials and any additional labour will have to be included in the cost in calculating what, in total, can be afforded. Provision should also be made in the affordable budget if it is anticipated that, at some date in the future, the household will need or be expected to add to the initial superstructure. For unless the household income can rise commensurately, commitments at a later date will be net additions to the present borrowing burden.

Contributions to off-site costs, on-site infrastructure and all the consequent design and management costs should be subjected to the test of affordability. Of these, none are dispensable, but the standards of provision can be varied according to the level of affordability that the particular target group of beneficiaries can sustain. Savings in costs usually mean sacrifices of standards; plot sizes cannot be increased after the initial development and to cut down on off-site costs may involve severing the serviced sites area or the improvement area from the prospect of being linked into the municipal services system. To reduce initial superstructure costs will require a greater financial effort on the part of the plot owner to provide for building materials and labour from his own resources at a later date; and to reduce the costs of design and management may imply the greatest penalty of all—the neglect of a project in terms of its supervision and subsequent management. To repeat, low-income group shelter provision has to be recognized as a very labour-intensive field of investment.

COST RECOVERY

The recovery of the costs of investment by the public sector falls neatly into two separate cases, each of which requires a quite different response. The cases are distinguished from each other by the fact that in the case of new construction and developement, ownership of property changes hands at a price, and in the second case of improvements to existing areas, property does not change hands. Cost recovery is much simpler in the case of new developments, such as a serviced-plot programme, than in cases where existing owners have to be induced by one means or another to finance improvements. Where new shelter is being provided, the cost of off-site infrastructure as well as the cost of land and on-site works can all be included as an integral part of the cost of a plot. Provided that the total cost of a project divided by the number of individal plots is affordable by the target income-group households, there is no reason why all of the cost: land, building, works capital, and management costs, cannot be recovered and reinvested. Whether the monies recovered can be reinvested to produce an equal number of equally serviced plots will depend on whether inflation in land prices and construction costs has diminished the real value of the original sum invested, and whether, as discussed earlier, subsidies are being provided in one form or another.

Subsidies in the form of charging the ultimate recipient less than the full economic cost can be applied either to capital items, to financing costs, or to recurrent expenditure on maintenance, repair and management. The ability to repeat or exactly replicate in the same volume a programme of low-income group housing requires that all costs are recovered, and particularly that allowances are made in the initial estimates of costs or in the financing arrangements so that the effects of inflationary increases—in capital and recurrent elements—can be eliminated. There is little doubt that in most circumstances in developing countries, low-income programmes for housing could not be successfully implemented in this manner; the actual monthly repayments would be too high because of the need to charge excessive interest rates, since this is the obvious means of combating inflation, and these rates would be politically unacceptable since they would inevitably be much higher than the rates being charged to other, wealthier elements of society than the rates being charged to other, wealthier elements of society for, say, commercial mortgages. Nevertheless, every increase in subsidization of a programme must inevitably diminish the number of possible participants; the available national resources would increasingly be concentrated in fewer hands to give, usually, higher standards. It is to the immense credit of the World Bank and its staff in the 1970s that long, hard, and sometimes bitter arguments were pursued in an attempt to persuade borrowing nations to reduce their standards and costs, to increase the amounts which were charged to project participants, thereby effectively and progressively reducing subsidies, in order to spread the available resources over a much wider proportion and a greater volume of the population.

In one form or another, subsidies to the poorer elements of a society can only ever be eliminated totally if governments simply do not intervene in their social and economic well-being at all. All organized societies to some extent or other redistribute wealth from the advantaged to the disadvantaged, but the lesser-developed nations cannot emulate the extent of redistribution in their housing programmes that wealthier nations effect. The numbers of those in need, and their capacity to contribute financially, render this an impossibility.

It is of paramount importance, therefore, that where programmes and projects are being prepared, every effort must be made to identify the true economic cost of all elements and to ensure that whenever conceivably possible all subsidies—hidden or otherwise—are revealed and eliminated if they are not judged to be absolutely essential and indispensable. The word 'judged' is used deliberately; ultimately it is an internal political decision as to where to strike the balance between costs, subsidies, standards, and numbers of participants. However, whether the resources of the developed world, particularly in time of severe international economic recession, can be expected to be diverted to finance overly subsidized social programmes in the developing world is at this time becoming increasingly uncertain and unlikely.

In cases where no property or other interest changes hands, and a public body makes improvements to the surrounding area, which are directly beneficial to property, for example by the provision of a power supply or water line, charges can be made either to those property owners who connect to the new supply or to all owners. These can be initial capital contributions for the right to connect to the supply, and recurrent charges for consumption. There are two problems encountered with this form of cost recovery. Firstly, illegal connections are sometimes made which remain undetected for substantial periods. Secondly, it is very often difficult to predict with any real degree of accuracy the rate of take-up of the new supply once it is made available, and in circumstances where connections are voluntary and not obligatory it is, as a consequence, difficult to forecast with precision the cash flow of the relevant utilities.

In cases where the improvements which are provided are of indirect benefit to property, such as the provision of an efficient street-cleaning system, the method of cost recovery usually has to be found in taxation measures, and usually, but not always, in the form of property taxes. To enable this to happen, the authority responsible for the improvements, whether they are capital works or an improved service-delivery system, has to possess fiscal powers. In some instances legalization enables local taxation authorities (municipal corporations, usually) to impose social taxes or rates, called variously betterment taxes, *impuesto de valorizacion* or *baatbelasting*. These are special both in the sense of applying to particular areas only, and in the sense of being in respect of, and as a means of, recovering the cost of specific improvements. Calculations can be made as to the extent and intensity of the benefit of the improvements and the resultant proportioned costs shared out between the properties lying in the affected area.

Professional judgements have to be made about the varying degrees to which different properties benefit from particular improvements, and there are no simple or universal rules. Where provisions for special taxation do not exist, but the implementing authority is empowered to raise general taxation, special legislation may be appropriate. As an alternative, if the fiscal route is not available there may be case for acquiring the principal title to the land and letting it out on long lease but at an enhanced rent that reflects the cost of the improvement works. This is, however, a fairly draconian measure, and presupposes powers of eminent domain or compulsory purchase. Sometimes, too, the acquisition of the superior title to land can lead to unforeseen consequences such as the destruction of the authority of the chief in a tribal system, where the authority derives in large part from the holding of tribal lands by the chief in trust for the members of the tribe. In West Africa particularly, a landlord system that is linked to tribal land ownership often provides a satisfactory degree of security of tenure and a means of providing shelter for new entrants to the urban housing market, and should rarely be disturbed.

Loan repayment periods, discussed earlier, are of course a principal determinant of the rate at which the initial fund can be recovered and recycled. They should therefore be as short as is acceptable, given that the shorter they are the more expensive the loan becomes in recurrent outlay terms to the borrower. Any capital contribution that can be made to the cost of new shelter or infrastructure improvements by occupiers from savings again will speed up the rate of recycling funds. It will also tend to ensure that the new occupiers will be bona-fide borrowers if they are willing to invest capital as equity into the project. But in many cases, ranging also from culture to culture, the larger part of the target population will have little if any capital to invest from savings. Deposits for the purchase of new shelter units should not therefore be the subject of rigid rules; the ultimate objective of low-income group urban development projects is to enable the poor to gain access to better living conditions. If deposit requirements on however small a scale prove, after investigation, to be an effective barrier to a significant proportion of the target households because of the absence of any really practical means of amassing the necessary lump sums, then they should not be made mandatory. Other means, such as restricting or forbidding the resale of the unit, should be devised to ensure that as soon as possible the occupant/borrower will feel a real commitment to continue his repayments. The evidence that exists about the behaviour of very low-income borrowers, however, tends to suggest that the need to formalize this sense of commitment is probably over-emphasized; the default rate, as reported earlier, is frequently low and exemplary.

SUMMARY

It would be difficult and pretentious to end this chapter with a 'conclusion' since the lessons of how to finance the provision of shelter to the poor of the developing world are still being assimilated and absorbed. Some of the issues are becoming clearer, however, and there is a growing awareness of the need to seek pragmatic solutions to the problems that arise, and to listen and learn from the people themselves about how they would use the resources being made available. The location of the dwelling is now accepted as being of critical importance; if it is far away from the sources of income then economic disaster on the family scale is not far away.

The poor are, like the rich, good at evaluating and ordering their own needs and priorities. To formulate designs and financing proposals without consulting them is now seen to be courting failure. Except in cases of extreme pressure of numbers on the supply and availability of land, the locational decision that the poor make in siting their meagre shelter will usually turn out to be one that maximizes the short-term economic advantages — price paid for land, closeness to work, schools (if they can be afforded), to others in similar circumstances, and perhaps most important of all, closeness to sources of supplementary income that other members of the family can earn to spell the difference between true poverty and the beginnings of an income surplus for very small-scale savings. It is as well to remember that in most countries of the developing world there is effectively no unemployment — to be unemployed is either to be living on savings, borrowings, or gifts from one source or another, or to be starving.

Dollar-for-dollar of investment there is now real evidence (see the Mexican case study, Chapter 8) for the belief that investment in improving the living and environmental conditions of existing shelter areas is more productive or cost-effective than investment in new shelter provision. The two are not, of course, always substitutable, and in conditions of extreme population pressure on rapidly growing urban centres, new provision has to be made. But land is the key to the success or failure of these institutionalized efforts to create new shelter. It is very rarely available in the right place and at the right price. Vast improvements could be made in increasing political awareness of how to tackle the problem of fair value assessment. There is a technology available, and professional codes of practice that can be relied upon to evaluate the issues. But there is always the overriding political issue of the concept of property and whether ownership and the freedom to use and dispose of land is an inviolable right. Urban land reform is not a particularly popular or indeed technically easy platform upon which to stand for election.

The purely technical problems of how to arrange in the most beneficial manner to all participants the financing of a new sites and services project or the improvement of a slum are well understood and should present no real problem. It is in the application of those techniques to the circumstances of real people with real, ever-present, and seemingly impossible claims on their financial resources that the problems begin to assert themselves.

All who participate in any way in the design and implementation of projects should be well aware of the need to look beyond, as it were, the figures, and to search for the facts: how realistic is it to presume that families could economically and socially be uprooted or diverted to the new project; on what grounds do families really order their consumption and investment priorities, and how do they view the prospect of a reorganization of these priorities? Sites and services as a concept and as a programme has not failed, but in some painful instances the projects simply have no market. The poor have their scale of values, too.

Low-income Housing in the Developing World
Edited by G. K. Payne
© 1984 John Wiley & Sons Ltd

Chapter 14

Land Issues in Low-income Housing

Roger Zetter

INTRODUCTION

The Vancouver Habitat Conference[1] in 1976 approved radical and extensive government intervention in land markets, recognizing that land is a pre-eminent issue in the provision of low-income housing needs. Yet many housing programmes still underestimate or avoid altogether the politically and technically complex question of land. Thus, shortages of land available for development in sufficient quantity and at affordable prices are still major barriers to the expansion of sites and services programmes. Similarly, land problems frustrate many upgrading programmes through complications in land tenure and transfer rights.

This chapter focuses on some of the major operational issues and barriers that land problems present in successful implementation of housing projects.[2] The provision of 'new' development land forms a major theme, since only in this way can substantial net gains in housing supply be achieved. The chapter concentrates as much on problem definition as prescription, because simplistic definitions of land issues have frequently constrained the implementation of housing programmes. Equally, there is the danger of generalizing prescriptions between countries, because cultural and political attitudes to land vary enormously, as do the structure and operation of land markets. To ignore these variations, or to use imported methods to intervene in land markets, may accentuate supply shortages, inflate land prices, and impair the best of housing programmes.

LAND OWNERSHIP—STRUCTURAL PROBLEMS AND RESPONSES

Land—its ownership, value, and use rights—symbolizes inequality, especially in the developing world, with its growing disparity between small, wealthy, landowning élites, and the mass of the urban poor. Ownership of land and the related issues of increases in land values (variously termed betterment, plus value, unearned increments) are here designated as *structural* problems, requiring fundamental policy changes. These are distinguished, in so far as two levels can be separated, from *procedural* or *managerial* problems; tax systems, land assembly, title registration. Procedural problems are probably best tackled by incremental change and reform.

221

Many countries are increasing public control over land in urban areas, since markets dominated by private landowners fail to supply land at an affordable price for low-income group housing. Greater public control can help to capture betterment in land values which communities have created and help in shaping urban growth patterns. It is argued that only through widespread public control rather than traditional land ownership patterns (and the social and political attitudes they represent) can rapid urban growth be accommodated.

Achieving these objectives through public ownership depends, in the last analysis, on political feasibility. Not surprisingly resistance is strong. Many countries, which have adopted radical programmes of rural land reform, stop short of similar measures for urban land and housing needs. To a large extent squatting is therefore the risk that a landowning élite accepts in order to maintain ownership and land values relatively unfettered by public intervention. The familiar sequence is to resist squatting at first, but eventually it is 'legalized', albeit within the framework of private ownership. This allows the surplus value to be capitalized by the owners either in compensation from the government or through higher rents on upgraded and titled land. Giving title, far from a radical process, is an eminently rational (if reluctant) reaction of capitalist landowners.

Funding agencies also have contradictory attitudes to the structural issue of land. Large-scale housing programmes cannot be separated from radical land policies and thus agencies may be investing, indirectly, in substantial social and political change. Equally, representing for the most part 'free-market' economic traditions, they may wish to steer governments away from radical land programmes. Such resistance may significantly limit the efficacy of internationally funded housing programmes.

Countries with strong private land interests often adopt incremental approaches, usually through fiscal policies and selective public acquisition; this political expediency means that little progress has been made in achieving the 1976 Habitat Agenda.[3] Those countries ideologically attached to state control, such as Sudan, Tanzania, and Zambia, tend to adopt stronger government involvement in housing land. Often national ownership policies adopted for modern urban needs are, in effect, a continuation of communal or customary land tenure traditions, colonial land law systems forming a temporary intervention. Any substantial public ownership of housing land will, paraphrasing Roberts,[4] need to address four questions:

(a) Why is housing land being taken into public ownership? It may be to eliminate delay or control land supply and price; but taxation and planning policies may be as effective, whilst the creation of alternative investment opportunities in industry or agriculture may help to reduce speculation in land.
(b) What form of public ownership is appropriate? The range could include use rights; development rights; freehold; all land or selected tracts. Different types of ownership will tackle different aspects of the housing land problem.
(c) How should land be taken into ownership? A range of financial and acquisition measures can be conceived with preferential conditions for housing development, all of which will have differential effects.
(d) What are the consequences for the public sector? There will probably be compensation, start-up, and management costs. There will need to be clearer coordination between housing, development, and planning agencies. The main point

is not the desirability of public ownership, but precisely how land will be held and developed for housing programmes.

Extensive public land ownership need not always facilitate a better supply of housing land. This is because it may be conceived for multiple political objectives rather than specifically for housing programmes. In some instances public ownership may allow greater control over the pace and shape of urban development; but a tax system may be a more effective control on land values and housing costs. Hong Kong and Singapore, with substantial public ownership and reasonably effective housing programmes, both have extremely high land prices since these are not directly controlled. In Zambia, all land is in public ownership but continuing shortages of housing, slow allocation of land, and illegal subdivisions mean that the cost of housing is still high. In Sudan, national ownership has substantially increased the supply of plots; but this has accentuated procedural problems elsewhere in the housing process, particularly access to finance, and shortages of building materials. National ownership therefore puts considerable pressure on administrative capability.

India (1975 Land Ceiling and Registration Act) and Nigeria (1978 Land Use Decree), allow land markets to operate under prescribed land-holding ceilings, with goverment expropriation rights. Illegal subdivisions or shadow transfer of holdings are used, however, to evade the ceilings. Equally, excessive fragmentation of holdings makes public acquisition for housing development far more difficult.

The urban poor understandably view private landowners as the main factor limiting their access to housing. Unfortunately, individual landownership is often an illusory concept hiding a complex and dynamic series of sub-markets and actors including developers, financiers, brokers, institutional investors, contractors, and so forth. Thus any system of public ownership will need to consider differing methods to tackle all these 'owners'.

Most forms of expropriation, however, directly benefit landowners. Thus an option more directly of benefit to the urban poor is simply to finance the provision of services and infrastructure. Clearly, governments take risks in the improvement of land they do not own. In addition, complex legal controls may be necessary to hold land values and ensure access by target groups. Experience suggests that private landowners invariably fail to supply land in the quantities required even with these 'incentives'. Extensive public ownership will generally only bring advantages if there is a clear relationship between ideological objectives and the detailed operational needs of housing policies. Otherwise it is unlikely that property wealth will be redistributed or that land will become more readily available for housing needs.

The complexities may partially explain why many countries adopt incremental or pragmatic adjustments. These encompass subtle differentiations in local land markets and housing agencies without fundamentally altering the distribution of power.

FISCAL POLICIES

Fiscal tools are important, but they only operate effectively in conjunction with other tools, such as zoning and planning policies.[5] Their attraction is also their weakness. First, in serving a variety of purposes there is a high 'leakage' of impact. Second, they leave land in the hands of the owner, seeking instead to influence his behaviour. Third, many land taxes are recovered at a national level, (e.g. betterment and transfer taxes). They have little impact upon land costs at the point of supply and may adversely affect investment patterns in local land markets.

Moreover, land markets become more complex with growing investment by financial institutions in land. It becomes exceedingly difficult to use taxation measures to release portfolios of 'commercially' owned land often held on long-term yield expectations.

Local property and land taxes are generally regressive since they form a disproportionately high element in low-income group housing costs. They also tend to increase land prices which the poor will have to pay. By contrast, they may be useful in managing development through differential rating. Ironically it is most difficult to levy land taxes outside city boundaries where speculation and future development occur. More importantly, these taxes are a vital source of revenue for service provision. Whilst urban administrations may be desperately trying to reduce land costs and values, they also have a vested interest in land values rising since, if taxes are efficiently levied, this will add significantly to the revenue base.

Nevertheless, there are some positive conclusions. Whilst capital transfer taxes operate against low-income groups by forcing land prices up, variable tax rates can be set with low-income group housing land incurring a lower rate. Certainly in Singapore and Korea high or total tax exemption on housing land seems to work with apparent success.[6,7] Alternatively, increasing tax liability as values rise, rather than after the surplus value has arisen, may be less 'injurious' to land prices. This may be linked to site value rating in conjunction with development plan designation, though efficient management and close coordination are necessary.

These tax systems combine a number of objectives in guiding growth, providing land, and stabilizing land prices. However, in very active land markets, or with rapid urbanization, they will only be effective if property valuations keep pace with escalating land values. In addition, the ethical desirability of recouping all betterment leads to protracted valuation problems and, in practice, a lower level will be more likely to bring land on to the market.

Taxes on the capital value of land, rather than annual value (or imputed rent) of property, are more likely to encourage house-building, although annual value methods are more common. Moreover capital value taxation methods tackle plus value increases more effectively; they are also more flexible and easily updated.

There has been little experimentation with the use of infrastructure charges to influence development. Colombian valorization, discussed below, in some respects exemplifies this principle in creating serviced development land and recovering costs. Great care would be needed in assessing how to pass on both the charging and the rising value of land if this system were to be used elsewhere to stimulate land supply. Differential charging for different income groups requires considerable managerial expertise to ensure that any effective cross subsidy works effectively.

Influencing the price and supply of land by taxation can have confusing and contradictory effects and it is extremely difficult to find a consistent balance between the objectives of penalty and incentive. In addition, taxation is rarely used to influence housing land markets alone. At best, the level or speed of land price increases may be reduced and investment released from land into more productive sectors.

Two other options for fiscal management are compensation and cross-subsidy. Compensation for land acquisition (and thus front-loaded development costs) creates complex cash flow and heavy borrowing requirements, thereby increasing housing project costs. But municipal/government bonds are used with some success in India and allow the agency an income before bond repayment falls due. Cross-subsidy mechanisms have also been used in a number of schemes (see Chapter 7) to reduce land or other costs for lower-income beneficiaries. This method is undoubtedly successful and avoids the stigma of creating wholly low-income estates.

Financial methods must operate consistently and continuously over relatively long time periods to introduce market stability, and this is clearly difficult in the developing world. In addition, changes to existing systems are more likely to be effective than importing methods used to tackle different economic and urban growth management objectives.

MANAGEMENT AND INSTITUTIONAL STRUCTURES

Weak institutional structures for land administration surveying and title registration accentuate market imperfections and create opportunities for speculation. Acquisition of land for housing projects is protracted where customary tenure systems are overlaid by European proprietary rights and where moribund legislative codes made compensation and thus affordability calculations uncertain. Multiple rights in the large areas of land needed for sites and services projects also cause delay. Yet relying upon land already in public possession is unjustified because of its limited quantity.

Lack of registration means that land tax collection will also be inefficient, impairing the flow of revenue to the authority and collection rates of 55% for Jakarta, 20% for La Paz, and 75% for Bombay have been noted.[8] If title is unrecorded, taxes will similarly go uncollected and there will be little restraint on land value and rent increases. Rent controls will also be ineffective. Registration of title is thus a critical element in the establishment of an orderly land market.

Artificially low or antiquated property and land valuations are also widespread in Third World cities with taxes incurred at rates too low to affect owners' behavioural to generate sufficient revenue for urban services. Inefficiency can occasionally be an advantage, as Ward's example of embargoing land by tax levy illustrates (see Chapter 8). More usually, however, the consequences are negative with substantial problems in other stages of the housing process. In Tanzania (see Chapter 6), despite extensive provision of land for sites and services, beneficiaries experience delay in registering title, and difficulties in obtaining housing loans and building approval.

Should there be specialized land development agencies? Should housing agencies be responsible? Should agencies be centralized or decentralized? Land acquisition tends to be centralized (since local authorities are weak) or vested with the general power of large urban authorities rather than the end user—the housing agency. Greater centralization may prevent inter-agency competition and enable land located in both urban and peri-urban administrative areas to be considered; but flexibility outside the largest cities will be sacrificed and delay, market uncertainty, and long lead times will add to housing costs. In addition, control of financial performance may prevent land costs being considered as part of a total housing cost with virement between the two; budgetary weakness caused the failure of such a land agency in Ankara (see Chapter 5).

Housing land must be carefully integrated into up-to-date strategic development plans. This helps to stabilize land prices, reduces delays in granting planning consent or agreeing development rights and compensation, and may thus help to accelerate land supply. It requires, however, a high level of coordination between agencies in the forecasting, location, funding, and phasing of development. Orderly phasing of growth may be very difficult and may seem peripheral to the main issues; but much of the success of Singapore's housing programmes can be attributed to continually up-dated development plans and inter-agency coordination.

Improvements in land management and development coordination are clearly essential in putting the land package together. The Dandora (see Chapter 1) and El Salvador case studies (see Chapter 2) show how tightly organized management can help to reduce rent default, maintain the pace of building, and assist cost recovery. It must be added that the basic profitability of the Dandora project to the beneficiaries is also an important factor. Land management processes that are easy to operate, open in method, and with the minimum of procedures, are desirable. Many of the remedies are labour-intensive and familiar shortfalls in professional manpower will need to be overcome. Stronger legislation with more direct and positive powers is desirable to inhibit manipulation by the landowning élite. Whilst this is unlikely to be subtle enough for all eventualities, it will hopefully not be the urban poor who suffer from inaccurate valuations or compensation calculations.

LAND AVAILABILITY, ASSEMBLY, AND SUPPLY

Housing programmes, as distinct from one-off projects, require a supply of land programmed on a rolling basis, in good locations, and in large quantities. These are precisely the problematic areas not often experienced in pilot projects. Moreover, many pilot projects contain a subsidy because the true land costs are hidden by lax accounting in inter-agency transfer, historic valuation, or simply concealment. This is a fundamental constraint to replication because housing programmes require acquisition and cost recovery at open market value—anything less clearly decreases affordability. Yet many housing schemes involve such high land costs that they quickly run into difficulty or are abandoned altogether.

Land is often held over long time periods to ensure continuity of supply, programme lead times, and to avoid speculation. But this imposes high management and interest costs and will thus alter affordability calculations. Offsetting these costs by revaluing land or writing them down as a subsidy will have to be decided upon.

Location and supply are also problematic. Large and cheap supplies of housing land are usually only available on the urban periphery. But this land is probably outside municipal administration and is thus more difficult to acquire. Frequent boundary reviews are thus necessary although these will affect land prices. In the medium term this may not be problematic, provided the projects are implemented as part of the city's spatial growth strategy. In the short term, beneficiaries are required to trade off lower capital costs of land against higher user costs. The development agency may also be trading off lower land costs against high initial capital costs for on- and off-site infrastructure to service remote or physically poor locations. This produces significant front-end loading and severe cash flow constraints together with longer execution and cost recovery periods. Smaller, more expensive land parcels, more easily connected into existing infrastructure, may generate lower overall costs. Thus whilst cheaper land may reduce direct costs the agency may simply be externalizing many of the costs, indirectly imposing higher travel costs on beneficiaries. Not surprisingly there is a high propensity for beneficiaries to return to squatter areas. These complexities must be made explicit in the supply of housing land and total project costs.

Up-to-date development plans are equally important in the locational context as in management. Where housing projects are discontiguous with the existing or planned built-up area, housing agencies may be 'inviting' illegal invasions, or gratuitously enhancing land values by servicing land at nil cost to the owners. Positive locational considerations may, however, actually generate benefits and as public sector housing programmes are likely to be major land consumers in many countries for some years to come, this provides development authorities with a significant choice of spatial strategies.

Next there is the problem of plot size and layout. In many countries land is inefficiently used with plot sizes more than double an 'acceptable' standard in low-income residential areas. This has effectively reduced the amount of land available for housing, increased development costs and created urban sprawl.[9]

Project layouts are determined by two objectives.[10] First is the need to achieve economy of layout to reduce infrastructure costs per plot. This will depend on plot dimensions, servicing thresholds, and a re-evaluation of technical design standards. In general a width to depth ratio of 1:2 or 1:2.5 is usually most effective for technical requirements. The second objective is to maximize the amount of site cover (or 'private') to servicing ('public') land. A 3:1:1 ratio for private, circulation, and public space (including facilities) respectively is a desirable target. This increases the number of households contributing towards recoverable land costs and thus reduces the unit costs per household. Maximum use should be made of every square metre since it all has to be paid for.

Rarely are costs-in-use considered as effectively as capital costs. Consequently, paying for maintenance and renewal is often a complicated issue. In addition, design for infrastructure inevitably creates monotony and rigidity of layout; the social and cultural needs of local users, as well as the needs of engineers, must be considered.

Of all the options for obtaining a continuous and cheap supply of land, land banking is one of the most widely advocated. It is used to help in shaping urban growth, reducing land prices, capturing plus value and ensuring a continuity of supply,[11] though it is unlikely, by itself, to affect land prices because of insider trading, political manipulation, and the need for extremely large amounts of land to be purchased. In complex or very active land markets, the precise situation where the procedure would be most desirable, it is probably least operable. Preferable conditions depend on large funds (higher than in most city administrations) and the purchase of very large amounts of land—effectively to flood the market.

An alternative is acquisition at existing use value, thereby appropriating both betterment and development value. To the extent that compensation is considered an inalienable right, this approach depends on political commitment to overcome strong private land interests; hence the modified versions in Korea and Singapore discussed earlier.

There has been successful experience with land readjustment schemes in Korea and Colombia in which the development agency, in return for creating a consortium of owners and servicing their land, expropriates a proportion of the land, (usually about 30%), as payment. The Colombian valorization method recoups development costs by charging them against increased value rather than by land appropriation. Both schemes permit effective control of land development and the recovery of betterment. These methods tend towards full cost recovery, but potentially offer considerable flexibility for meeting housing needs. For example, land appropriation could be varied in relation to land values and development costs. Land could be released at below market rates as a direct subsidy, or cross-subsidies designed within the scheme. Capital borrowing is reduced to short-term requirements, though such methods clearly place a premium on administrative efficiency and operate best over relatively short time scales.

A unique method of providing land through the spare plot method and at the same time reducing land costs to the development agency has been proposed in Mexico (see Chapter 8). Ankara's secondary market (see Chapter 5) is the illegal counterpart of this process. The Mexican experience seems to offer considerable potential, although the apparent 5-year grace period, selection of target beneficiaries, and control of land prices in the second phase, would appear to be among the main problems.

Another alternative, canvassed by the World Bank[12] is to acquire future development *rights* rather than full title initially. This process, although administratively complex, would make land less attractive speculatively and with high discount rates used in most Third World countries gives a low net present value. An important caveat in all these experiences is that housing land acquisition cannot be separated from taxation, issues concerning wealth distribution, planning strategies, affordability equations, and the tenure arrangements which the authority will subsequently have with project beneficiaries. Improved administrative capability is also necessary since, as in the examples already quoted, blockages may occur elsewhere in the system. Alternatively a vacuum is created where illegal subdivision pre-empts government possession; or squatting takes place immediately afterwards, which a track record of subsequent upgrading may accentuate.

TITLE AND TENURE

Title and tenure security are enshrined in most housing policies for the urban poor. The more regular operation of the land market is an important, if long-term and indirect, benefit. In the shorter term it permits project beneficiaries to be more precisely targeted and, through this tighter control, better cost recovery achieved. Title also gives security and thus collateral, enhancing access to mortgage finance as Tym shows in Chapter 13. Accordingly, how title and tenure are created is an important dimension of the land issue in housing policies.

The simplicity of the concept conceals many technical problems since title is often a confusing mixture of traditional and European hybrids. Housing programmes may be creating 'clear' title for the first time, and by breaking traditional forms will create new problems. The vital need is for clear and simple title, of relatively short initial duration.

Title has been an integral component of Zambia's upgrading programme (see Chapter 3), under which relatively simple, negotiable 30-year occupancy leases (or licences) are provided. Where precise cadastral surveys do not exist, a map is prepared from air photos, indicating the plots; the houses are numbered and a certificate of title given which is linked to the approved map.[13] Botswana's urban land policy provides for a Certificate of Rights to be issued which is also simple, quick, and cheap; it guarantees both dwelling construction and residence rights, but seems insufficient collateral for loan institutions.[14]

There is contradictory evidence about the precise significance of tenure in the process of consolidation. Although residents considered tenure their most important requirement in the Ismailia projects (see Chapter 7) a number of studies show that tenure may be a necessary but not a sufficient condition to encourage consolidation. Consolidation and development may depend equally on other factors such as education, income, finance, and social priorities.[15] *Perceived* security of occupation through *de facto* government, political and community attitudes can be as important as tenure *per se* in the consolidation process, though in Ankara (see Chapter 5) and Jakarta (see Chapter 4), implicit government acceptance, by providing infrastructure and development plan 'approval', was an effective consolidating mechanism.

Security of tenure in squatter areas may, paradoxically, encourage further squatting, as Tokman describes in Ankara (see Chapter 5). More significantly, improved tenure can create instability rather than consolidation; it will probably cause rents and land values to rise (accruing to landowners not necessarily squatters) and impose the additional costs of government land and property taxes with consequential effects upon affordability calculations (see Chapter 13). These are the conditions for the invasion of squatter areas by middle-income groups who can invest in affordable, now titled, land. This process, with the original squatters re-entering the urban system through further squatting, is widely documented.[16] The rather more subtle approaches in Zambia and Botswana may be more appropriate, combined with some form of progressive rather than instantaneous title. Issuing building licences with favourable options for renewal, provided they ensure collateral, is another option.

It is often difficult to create title. In Zambia giving title in upgrading schemes has been frustrated by lack of funds and staff and an inadequate information base. In addition, many squatter areas are on land held on private leasehold which the government must first acquire before upgrading. It is also difficult to ensure that title is in fact going to the 'right' person. Who then is benefiting from legitimization? Progressive title may be a 'solution' to ensure that injustices do not become institutionalized.

In sites and services projects attitudes to title are usually conservative to ensure cost recovery. The Dandora project (see Chapter 1) has simple but effective rent payment mechanisms with identity cards to discourage title reassignment. A progressive form of title, issued against completed stages of house construction, is quite widely used and is a positive incentive for completion. Indeed it could be argued that, since sites and services schemes distinguish housing from land, so long as unambiguous compensation codes exist, legally secure title may not always be vital.[17]

Most housing agencies prefer the greater control of freehold retention in order to capture gains in the value of the scheme. On the other hand, long amortization periods create long debt liability periods and may increase management costs and vulnerability to fluctuating interest rates. If fixed long-term leases are given, increases in value tend to accrue to the structure not the land — enhancing the process of subleasing or assigning to capitalize the enhanced values. Title need not be standardized, although this is administratively more simple. Indeed the overall design and financing of the project may require different recovery mechanisms and therefore different title mechanisms.

Assignment, through subleasing, room rental, or sale of freehold, is a contentious issue. Although widespread in practice, plot subleasing or sale is 'officially' prevented in many projects. Conversely room rental may be explicitly built in — it generates an income stream which may reduce repayment defaults and provides additional accommodation to even lower-income groups (at extortionate rates). Overcrowding, social problems, and infrastructure overload are the usual objections, yet in Zimbabwe, with occupancy rates twice the planned capacity in some schemes, these problems have not arisen, despite some of the most rigorous cost and design controls in Africa.

Sub-leasing and sale of freeholds are often strongly resisted to ensure that: the target group is the beneficiary; land and housing is not traded up to higher-income groups; and appreciating value is not lost to the agency. Nevertheless more relaxed policy on assignment is increasingly canvassed.[18] The most immediate advantage of selling freeholds by the project agency is the relief from debt burden, but it is important to find out why it is required and what the likely consequences are. Increasing rent in upgrading projects and external costs in sites and services commonly cause 'trading up', confirming that surplus value and overall costs have not been fully exposed in project planning and that proposals are not affordable by the target group.

If assignment happens, the transfer, being illegal, will probably be at sub-market value. Legally permitted, it will at least allow the allottee to capitalize at full market value—a pragmatic answer merely underlining the failure of the housing projects. Next, if it *is* middle-income groups who benefit then provided the agency can recover a proportion of the enhanced value (a 5-year period is often cited), then greater flexibility could be allowed. Differences between market and capital value can be recovered on a declining percentage basis—for example 100% of the difference in year one to perhaps 10% in year five. This is an incentive for the allottee to remain as a project participant or allows the agency to recover the big jump in values characteristic in the early years of a project.

Above all it is important to get away from concepts of European land law which perceive of title as absolute. Such assumptions should not blind us to the fact that, in many countries, individual title is something new to the urban poor.

CONCLUSIONS

There are no easy solutions to the problems of housing low-income groups in the developing world. Nowhere is this most obvious of conclusions more relevant than in a review of land issues and this is partly because land has been an insufficiently considered element in housing policies.

Whatever is done to open up the supply of cheap, developable housing land, raises many formidable consequences, irrespective of whether the state owns freehold or restrains the use and development rights of privately owned land. Even with some headway being made on the land issue, inequalities and bottlenecks may be accentuated elsewhere in the housing process. Nothing in ownership, tenure or land supply is fixed, however, and Third World countries are clearly beginning to break out of the mould of European conventions and attitudes.

Social, cultural, and economic issues are the parameters constraining the precise ability of housing agencies to tackle the land issues as they perceive them. Consequently it is not surprising that radical remedies are grasped by the urban poor. For them it is only in this way that soical and economic traditions pertaining to land will change fast enough to accommodate their acute demand for housing in expanding cities.

NOTES AND REFERENCES

1. UNCHS Habitat, *Report of Habitat Vancouver*. UN Ref. A/Conf/70/15.
2. For a comprehensive review see:
    (a) World Bank, *Urban Land Policy Issues and Opportunities*, World Bank Staff Working Paper, No. 283 (2 vols), (ed. H. Dunkerley). Washington, 1978.
    (b) United Nations, *Urban Land Policies and Land Use Control Measures*, Seven volumes, Summary Volume VII. Global Revies, ST/ECA/167/Add.6. New York, 1975.
    (c) M. Cullen and C. Woolery, (eds), *World Congress on Land Policy, 1980*. Lexington, Mass: D. C. Heath, 1982.
3. J. Hardoy and D. Satterthwaite, *Shelter Needs and Responses*. London. Wiley, 1981.
4. N. S. Roberts, 'Workshop 2: Public land ownership' In M. Cullen and S. Woolery (eds), *op. cit.*, 2 (iii), pp.89–90.
5. For a comprehensive review see:
    (a) Schoup, D. C., 'Land taxation and government participation in urban land markets. In World Bank, *op. cit.*, 2 (i), vol. 2, pp.1–84.
    (b) *The Taxation of Urban Property in Less Developed Countries*. Madison: University of Wisconsin Press, 1979.
6. P. M. J. Motha, 'Land for low-income housing in Singapore'. In R. P. Pama, S. Angel and J. H. De Goede, (eds), *Low Income Housing: Technology and Policy*. Asian Institute of Technology, 1977, chap. III, pp.469–483.
7. H. C. Hwang, 'A search for low-cost land development technique'. In R. P. Pama, *et al.* (eds), *ibid.*, 6, chap. III, pp.485–502.
8. UNCHS Habitat, Human Settlement Finance and Management, Director's Report to Third Session, Mexico City HS/C/3/5 (1980), p.28.
9. R. W. Zetter, *Housing Policy in Cyprus—A Review*. Habitat International, vol. 6, no. 4 (1982).
10. H. Caminos and R. Goethert, *Urbanization Primer* Cambridge Mass: MIT Press, 1978.
11. H. L. Flechner, *Land Banking and the Control of Urban Deveopment*. New York: Praeger, 1973.
12. W. A. Doebele, 'Selected issues in urban land tenure development'. In H. Dunkerley (ed.) *op. cit.* 2 (i), vol. 1, pp.99–207, esp. p.158.
13. G. H. Mutale, 'Statement on land policy in Zambia'. In USAID, *Fourth Conference on Housing in Africa*. Washington, 1977, pp.95–100.
14. B. K. Temane, 'Land tenure and land reform in Botswana'. In M. Cullen and S. Woolery (eds) *op. cit.*, 2 (iii), chap. 24.
15. P. Ward, 'Self-help housing in Mexico City: social and economic determinants of success. *Town Planning Review*, **49** (1978), pp.38–50
16. A. Noorduyn, *The Functioning of the Urban Residential Land Market Within a Third World Context*. BIE, Staff Paper, Bouwcentrum, Rotterdam, 1981.
17. S. Yahya, *House Registration Handbook: A Model of Registering Houses and Plots in Unplanned Settlements*. Urban Development Department, Technical Paper No. 4, World Bank (1982).
18. Doebele argues that assigning title would permit allottees to capitalize their holding and transfer the investment to other productive uses, for example informal sector employment. This optimal investment function would be completed by the higher market value of housing to middle-income groups. This kind of intersectoral mobility of capital is a conceptually attractive, if politically divisive, use of housing funds for the urban poor apart from requiring a level of economic management not available in most Third World countries. See W. A. Doebele, 'Some unexamined aspects of urban land markets', in M. Cullen and S. Woolery (eds) *op. cit.*, 2 (iii), chap. 22.

Low-income Housing in the Developing World
Edited by G. K. Payne
© 1984 John Wiley & Sons Ltd

Chapter 15

The Provision of Infrastructure and Utility Services[1]

John Kirke

BACKGROUND

The design and provision of appropriate infrastructure and utility services for both sites and services and upgrading projects in developing countries is a relatively new and inexact science. The World Bank has only been involved in this sector for 10 years and only a few countries can claim experience of more than 20 years. In essence the World Bank, other donor agencies, the recipient governments, and designers are therefore still learning in this very complex field. Many important lessons have been assimilated, including the need to provide security of tenure to the beneficiaries and to avoid subsidies by designing appropriate and affordable facilities. Most of the significant conceptual issues associated with the provision of affordable low-income housing have been identified and addressed. Problems still remain however, particularly in the areas of physical cost necessary, administration, and maintenance.

Previous chapters have described individual experiences and the major factors to be considered in identifying and preparing projects. This chapter will seek to review the changes which have taken place in the approach to the provision of basic infrastructure and utility services in both sites and services and upgrading projects and to provide some basic guidelines for those involved in their design, implementation, administration, and maintenance. It is, of course, in the context of enormous pressure on the towns and cities of the lesser-developed countries that the provision of infrastructure and utility services to low-income housing areas must be seen.

The traditional approach to the provision of services has been, and to a large extent remains, that of giving an already agreed layout to the engineers with instructions to design the various infrastructure networks to fit the plan and to meet existing design standards. These standards are frequently arbitrarily laid down on the basis of current practice in one or more of the industrialized nations of the Western World. Not only are such standards generally inappropriate in relation to the real needs of the likely beneficiaries, but they are usually unaffordable. It is a matter of record that in one early sites and services project a major road was laid out with a 60 m wide right of way. This colossal waste of high-value land was to some extent remedied by new squatters who set up an informal shopping strip some 20 m wide down the centre of the right of way. In real terms, however, there remained a net land wastage of at least 20–25 m in overall width which could have been developed for housing or other revenue-generating use.

More frequent examples of over-design are to be found in the provision of water supply where demand, in both sites and services and upgrading areas, is so often based on estimates of consumption made by international consultants who have prepared a water supply 'master plan' for the city. In Cairo, for example, the approved master plan envisages the supply of treated water for domestic consumption to reach in excess of 500 lcd (litres per capita daily) within 20 years. This standard presupposes that every dwelling unit would have multiple taps, baths, showers, and cistern flush toilets. In reality almost 50% of the existing housing stock has wet areas (kitchen/toilet/shower) of less than 3 m², and the majority of these are not connected to the piped sewerage system. The cost of physical improvements to existing dwellings to enable them to use the water proposed to be delivered are totally unachievable. Overriding these problems is the vast investment in sewerage improvements which will be necessary to remove the inevitable high level of waste-water flows from the urban area. Indeed major sewerage investments are now agreed as part of the waste water master plan based on the assumed need to convey and treat the increased flows envisaged by the acceptance of the water supply master plan. Within the mainly unsewered, high-density, low-income areas of Greater Cairo, which are currently estimated to house over 4 million people, the maximum level of upgrading likely to be affordable would consist of a single tap serving each building (average four to five apartments per building). At this level of supply, water consumption is unlikely to exceed 100 lcd with resultant waste water flows of around 80 lcd. These figures are far removed from the currently accepted design standards of 500 lcd and 350 lcd respectively. The cost implications on infrastructure networks in designing an upgrading scheme to meet these totally inappropriate design standards must be obvious, as must the capital cost implications of water extraction and treatment and sewerage treatment plants. It is worth pointing out that water consumption in Greater London in 1980 was only 346 lcd, whilst combined stormwater and sewerage flows were only 302 lcd.

PLANNING INFRASTRUCTURE AND UTILITY SERVICES

The major services which may reasonably be required to serve any existing or proposed low-income urban housing area and which particularly affect the cost and affordability of individual plots are:

(a) access and circulation (roads and footpaths);
(b) storm-water drainage (where rainfall is significant);
(c) water supply;
(d) sanitation;
(e) electricity and street lighting;
(f) solid-waste collection.

The level of service which can be provided under any individual heading will be dependent to some extent on the quality and capacity of off-site or existing city infrastructure.

Additionally the need for wage-earners from the beneficiary families to have reasonable and affordable access to employment opportunities needs to be carefully evaluated, as failure will result in families moving back to squat illegally near their original homes.

Each individual service listed above has traditionally been designed by one specialist engineer. It is only now becoming accepted that the various sectors are closely linked, and that decisions taken in respect to standards of provision in one sector may well impact adversely on other sectors. Water supply and sanitation are perhaps the most obvious examples. Increases in the level of water supply to individual dwellings, unless matched by similar improvements in waste-water removal, may well result in poorer sanitation and an increase in health risks.

Less frequently appreciated is that failure to provide facilities for solid-waste collection often results in the dumping of waste in sewers and storm-water drains with resultant blockages and flooding. Inadequate provision or maintenance of storm-water ditches and culverts can cause the flooding of circulation routes with resultant structural damage to roads and even bridges.

There is thus a need to treat the provision or upgrading of infrastructure and utility services to low-income housing areas as an integrated planning exercise. In this respect it is also necessary to emphasize that the infrastructure engineer or engineers have a substantial role to play not only in detailed design but also in project identification and preparation. Site selection has a particularly important influence on infrastructure costs, firstly in the directly recoverable on-site costs, where site conditions and topography will influence design alternatives and construction costs, and secondly in the indirect and frequently non-recoverable costs of off-site works. These may include expensive extensions to existing infrastructure networks such as roads, water supply, sewerage, storm-water drainage, electricity, and even solid-waste collection. Site selection will also affect the level of disposable income of the beneficiaries by increasing or decreasing the cost of travel to existing or proposed employment opportunities.

If low-cost housing programmes are to be replicable on any substantial scale it is readily apparent that non-recoverable off-site infrastructure costs must be reduced to a minimum. Failure to do this must result in escalating public subsidies to meet the required capital expenditures, and in a reduced capability to provide adequate funds to cover the subsequent annual costs of administering and maintaining the services provided.

The role of an engineer as a member of the planning team for sites and services should no longer require detailed definition. The following basic concepts may serve to illustrate his importance in the overall planning task:

(a) The opportunity cost of developable urban land is often the largest single element of project costs. Thus a small percentage reduction in land retained for non-revenue-earning public use (especially circulation space) will represent a far greater cost saving than any which may result from decreases in infrastructure costs, or even from reductions in standards and improved network designs.

(b) The major savings in the physical costs of infrastructure and utility provision will be made by reducing network lengths to a minimum. This is a function of site planning and layout.

(c) The actual on-site cost of any individual infrastructure item, once an optimum layout plan has been developed, will depend primarily on the level of service to be provided and on the ability of the engineer to develop the most cost-effective physical design solution to provide the required service.

The acceptance of these concepts by the planning team will not necessarily guarantee their incorporation into any particular project, unless they can be fully debated with the client bodies representing aid donors, national governments, and local implementing agencies. They must clearly be shown to be compatible with short- and long-term political, social, and economic objectives.

In the case of upgrading schemes, the concept of land value as an influencing factor on infrastructure and utility design is obviously less appropriate than in corresponding sites and services projects. However there are often opportunities, particularly in parts of South-East Asia, where existing timber-frame buildings can be resited within any particular upgrading area without damage to the existing structures. The use of this technique may result in considerable improvements to site layouts with resulting reductions in infrastructure costs, improved access, clearer definition of plot boundaries, and even in the provision of new plots. The sale of any additional plots can then provide a cross-subsidy to reduce the cost to be recovered from the upgraded households. The major task for the engineer, however, when planning the approach to upgrading existing low-income housing areas is to identify those improvements to basic services which are affordable to the existing inhabitants, technically and politically feasible to implement, and which are perceived by the inhabitants to meet their most immediate needs. The ultimate improvements to, and enhancement of, any low-income urban area will depend on the decisions of the inhabitants to carry out self-help improvements to the housing stock (see Chapter 12). Whilst the provision of material loans may assist them, their energies will only be harnessed in this direction where they are provided by the project with security of tenure. This issue is discussed in Chapter 14, and is raised here only in so far as it affects the ability of the client authority to recover from the beneficiaries the cost of infrastructure and utility improvements. For this reason, the upgrading of squatter areas must tackle land ownership, the registration of titles and definition of institutional responsibilities if the catalytic action of providing new or improved infrastructure and municipal services is to achieve the maximum health, safety, social, and environmental benefits.

DETERMINATION OF INFRASTRUCTURE STANDARDS

For most projects, the major infrastructure and utility services under consideration should include access and circulation (vehicular and pedestrian), storm-water drainage, water supply, sanitation (waste-water removal), electricity and street lighting, and solid-waste collection. The standard to which any or all of these services can be provided in any particular project, and hence the appropriate design details, will depend on the interaction of a number of basic parameters. These will include:

(a) site location, especially land cost and accessibility to employment;
(b) access to, and adequacy of, off-site infrastructure;
(c) socioeconomic profile of existing or proposed beneficiaries;
(d) priorities and perceived needs of beneficiaries, especially as expressed by their willingness to pay;

(e) physical on-site conditions, including topography, geology, water-table, propensity to flooding, and existing services in upgrading areas;
(f) the absolute need to provide a minimum level of services in terms of public health and safety, including the provision of suitable access for emergency vehicles;
(g) the maintenance capability of the relevant central and local government agencies;
(h) the need, where minimum standards are proposed initially, to provide flexibility in the detailed design for subsequent enhancement;
(i) the existing and proposed site layouts and densities.

It is frequently found that the socioeconomic profiles of low-income urban households are in direct conflict with the need for cost recovery and the aspirations of politicians and key agency executives, as evinced by the general planning standards for utility provision which are in current use. In such instances, establish a set of acceptable, appropriate, and affordable design standards for any urban housing project will not be easy.

There are two other issues which have seldom if ever been satisfactorily resolved in low-income urban housing projects. The first relates to the need to provide compatibility between selected design standards for infrastructure and utility services in new or upgraded urban areas and those which already exist in the rest of the urban areas. Anomalies can quickly become apparent where the design standards in new or upgraded low-income areas are higher than adjacent urban areas. There is no point in designing a scheme which is dependent on daily solid-waste collection or monthly emptying of septic tanks if the only services available are weekly and annual. Similarly, if the majority of the existing urban form consists of small housing fronting onto narrow streets, the provision of 20 m rights of way as part of an upgrading project will obviously appear inappropriate. The design of sewerage, water supply, and electricity networks in sites and services and upgrading projects frequently assumes a level of demand greater than that being met throughout the town or city as a whole, and sometimes beyond the delivery capacity of the concerned agencies.

The second issue is concerned with defining the proportion of total site development and infrastructure costs which should be recovered from beneficiaries. Whilst the principle of cost recovery is generally accepted, there is an obvious need to differentiate at an early stage of project preparation between those elements of basic infrastructure and utility services costs which should be removed from the low-income beneficiaries and those which traditionally are provided without charge. Generally the distinction has been made that off-site costs are not recovered but anomalies remain, particularly where on-site streets will form part of the expanding urban network and will carry an element of through traffic, or where a proposed sewerage network and treatment plant will be incorporated into the urban sewerage system in order to serve other areas. On-street solid-waste containers are often included in the costs to be recovered from beneficiaries even though they are provided free of charge to areas of public housing and to privately built middle- and high-income developments.

Thus before the planners, architects, and engineers can begin to assess physical design alternatives for any project site, a complex series of surveys and technical, political, and community consultations will need to be undertaken. As a first priority, all relevant data on existing infrastructure services within and adjoining the site will need to be collected and collated. Physical surveys of the site must also be undertaken and, for upgrading areas, these must include property boundaries, rights of way, and ownership details. Socioeconomic surveys of existing or proposed beneficiary households are also essential together with cultural, behavioural, and health assessments of the target population.

At the same time the project objectives need to be reviewed with the client and discussions held with the various agencies involved in the delivery and maintenance of infrastructure and utility services. The financial, technical, and administrative capabilities of these agencies will need to be examined and all existing deficiencies and committed development plans impacting on the proposed project must be clearly defined. The legal and administrative framework which affects infrastructure standards and cost recovery procedures must be clearly understood, as must the way in which the infrastructure services for the proposed projects will affect other sectors in the urban area.

From these surveys and consultations, the many frequently conflicting parameters which will affect the design of the basic infrastructures and utility services will emerge. There will invariably be alternatives and trade-offs to be considered. For instance, a reduction of 5 m^2 in average plot size might enable full cost recovery from a project which included water supply to every house and a conventional sewerage system. Alternatively to provide sufficient space for on-plot sanitation facilities might require a 10 m^2 *increase* in average plot size, thus rendering the plots unaffordable to those most in need. For the majority of sites and services and upgrading projects it is safe to assume that, for the foreseeable future, it will be essential to achieve minimum standards of design and reasonable provision of infrastructure networks commensurate with public health, safety and environmental considerations.

Whilst initial design efforts should concentrate on the twin aims of appropriate standards and affordability the engineer must not lose sight of possible longer-term enhancements of these standards which might be affordable and desirable at some future period. The plots themselves, once designated on a layout plan, cannot be increased in size in the future, although two or more plots could theoretically be combined to provide a larger plot. Similarly, road and footpath reservations could only be increased at the expense of plots or land in residential or other designated use. Savings can be made, however, by providing an appropriate surfaced road width within a reservation more appropriate to some future stage of economic growth. The structure of the road can be similarly laid out for incremental development by starting with a gravelled surface, increasing this by a more permanent or thicker base, and eventually by adding a concrete or asphalt surface as traffic volumes increase. Street lighting can be installed as security lighting initially and be increased through time as the wealth of the areas increases.

Other infrastructure services can be designed for incremental development provided that common-sense approaches to initial costs and future needs are clearly established. Sites and services schemes can be designed to the lowest standards of utility service delivery with no on-plot electricity or water supply and including on-plot latrines or communal toilets. The provision of reasonable (30–40 lcd) supplies of potable water via well-located public standpipes or by tanker with carefully designed on-plot or communal sanitation facilities, can represent a major improvement to families whose homes have previously had access to neither of these facilities. Where septic tanks are used initially they can be designed to be connected to a small-bore sewerage system as increased supplies of water lead to increased water usage, on-plot connections, and larger volumes of waste water.

Generally, however, where land is expensive, densities will be high and plot sizes small. On-plot pits or septic tanks will require excessive space and waste water will tend to create problems of ground-water pollution and of maintenance. As most countries now have on-plot water supplies as either an initial or early objective, the removal of waste water will tend to require a piped sewerage system. In these cases the use of sensible design standards will be essential. Small plots will remain small plots and water supply figures for design purposes can sensibly be taken at 80–100 lcd.

The sewerage system can also be designed for this level of consumption and costs can be kept to a reasonable level. Consultants must avoid the common error of designing for 300–400 lcd because a city water supply master plan calls for it. These levels will only be reached in the larger houses or flats of middle- or higher-income families and then only if tariff charges are artificially low as a result of sectoral subsidies. Sewage treatment can be improved incrementally as volumes increase or effluent standards are improved.

Thus the possible approaches to achieving standards which are both affordable and appropriate in the short term and capable of upgrading within a reasonable design period, as well as being technically, culturally, and politically acceptable over time, will differ from one situation to another and will also vary from utility to utility. The alternative approaches to the design of individual infrastructure services are briefly discussed in the following paragraphs.

ACCESS AND CIRCULATION

The minimum level of service in the provision of on-site roads and footpaths should relate primarily to the provision of reasonable access to all buildings for pedestrians. Paths or walkways provided for this purpose should be well compacted, not subject to flooding during regularly occurring wet periods and, in dry areas, should be provided with at least a sealing coat which will keep down dust. The width will vary with density of anticipated use but should not normally be less than 1.5 m. For vehicular access, the minimum standard will generally relate to access required for emergency vehicles; in this respect no plot or dwelling should be further than 75 m from a vehicular road. Access for private vehicles is most unlikely to be required to the majority of plots and those requiring access can be located along the main vehicular access and circulation routes.

The main guideline to cost-effective provision for access and circulation is in the percentage of the total project area taken up by roads or footpaths. In early sites and services projects this was frequently in excess of 40%. In the Philippines, and elsewhere in South-East Asia, projects are under preparation with circulation space reduced to less than 20% of the site area. As a general rule the most efficient layouts will usually result from providing a number of housing groups served by footpath access from vehicular access culs-de-sac, which are in turn connected to vehicular circulation routes (see Figures 15.1 and 15.2).

Rights of way and construction standards should reflect the likely level of use and a reasonable forecast of traffic volumes. Some savings in foreign exchange and physical construction costs, apart from keeping constructed and surfaced widths of designated rights of way to an appropriate minimum, can be made by use of suitable locally available

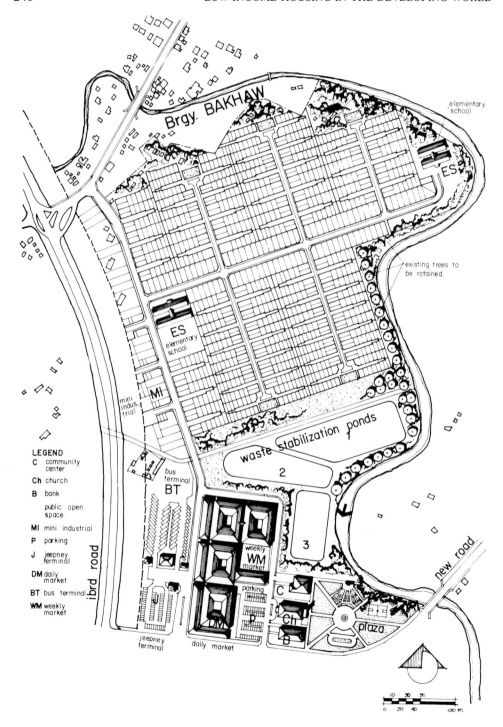

Figure 15.1   Part of a site and services project at Iloilo in the Philippines, showing the layout
of plots, major facilities and waste stabilization ponds

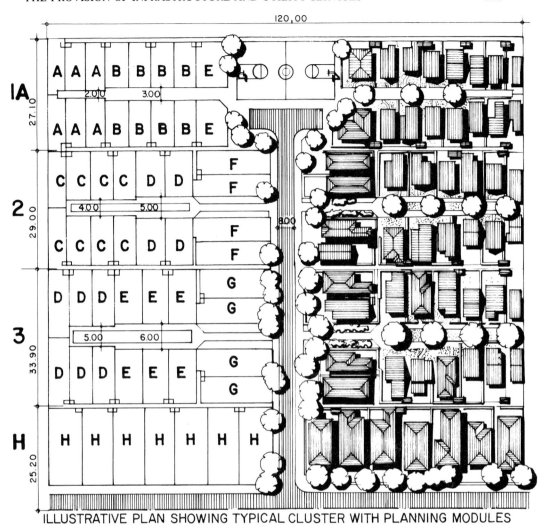

ILLUSTRATIVE PLAN SHOWING TYPICAL CLUSTER WITH PLANNING MODULES

module type	plot types	plot areas	numbers of plots	module type	plot types	plot areas	number of plots	Land costs per m^2
1A	A	60m^2	12	2	C	70	16	A — 30 pesos
	B	65	16		D	80	8	B — 45 pesos
	E	90	3		F	110	8	C — 70 pesos
	F	110	1					D — 90 pesos
				3	D	80	12	E — 110 pesos
1B	A	60	12		E	90	12	F — 130 pesos
	B	65	16		G	130	8	G — 130 pesos
	F	110	8					H — 135 pesos
				H	H	150	14	

Notes: standard housing modules

Figure 15.2 Typical compound and plot layout in Iloilo, project showing how plots are priced and the types of development anticipated. On-plot development costs (sanitary costs and connection charges) were 2340 pesos for all plots

materials, by application of labour-intensive construction techniques, and particularly by reducing the use of kerbs.

It is unlikely that low-income families will generate more than a minimal demand for private-vehicle ownership, but careful provision must be made for public transport access. In upgrading areas the provision of improved access may also be required in order to create firebreaks in densely packed areas of squatter housing. These will then serve the dual purpose of providing reasonable access for emergency vehicles and public transport whilst reducing overall density and fire risk. The need to minimize requirements for demolition and relocation may well influence the location, right of way, and spacing of access roads in upgrading areas.

STORM-WATER DRAINAGE

Storm-water drainage provision standards, together with the resultant maintenance and cleaning operations, impact directly on both the capital and recurrent costs of access and circulation. The provision of an efficient network of earth ditches adjoining the main access and circulation routes may be justified simply by the resultant reductions in initial construction costs and lower annual maintenance cost of the roads and footways. Recent requests for World Bank loans from one government agency in South-East Asia included requests for substantial funds to carry out extensive reconstruction and resurfacing of major city streets. Subsequent investigation revealed that these same streets had substantially deteriorated over a 2–3-year time-scale. This deterioration was due almost entirely to flooding resulting from the inadequate provision and maintenance of storm-water drainage. A significantly lower level of investment to improve drainage has enabled lower cost and more appropriate repairs to be carried out to the roads, and considerable increases in surface life are now forecast.

Where storm-water drainage is required, networks should be developed to meet realistic climatic, and design criteria. In small upgrading areas, and in many sites and services developments, it may prove unaffordable to design for more than a 1-year storm. The engineer must assess the likely incidence and resultant cost of anticipated flooding to both the project site and the urban area in general. The capacity of receiving water-courses and rivers must also be carefully checked to ensure that the project area will not be delivering more storm-water than they can reasonably accept.

Particular problems arise where storm-water and sewerage are combined. In most developing cities urban sewerage networks are both limited in scale and heavily overloaded. Where any risk of surcharging exists, or can be forecast, the addition of the storm-water to the sewers will simply result in untreated sewerage being spread over a greater area of the city streets. Standing water on hard surfaces will generally evaporate in a few hours and in itself, unlike diluted sewerage, presents few if any health risks. Where storm-water drainage is required the first consideration is to design an appropriate network. Open channels constructed in earth or suitable local materials will generally provide the most appropriate, least-cost and most easily maintained solution. Covered channels or piped networks should only be considered where other cost, environmental, or health considerations dictate; for instance where covered channels are part of the footway network and for culverts under roads.

WATER SUPPLY AND SANITATION

The need for, and benefits of, appropriate standards in the provision of potable water and sanitation to the urban poor have been more effectively researched, reviewed, and debated over the last few years than any other aspect of urban infrastructure or utility service provision. The results of this research, with detailed conclusions, cost comparisons and design criteria, are contained in recent publications of the World Bank under the general title of 'Appropriate Technology for Water Supply and Sanitation'.[2] These publications are extremely comprehensive and provide a most clear design guide to the engineer concerned with sites and services and upgrading projects. It is perhaps worthwhile to emphasize that levels of provision and standards of design for these two services are irrevocably linked. Almost all the water delivered to and consumed by any household will re-emerge either as sullage (kitchen and sink wastage) or in sewage. Thus any level of water supply to dwellings must be matched by appropriate facilities for waste removal.

The provision of potable water from on-plot or nearby wells will seldom be a feasible option in sites and services projects in densely populated and rapidly expanding urban centres. The available alternatives, once an optimum site layout has been agreed, will thus generally be limited to:

(a) public standpipes;
(b) courtyard taps;
(c) single tap on plot for sites and services;
(d) single tap to multiple occupancy building (upgrading areas);
(e) multiple taps to all dwellings.

It is generally accepted that, where public standpipes are the only source of potable water, consumption per capita will be in the region of 20–40 lcd. Whilst this is sufficient to meet the essential basic needs it is usually inadequate to meet all in-house demands for water even from the poorest families. Where water supply is by public standpipe the overriding factors which most influence resultant levels in personal consumption are:

(a) Residual mains pressure

If residual pressure is low supplies will be intermittent, the time taken to fill containers will increase, and consumption will decrease.

(b) Number of persons per standpipe

This factor is more important in urban areas than standpipe spacing. The average demand of around 30 litres per person can be met by filling two 15-litre buckets. Thus for an average family of six persons some twelve buckets of water will have to be fetched each day. The average filling time (including time spent in 'swilling out' the bucket and turning the tap on and off) was observed in Cairo to be approximately 3 minutes. Standpipes are generally in use for about 12 hours per day indicating that, at 6 minutes per person per tap, each tap could supply 120 persons under constant use and reasonable pressure conditions. Where densities are around 600 persons per hectare (a figure often exceeded in low-income urban areas) some five taps would be required per hectare. With four tap standpipes and a high mains pressure, each standpipe would serve only 0.8 hectares and all households would be within 50 metres of the nearest standpipes. For increased densities or higher levels of consumption more standpipes would be required.

(c) Maintenance

In most developing cities, public standpipes are provided at the public expense and, although frequently metered, are seldom adequately maintained. Lack of maintenance results initially in water wastage, as standpipes deliver water continually, and ultimately in a cessation of supply. As each standpipe ceases to operate, increasing demand is put on the remainder with resulting increases in carrying distances and waiting times and decreasing levels of individual consumption.

The difficulties in obtaining reasonable and equitable cost recovery from or adequate levels of supervision and maintenance to public standpipes generally militate against their widespread use in sites and services projects. Additionally, where good planning results in minimum lengths of infrastructure networks, the cost of providing an on-plot single tap will be little more than the cost of providing adequate standpipes, particularly if the need to design the distribution network to deliver at least 100 lcd ultimately is accepted. The design of the system on the basis of multiple taps in every dwelling is also unreasonable as it will presuppose a size of dwelling, household income and water extraction/treatment capacity far beyond the affordability level of low-income families, and indeed to most developing countries within the design lifetime of the project.

Thus a design based on the delivery of around 100 lcd through a single tap outlet on each plot is the most commonly applicable and affordable level of service in sites and services projects. The design of minimum-length networks and the provision of block metering systems (rather than individual plot meters) will help to keep the physical costs to a minimum.

The design of a system to deliver an affordable supply of water to upgrading areas is often more complex. Whilst the solutions listed above for sites and services are still possible, there are often cases where mains supply will not be available for some years. In these cases alternative delivery systems may have to be found. In a low-income squatter area of one large South-East Asian city, agreement is being sought to use the Fire Service water trucks overnight to fill prefabricated water storage tanks specially constructed within the squatter area. These tanks will then be able to deliver a greater quantity of better-quality water per capita to the inhabitants than they are currently able to purchase from water vendors. The charge levied per household will be less than 50% of the average cost paid to vendors. Full cost recovery will result in additional funds being raised for the Fire Service. Careful attention is being paid to the night-time delivery service to ensure that the Fire Service's ability to respond to a fire in any location of the city will not be adversely affected. The basic criterion to be met in providing potable water to urban households remains the need to deliver at least 20 lcd. Significant health benefits result if this can be raised to 50 lcd, but benefits are less easily quantified above this figure. The cost of public standpipes to deliver 50 lcd in high-density urban areas is not significantly less than the cost of provision of a single tap supply to each plot or building.

Single tap outlets can be expected to provide a level of consumption of around 100 lcd and will significantly reduce public costs of administration and maintenance.

The final decisions on water supply standards will rest with the politicians and senior executives of the concerned agencies. The greatest danger therefore will continue to be the acceptance of demand values and design criteria financially and economically beyond the reach of the household, community, city, and country resources. Whichever level of service is ultimately accepted, there remains an absolute necessity to accept that most of the water delivered to individual dwellings will reappear as waste water. Provision must therefore be made to dispose of this liquid waste without causing increased levels of public health risk. In this respect the primary requirement is to make adequate, affordable, culturally acceptable and technically feasible provision for appropriate sanitation facilities. The alternatives can be broadly divided into household or on-plot solutions and community or off-plot solutions.

Entirely on-plot solutions include pit latrines, aquaprivies, pour flush toilets, septic tanks, and composting toilets. Community or off-plot options (including those on-plot solutions requiring extensive off-plot services) include bucket latrines, vaults with vacuum cart collection, sewered aquaprivies, communal toilet facilities and conventional sewerage systems. Detailed analysis of these alternatives would not be appropriate here and is more than adequately covered in the World Bank Sanitation Manuals referred to previously.

General guidelines for sites and services and upgrading schemes in urban areas are mainly matters of common sense and are related to the design quantity and method of water supply. Where water will be hand-carried to the dwelling from public standpipes, sanitation options will be restricted to those requiring either little or no household water such as pit latrines, composting toilets, bucket latrines, and communal toilets. Single tap provision on-plot or within a multi-rise building will permit pour flush and vault toilets and, providing delivery exceeds 60–80 lcd, will also permit cistern flush toilets to be used. Where pour flush toilets can be used to reduce water wastage, consideration should always be given to utilizing sullage water from an adjoining tap or sink to be passed through the toilet to provide additional flushing and reduce the likelihood of blockages.

The possibility of providing a phased upgrading programme for sanitation is often overlooked. Where increasing population density and water use causes soakage problems, septic tanks and aquaprivies may be improved by the addition of a small-bore sewer system which will carry away excess liquids, thus reducing the frequency of flooding. Subsequently, as incomes increase and improvements in water supply are made, the system can be upgraded to conventional sewerage standards. Where falls are limited, the small-bore pipes might be connected to standard sewer pipes in the roads to reduce pumping costs and subsequent costs of system enhancement.

Whilst conventional sewerage systems are often considered financially unaffordable in sites and services and upgrading projects, it is in this field that major cost reductions can be made. The majority of developing countries have climatic conditions well suited to the successful operation of waste stabilization ponds. The use of such ponds for effluent treatment can reduce treatment costs to less than 10% of the costs of a traditional sewage treatment works. In carefully planned sites and services developments, four-way toilet or ablution units can be provided at the rear of the plots in such a manner as to sit almost directly over a sewer pipe. If the single on-plot tap adjoins the toilet then waste water can be used to aid flushing and for transporting sewerage. The careful design of this type of on-plot service can provide a conventional sewerage solution for less than the cost of sewered aquaprivies or septic tanks. Additional benefits, although difficult to quantify, will result if the final effluent from the ponds can be re-used for aquaculture or agriculture.

In a recently appraised shelter component of an urban development project in Iloilo in the Philippines,[3] the consultants[4] prepared preliminary planning and costed engineering layouts for some 1860 plots varying in size from 60 to 150 m². The detailed estimates for the sewerage system and sewage disposal by waste stabilization ponds inclusive of design, price and physical contingencies was 5,461,000 pesos, i.e. a cost per plot 2940 pesos, or (US$390). Recent reviews of on-plot sanitation provision undertaken by the UNDP/World Bank TAG project have disclosed that on-plot ventilated improved pit latrines can be provided in Tanzania, Lesotho, and Botswana at an average cost of US$400 per plot.

These figures serve to emphasize that piped sewerage systems can be provided at costs similar to those for well-designed on-plot facilities. Operation and maintenance problems are different, but the short-term benefits of low costs for on-plot units must be seen against the need for costly maintenance or replacement at regular intervals and increasing public health hazards over time.

ELECTRICITY AND STREET LIGHTING

The capital cost of electricity generation and primary transmission networks is extremely high and investments by major aid donors have almost invariably been tied to improvements in the institutional structure and financial viability of the concerned agencies. Electricity supply agencies have become generally independent of direct central government subsidies and in most urban centres the growth of residential electricity connections over the last 15 years has far outstripped the growth in water supply or sewerage connections. Electricity connection costs and tariff charges seldom provide for full economic cost recovery, but they are invariably far more realistic than for water supply and sewerage. This is probably due to a perception by governments that electricity is a luxury for private households and its cost should therefore be fully recovered from the users.

Not only do beneficiaries in sites and services and upgrading projects appear to put a high priority on achieving their desire for in-house electricity, but in almost any urban slum area in the world there will be a significant number of dwellings connected legally or illegally to the electricity network.

It has been common practice for lending agencies and Governments concerned with low-income urban housing to provide, as a cost item recoverable from beneficiaries, only street lighting. The design for the electricity distribution system is then left to the concerned agencies on the basis that costs will be recovered from the connection and tariff charges. As a result of this approach little effort has been made to evaluate low cost alternatives for the distribution networks or individual connections.

Costs of basic urban networks and house connections can be significantly reduced without detriment to standards of public safety, if a more pragmatic approach to design is accepted. The greatest savings can accrue from three sources: firstly by designing systems to meet a more realistic and affordable level of demand. It is common for agencies to assume a domestic demand of about 1.5 kW per plot. This is between three and six times greater than the actual demand from most low-income households, and will, when applied to network design, dramatically increase costs. The second major area of cost savings will stem from the provision of an above-ground medium-voltage distribution system with post-mounted transformers connected to above-ground radial or ring low-voltage distribution networks in a combination of three-phase and single-phase mains. The third source of cost savings can come from the use of circuit-breakers to control levels of supply to individual plots. Not only are these cheaper to install than meters, but the removal of the administrative burden of regular meter readings will result in enormous savings in annual labour and maintenance costs. With well-planned site layouts, adequately spaced street lights can be fed from the single-phase house supply mains.

SOLID-WASTE COLLECTION

The need to provide some system of solid-waste removal from urban residential areas has already been discussed. Unfortunately it is unlikely that any city or municipal council will have the resources to provide a full solid-waste collection service during the early years of a project. With careful planning, however, and good community participation, the provision of a daily road cleaning and solid-waste collection service is feasible. Space should be provided in central locations, where other community facilities are to be provided, for the storage of suitable hand carts, brooms, and large containers. Funds can be provided within the project for a small building and the appropriate equipment.

The community should then be able to appoint and preferably be provided with funds to pay individuals who would sweep selected routes daily, collecting household refuse at the same time. The collected waste would then be transferred to the central containers, which would be collected weekly by the Municipal or City Council who would leave empty containers in their place. The provision of equipment including containers and, if necessary, extra vehicles will represent less than 5% of total project costs and it is arguable that only a relatively small proportion of this should be recoverable from the beneficiaries.

COMMUNITY PARTICIPATION AND MAINTENANCE

This chapter has attempted to illustrate that the lessons already learnt by many different agencies undertaking sites and services and upgrading projects in a wide variety of countries for low-income households of many cultures and nationalities provide a solid base of experience for the future. In every case, however, the engineers responsible for the design of infrastructure and utility services must adapt their traditional approach to infrastructure design to provide appropriate, affordable, and maintainable levels of service.

If these goals are to be achieved, the maximum possible time must be spent with the communities expected to benefit from the proposed projects. Firstly their own perception of their priorities and existing patterns of cultural, social, and economic behaviour must be clearly understood. Secondly the trade-offs in cost affecting alternative levels of provision between different infrastructure items must be explained. Finally the detailed design of the proposed services must be agreed with the responsible agencies and the ability of those agencies to administer and maintain them must be ascertained. The maximum possible role for the community in administration and maintenance at the local level must also be defined.

In most Third World countries, adequate well-trained and competent local engineers are available to undertake detailed design and construction supervision of infrastructure networks. Guidance from foreign consultants will generally be essential if the design standards are to be appropriate to the needs of, and affordable to, project beneficiaries from amongst the urban poor. Further training and exposure to innovative solutions is required as local professional solutions will usually derive from previous experience or training in developed countries or from working to long-established inappropriate government standards.

Only when the engineer is able to match the needs of the beneficiaries to the provision of culturally acceptable and affordable levels of infrastructure services, which are in turn compatible with the administrative and maintenance capabilities of the responsible agencies, will these much-needed urban projects become truly replicable.

NOTES AND REFERENCES

1. For the purposes of this chapter, utilities are taken to include services supplied by public utility agencies, such as water supply, sewerage and sewage disposal, electricity and telephones. Infrastructure includes all utilities plus roads and footpaths, refuse collection and disposal, street lighting, and cleaning and drainage.
2. *Appropriate Technology for Water Supply and Sanitation: a Planners' Guide.* Published as volume 2 of a series of manuals on utilities provision by the Transportation, Water and Telecommunications Department of the World Bank, 1980.
3. Regional Cities Development Project, to be funded by the World Bank Fourth Urban Loan.
4. Gilmore Hankey Kirke Partnership, London; Roger Tym & Partners, London; and P.M.D.S.I., Manila.

Low-income Housing in the Developing World
Edited by G. K. Payne
© 1984 John Wiley & Sons Ltd

Chapter 16

Building Materials and Construction Systems

John P. M. Parry

CULTURE AND PRAGMATISM IN DESIGN

Construction systems in the modern context reflect a very wide array of influences. They range from the entirely pragmatic use of the materials locally to hand (which in turn largely dictates method of erection) to the other extreme, frequently related to population movement or previous colonial rule, by which the choice of materials and methods obviously stem from the country of origin of the people concerned and not to indigenous influences.

Transposed building technologies are less interesting to study away from their original context. More can be learned from the heritage of ingenuity and application by the people for whom economy is not a preference but a necessity, the low-income groups or people living in isolation.

The first consideration is to recognize how important the available raw material is in determining the construction system. It is at least as important as climate, which most people assume to be the main governing factor, and more important than culture which is often judged, erroneously, to be the principal factor in building design. The African people who build round dwellings do not do so because of a liking for round shapes and an abhorrence of rectangles. They do so because bundles of tall thatching grass cut directly from the field provide the most effective waterproof cover if formed together into a conical canopy.

Once the village-dweller has the income to enable him to buy tiles or corrugated iron sheets, he cheerfully changes his house shape from a circle to a rectangle to accommodate this new type of roof. Wall building materials can also influence styles. If burnt bricks or sandcrete blocks become available but the roof is still thatch, the awkwardness of trying to build circular walls out of oblong objects usually results in the rectangular plan being adopted even though this causes more work in building the roof. It therefore may seem to be an inevitable process that one high-technology material brings others with it. Switching from thatch to sheets also brings into question the use of rough pole timbers cut from the local bush. These poles, frequently originating from gum, eucalyptus, or teak saplings which grow in 2 or 3 years, are a cheap material. However, they are often not straight enough to build a satisfactory sheet roof although perfectly adequate for holding up grass thatch. The substitute, sawn timber, comes from

249

full-size trees, a much scarcer commodity than saplings. It is also more difficult to renew and considerably more expensive.

The more irregular in shape or quality the material used, the more important it is to have access to special skills in relevant trades. These trades of course exist in less developed countries, where the 'maestro' of Latin America, 'fundi' of East Africa and 'tukang' of the East Indies are respected members of the community, though they are merely better at doing the work done by most other people. Only some of the new, highly educated elite would feel embarrassed to pick up a hammer or trowel.

Nevertheless there is an important area increasingly in common between all building industries, as traditional building materials are progressively made by someone other than by the end-user. Whereas the householder in the remoter areas of the world still sends his family out to cut bundles of thatch or palm leaves for thatching, as the money economy expands and simultaneously traditional materials get scarcer, it is now normal for him to save up to buy galvanized corrugated iron sheets instead. The same applies to walls and floors as manufactured materials displace the adobe or wattle and daub that would normally be made from locally gathered materials.

The international recession has caused special problems for the building needs of poorer people, especially those who had begun to switch to store-bought in place of indigenous materials. They may have begun to use straight sawn timber bought from the store in place of the more irregular poles and saplings cut from the surrounding bush. This in turn involves fixing things together with iron nails instead of traditional thongs or ropes. As mentioned earlier, the use of sheets more or less compels the housebuilder to adopt a rectangular plan in place of the round shape of house, which in turn affects wall building methods. Wattle and daub construction is more difficult to use in a house with corners than it is for round walls, so bricks, blocks, or sawn timber planks begin to appear. Even if natural resources remained abundant it would not be easy to go back to using materials in their original form once the benefits of permanent construction have been experienced. So 'modern' methods tend to stick. Yet shop prices continue to rise, causing hardship when the need arises to extend or repair. The assumption is normally that there is nothing that can be done to counteract this squeeze from both directions, but of course there has to be.

Three types of activity will be discussed in subsequent paragraphs:

(a) Whether it is possible to achieve the desired amenities of comfort, durability, cleanliness, and aesthetic/visual acceptability while consuming less of the resources which are scarce.
(b) What might be achieved by innovating processes which concentrate on using the materials which are abundant in substitution for those which are scarce.
(c) What prospects exist for eliminating many of the costs of purchased items which are associated with centralized manufacture and distribution, by instead manufacturing on a very small scale with the end-users or their close associates undertaking the actual production processes, possibly at the building site itself.

CUTTING BACK ON MATERIAL USE

Taking first the roof of the building, which is usually the most costly item, a designer can always achieve more covered room space from the same area of canopy by building upwards and building flatter. But this brings with it other problems. Multiple-floor buildings place more load on foundations and bottom-storey walls, which become more expensive as a result. The implications are even more serious in areas which are subject to high winds or earthquakes. Similarly, the flatter the roof (unless it is a reinforced concrete slab) the more susceptible it is to hurricane damage. Building taller buildings also brings in new components such as stairs or mechanized elevators, and requires more pressure in the water-supply system. Nevertheless, many cultures already use two- and three-storey buildings for their traditional accommodation, so this option should always be looked into as an early priority.

Looking at the materials themselves, producers have examined the manufacture of thinner grades of corrugated iron sheeting to reduce costs but this has also reduced the potential lifespan of the products. Manufacturers have devised huge 7 m long components—'W'-shaped sheets which provide both cladding and self-supporting structure. These can be made of steel, aluminium, or asbestos cement, although this last material is coming under close scrutiny due to health hazards, particularly during manufacture and cutting on site. Tilemakers have progressively introduced products which provide greater areas of cover for the amount of material used. This has been done by increasing sizes and using interlocking edges to cut down the overlap between adjacent tiles. The timber trade has devised systems of trusses which minimize the volume of wood required to support the required load and withstand high winds. All these

Figure 16.1   Roofing elements performing the role of both structure and cladding of flat roofs in Peru

measures represent modest technical breakthroughs, but the scope for further advances is not all that great. Perhaps the area which warrants closest attention is the combination of the role of both structure and cladding. This might sometimes be fairly sophisticated but humbler solutions will also be needed. Use of sheeting in self-supporting structures could be developed for pitched roofs and in areas of low seismic activity, whilst low-cost vaults and domes have considerable development potential.

In wall construction, manufacturing industry has gone to considerable lengths to reduce to a minimum the volume of expensive materials needed for components. Prime examples are the various forms of cavity and perforated masonry. Extruded burnt clay blocks are made in numerous countries and their composition is frequently more than 50% void. Some concrete blocks are hollow shells with the actual concrete material about 2 cm thick. The other approach to material saving has been to introduce random voids by aeration—gas concrete made with the help of aluminium powder; or no-fines concrete. This latter takes the opposite route from normal concreting which endeavours to pack the particles closely. In no-fines concrete an open matrix of stones is 'glued' together with a film of cement and the spaces which would normally be filled with smaller aggregate are left empty. If prepared properly this masonry is a potential cement saver but is more effective for *in situ* concreting than for precast elements, as compressive performance will inevitably be better than flexural or impact resistance.

More work needs to be done on researching ways of selecting and grading material by size and shape to achieve natural dry packing without cement. It may be that the correct formulation could produce a wall which only needs protective surface and little or no internal stabilization. Low cement contents are being achieved with stabilized laterites and other soils but here materials are used as dug without modification to the natural grading. In nature itself rock is usually formed by compression or heat, or a combination of the two. Red bricks derive from a similar heat treatment, but no technology is in widespread use which produces a stable masonry unit entirely by compression, although this is theoretically perfectly possible.

Regarding the development of blocks and bricks with perforations or cavities, it needs to be mentioned that it is not altogether a desirable objective to eliminate mass in walls indiscriminately. Mass is an important feature in acoustic insulation. More important still, in continental areas with wide diurnal range (night-time temperatures uncomfortably cold and day-times hot) massive walls can operate as 'thermal flywheels', keeping the inside of the building at a reasonable temperature at all times. Introduction of light-weight construction in these circumstances will result in the need for day-time air conditioning and artificial heating at night.

Floors present a fresh series of problems. They are subject to constant impact and frequent contact with water, and in most buildings have to be frequently cleaned, which may involve contact with abrasive action and attacks by deliberately penetrating chemicals. Upper floors are a serious expense, either involving an all-timber construction or a concrete slab reinforced by steel which has to be prefabricated and moved by a heavy-duty crane. If prefabricated beams are used, these can be manhandled into place but the components, such as 'pots' and 'T' blocks which fill in the space between the beams, and the beams themselves all have to be purchased, adding to the material cost of the building. If built *in situ*, a long and elaborate process of shuttering, usually timber, has to be used to support the slab while it sets. It used to be the practice to construct upper floors using a vault system with a series of brick arches carried on large steel beams. This method has largely been abandoned because of the labour cost in building the brick vaults and the expense of the steel beams, but it is still used in a few regions, such as the Indian subcontinent.

ENHANCING THE PERFORMANCE OF
INDIGENOUS BUILDING MATERIALS

There is no such thing as a completely permanent building material because even the hardest natural or man-made substances wear away with the passage of time. However, there is a big difference between the economic aspects of materials such as granite which will last for centuries in exposed situations, compared with organic materials such as grass or wood, which in a similar position may deteriorate in months or a few years.

The characteristics of building materials which deteriorate rapidly are that they are either organic, derived from animal or vegetable products, or otherwise are mineral but in an unconsolidated form so as to be vulnerable to shock, thermal movement, or biochemical attack. In a special category are also a few materials which are vulnerable to contact with water, i.e. they soften or change their form or volume. Bearing in mind that the different forms of attack will affect different parts of the structure, the procedures necessary to protect the building will not all need to be applied universally to every part of the structure.

Even buildings constructed to modern specifications using factory-made materials are in part very vulnerable to one or other form of deterioration. Taking the interior in particular, there are many features such as plaster, papering, metal connections, and timber work which would rapidly be destroyed if they were exposed to the elements. The whole concept of building construction takes into account the different forces which apply in different areas. The principal contrast between a mud hut and a modern Western dwelling is that while the latter contains degradable materials within the canopy, these are protected by the more durable outer surfaces; in the former, both outer and inner materials are degradable and so after a time, once the external fabric has been destroyed, the interior is no longer protected and that goes too.

The approach which we suggest, therefore, is to concentrate upon upgrading the surface protection. Much work has been done on improving the durability of the commonest material of all, mud. If it were possible to make an unfired mud brick wall behave as durably as concrete brickwork or burnt bricks, it would be a most significant development, with potential to improve the lifestyle of the majority of the world's people who live in houses with walls of this material. The approach taken by most researchers has concentrated on stabilizing the *whole* of the material rather than just protecting its surface. The substances most commonly used for stabilizing mud are cement, lime, or bitumen, none of which are low-cost.

Where the traditional builder tries to prolong the life of the material, however, he just attends to the surface by applying paint or plaster. Modern researchers had rejected this approach because past evidence had shown the effect to be only temporary and unless renewed the coating or plastering fell away after a time and the deterioration began again. However, this does not mean that a coating technology for a mud wall was completely impractical, and some promising new research has begun to indicate the potential for providing an adequate bond between a cement plaster and a mud brick wall. Only time will tell whether this new approach will produce a 'permanent' solution, but so far the performance has been good for over 5 years.

The approach taken has been to use a common woodworkers' adhesive, diluted with water to penetrate and seal the outer surface of the mud brickwork and provide a suitable skin to which the cement can bond. What happens with the traditional plaster is that the cement does its normal job of adhering to the mud brick's surface but the surface itself comes away from the brick in the form of a layer of dust. The solution appears to be effective in temperate and humid, tropical climates but has not yet been tested in areas with a high diurnal range.

A further approach in extending the life of a mud brick wall is to take pains to prevent contact by heavy rain either falling direct, running off the roof, or splashing up from the ground. This can be prevented either by extending the overhang of the roof or by installing guttering and downpipes. This of course applies to pitched roofs. Where flat roofs are concerned the approach is usually taken to project short pieces of piping out from the walls and to channel all the water into these guttering spouts.

The solution is not so easy for the roof itself. While a protective coating for a natural material such as thatch might be devised, much of the biological attack starts from underneath and the agents responsible are frequently already in the material at the time of installation. It is not out of the question to try to kill off the insects or other organisms in the straw or reed beforehand, but if this involves chemicals or heating the costs begin to rise. A better approach is to be selective in the basic material where it is possible. One type of reed or straw may be naturally more resistant than another. In Britain,

Figure 16.2   Agriculture building in Devon, UK, with experimental plaster over mud walls, in excellent condition after 5 years exposure

where thatching was once the major roofing material, people would deliberately cultivate the best species of reed that had proved to have greater natural durability.

Thatching technique can also help a great deal. By capping the upper ends of the straw or reed bundles with impervious materials it is possible to restrict the incursion of rain water, while tightness of the packing also helps to deter biological attack. For preserving the supporting frame, treatment or selection can be effective. Bamboo is the most cheaply preserved material because where suitable stretches of running water are available, the edible starches which attract destructive insects can be washed out without weakening the material. Ordinary wood may be naturally durable, but if not, chemical preservatives need to be forced into the grains under pressure to achieve prolongation of service life. Surface treatments have to be renewed from time to time.

Mention needs to be made of the most passive method of protecting materials—the use of physical blocks. Far better to deter animals such as termites by barriers such as projecting strips of metal sheet around the footings than to try to kill them off with poison. The well-known practice of putting discs of wood around ship hawsers when tied up at the dockside, demonstrates the same approach used to prevent rats from climbing aboard. The author once terminated the tenancy of a large family of rats in the roof of his house in Borneo, by partially driving a six-inch nail into each upright post of the building's timber frame. The task of scrambling up and down to the ground became so awkward that they simply went away to live somewhere else!

PURCHASE OR SITE MANUFACTURE OF ELEMENTS

Most technological commentaries make frequent reference to efficiency in production of components and elements such as bricks and window frames. By 'efficiency' it is normal to mean the quantity of resources such as labour and materials used, or the output achieved from a plant compared with its notional capacity. It would be surprising, indeed something would be wrong with the local manufacturing industry, if in these terms products could be made more 'efficiently' on a small scale on the building site. However, this does not mean that there are not strong arguments for organizing production on site. On the contrary, in self-help schemes such as sites and services projects there are hugh gains to be made from scaling down and localizing many manufacturing processes.

In terms of sheer efficiency in the wider sense site work, though less 'productive', may be cheaper when there are rationalizations in the transport of individual materials such as sand, cement, aggregate, and steel so that the trucking costs are lower. If one of the materials (say, sand) can actually be obtained on the site itself the transport savings will be even greater.

More important still are the savings in suppliers' wages and associated overheads when self-help conditions apply. These will vary for different countries, but it can generally be assumed that for the majority of building elements the raw material ingredients' original costs only constitute about 10–20% of the final price of the manufactured component. The rest goes to the other costs of running the business and to making a profit. A specialist component producer such as a concrete blockmaker does not set himself up in business to reduce builders' costs. He welcomes the inertia or lack of technical knowedge or suitable equipment which prevents his customers from making blocks for themselves. The only constraints on his pricing are the availability of competing

Figure 16.3 A simple breeze-block making machine in Ankara, Turkey, capable of producing 400 blocks per man-day (photo by G. K. Payne)

blocks or alternative materials which can substitute for them. The importer is even less concerned with anything other than selling his goods and must harden his heart to the burden his activities place on a country's foreign exchange reserves. Transport is an important cost element which could be reduced by initiation of local manufacture. Another benefit of on-site production is that it generates local employment and raises incomes.

Concrete blocks do not necessarily need a sophisticated producer. In Ankara they have small blockmaking machines which can produce very large numbers of blocks on site, as shown in Figure 16.3.

If on the above evidence there may be a considerable potential for building cost reductions by self-help builders undertaking their own production on site, why is this practice not already more prevalent? There are probably several answers but the singularly most important is the combination of two factors:

(a) the self-help builder is usually undercapitalized and with only one project in view he sees little justification in acquiring capital plant if the cost savings can only be achieved once;

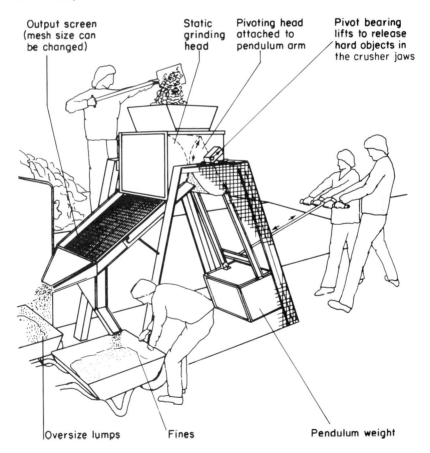

Figure 16.4   The principle of the clay crusher. For continuous operation a team of four is needed.
(Drawing by J. Parry.)

(b) as the trends in manufacturing technologies have been to scale up so as to secure 'economies of scale' (the 'efficiencies' referred to at the beginning of this discussion) the plant manufacturers have usually left a gap in the range of equipment offered.

Our Building Materials Workshop in Cradley Heath has been developing equipment that helps to remedy this situation. Effective manually powered machines have been designed to serve the small-scale producer of clay-based components. For example, a moulding machine for clay bricks, simple in its construction, is entirely built with the type of timber and metal sections common all over the world. It is therefore easily maintained and repaired. With it an operator can make standard hand-moulded bricks at a rate of up to four a minute. The latest development of the Workshop has been a manually powered, pendulum clay crusher (see Figure 16.4). This offers relief from the drudgery of hand-pounding and foot-treading of clay, necessary in the manufacture of various clay-based products, as it produces a high output of crushed fines from most dry clays or shales. It can also be adapted to handle a wide range of materials that have to be crushed, ground, or milled.

   The other gap in technology appears in the application of truly indigenous local or site materials for construction. Any review of self-help building techniques needs to make some reference to the traditional building techniques which by their nature were truly 'self-help'. There were few equivalents of contractors or specialist component suppliers in the poorer rural economies from which people were drawn into the new urban conglomerations. Again technologies have largely ignored traditional construction materials and methods such as adobe brick or wattle and daub walls, pole timber, bamboo and split palm, roof structures with thatch for cover, and compacted earth floors. Primitive and inconvenient though some of these are, they cannot be ignored, especially as the costs are sometimes a small fraction of that for modern materials. The technological gap here relates to methods of improving these primitive technologies and upgrading aspects such as cleanliness/hygiene, general appearance, and durability. For instance it seems to transform a government officials' sceptical attitute to sundried bricks if those are made sharp and regular in shape and size; in other words if they seem to be 'manufactured' products rather than made by people grubbing about on the ground. A complete intermediate technology brick plant producing up to 10,000 baked bricks a week is illustrated in Figure 16.5.

INTERMEDIATE TECHNOLOGY APPROACH

The description 'intermediate' is chosen deliberately to describe the methods aimed to fill the gap between the traditional and modern mechanized systems of producing building materials. More frequently commentators classify these under the generalization term 'appropriate technology' but this begs the question, 'Appropriate to what circumstance?' The appropriate technology for constructing a base on the moon might well be to use robots and eliminate manual work as far as possible. Intermediate technology describes the level of capital investment and associated labour requirement which seem to best meet the people's needs of many areas of the developing world, with their rising aspirations but scarce capital resources. Intermediate technologies have been in operation long before the founding of the Intermediate Technology Development Group (ITDG), and numerous examples which fit this description are being evolved spontaneously in

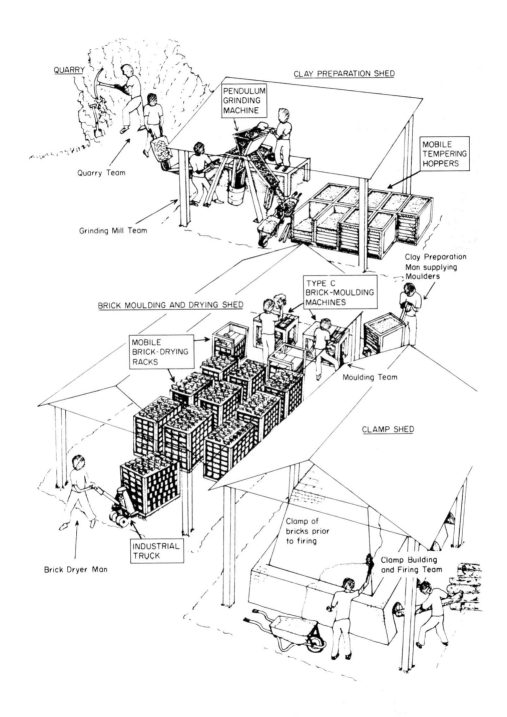

Figure 16.5   An intermediate technology mini-brick plant. Capacity 10,000 bricks a week, with 10 good men. (Drawing by J. Parry.)

small workshops all over the world, without institutional sponsorship of any kind. Two items of equipment which in their function best fit the description are the bicycle and the wheelbarrow.

Some important new equipment has been developed to fill gaps in the range of technologies available to low-income builders in, for example, the manufacturers of elements used for constructing their roofs, walls, and floors. These examples are examined in detail below.

Fibre-cement roofing sheets

Of all the difficulties facing self-help builders the cost of buying the roof cladding is probably the worst. The principal material in present-day use, the galvanised corrugated iron sheet, is also, for most countries, an imported product costing about US$4 a square metre. Even with this cost penalty there is no guarantee of durability. Some of the poorest-quality sheets corrode and begin to leak after 3 years in coastal or polluted climates. Small-scale manufacturing technology is already employed in localized production of clay and concrete tiles. Neither are to be encouraged where lack of skill or expense of sawn timber puts the possibility of constructing the roof framework to support the tiles beyond the economic reach of low-income people. However, tiles are still very appropriate in some areas.

A relatively new intermediate technology has been developed for producing sheets, thinner but much larger than tiles. This technology emerged from the various efforts by researchers to use organic fibres such as sisal, coconut coir, and date palm fibre to reinforce concrete—FRC. Corrugated roof sheets of natural fibre reinforced cement first began to be manufactured experimentally in 'village-scale' production plants in 1977–78. Since then production has grown considerably and it was estimated that, by the end of 1981, the combined output from small scale plants, in 15 countries, exceeded 3000 m² per month.

The production process in most widespread use for the manufacture of corrugated sheets from FRC was developed by the IT Building Materials Workshop in Cradley Heath

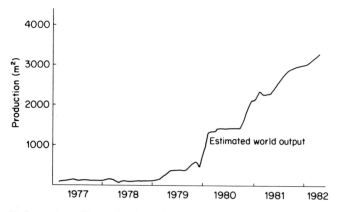

Figure 16.6   Estimated world production of FRC roof sheeting. (*Development and Testing of Roof Cladding Materials made from Fibre Reinforced Cement*, by J. P. M. Parry. Published 1981 by the IT Workshop, Cradley Heath)

Figure 16.7   Producing FRC sheets by the I.T. method in Sri Lanka. Products in use on a low-cost self-build house which, incidentally has sundried brick wall protected with fibre cement plastic

in Britain, with development funds provided by the UK Government through Intermediate Technology Industrial Services. It consists of a simple tilting table on which a wet screed of proportioned cement, sand, and natural fibre is prepared inside a steel frame, resting on a polythene sheet (see Figure 16.7). When level and tamped to remove air bubbles, the screed is transferred from the laying-up board by a tilting action which enables it to slide onto the corrugated mould. It is left to set hard for 24 hours before removal to begin curing.

The process is deceptively simple, a feature which caused some counterpart teams pioneering projects in the early days to forget to apply normal workshop techniques of process and quality control. This led them into serious trouble with porous, cracking and badly fitting sheets. Another early mistake was to ignore the importance of erecting firm, regular roof frames to carry the new products which, being concrete, are brittle with little capacity to flex. Nevertheless, after the early growing pains, sheet-producers in countries as diverse as Zimbabwe, Honduras, Sri Lanka, and some Pacific islands began to settle into regular production and to gain considerable economic benefit out of the low costs involved. Meanwhile, as time passed the potential longevity of the roof sheets began to be established. The earliest test samples, after 5 years exposure to alternate periods of frost and snow, heavy rain, storm-force winds, and hot summer spells, show no sign of deterioration. Minor discoloration in industrially polluted atmosphere was noted as well as rust staining around fixings, but otherwise no defects had emerged in the early years.

Other FRC-based products suitable for self-builders, developed by the Cradley Heath Workshop, include arch shells as permanent shuttering for floors to save the inordinate consumption of timber used for this purpose, as described earlier. Also in the role of formwork, FRC shells have been used successfully in the installation of otherwise conventionally constructed brick arches. In these applications the FRC occupies a structural role only in the few hours following the installation of the masonry superstructure. After that the masonry itself, acting in compression, takes over the role leaving the FRC formwork components just to provide a tidy finish.

Table 16.1   Materials consumed per square metre of flat screed (thickness)

Material	6 mm	8 mm	10 mm	12 mm
Cement (kg)	7.5	10	12.5	15
Sand (kg)	7.5	10	12.5	15
Fibre (g)	225	300	375	450

For the purpose of calculating the cost of FRC sheet composites, Table 16.1 provides a general guide to the quantities of materials used. The thickness chosen for most of the corrugated roof sheets currently being produced is about 8 mm. Arches used as formwork are usually made to a thickness of 10–12 mm. With a fully manual process a three-man team can prepare a square metre of material in about 15 minutes. A vibrating table can cut the time down by as much as half.

From the viewpoint of self-builders, the greatest advantage of the new FRC technologies is portability of the plant and its independence of normal services. These features make it possible to undertake production on the building site, reducing both transport costs and breakages.

Clay soil-based products

The best-known of the portable simple-function machines is the Cinva-ram developed and first used in Latin America. This machine has received strong support in its wider dissemination by US and international agencies. Manually operated, the Cinva-ram uses a long lever to provide compression of the block inside a steel mould box, a clever system of linkages to apply the necessary force, and also to eject the finished block (see Figure 16.8). Cinva-ram operation is a team effort and production usually takes place on the building site.

The system is probably at its best in production of stabilized-soil blocks where compression is important. If the material used a heavier clay-based soil, and if the bricks or blocks are subsequently to be burned, a wet moulding system is preferable. Most of the world's hand-made bricks are 'slop' moulded, cast directly on to the ground from an open frame with the clay in a saturated semi-liquid state. They are generally irregular in shape and size and as a result can be inconvenient to use. In a project supported by the UK Building Research Establishment (BRE), the IT Building Materials Workshop followed up its earlier development of a 'hinged-bottom mould' (already in fairly widespread use in eight countries) with a table-mounted moulding machine. While still

Figure 16.8   Cinva-ram in operation on a building site in Somalia

producing what is essentially a hand-made brick, the Type 'C' cutting-off and ejection mechanism makes it easier for a newly trained worker to produce accurately formed bricks at a rapid state. Burnt bricks are more usually made in a plant rather than on a building site, but this may be a missed opportunity. In a few southern African countries, most notably Malawi, it is fairly common to see a house-building project commence with the firing of a clamp of bricks made from the site soil. With the availability of equipment like the Type 'C' moulding machine, it should be more possible for this economical practice to develop elsewhere.

A problem outstanding in many areas is a means to break down hard clayey soil to a powder suitable to be tempered with water before moulding. Experienced brickmaking teams have the capability to undertake the strenuous and dirty activity of treading clay with their bare feet to produce the brickmaking raw material. However, in this form it is too wet for moulding a brick which will keep its accurate shape during handling. Moreover it requires work which would be uncongenial for most ordinary people involved in a housebuilding project.

Clay can be tempered satisfactorily without treading or mechanical mixing. After being reduced to a fine enough powder (below 3 mm diameter) clay, if layered with a correct proportion of water, will blend, in a few hours, into a paste suitable for brickmaking. This paste can be made dry enough for good quality-moulding. Necessary to this process was a way of grinding the clay efficiently.

A further new machine under development in the Cradley Heath Workshops, although not yet in widespread use, shows promise of filling this gap. Based on the use of a heavy pendulum, the new device grinds lumps of clay to a suitable powder using one static head and a movable one which pivots near to the fulcrum of the pendulum and thereby exerts great leverage. Its output, depending on the hardness of the clay is between 10 and 30 kg per minute when worked by a team of three or four men; ten times the productivity of pounding it with hand tools.

The machines and processes described above are far from a comprehensive list, and may be disproportionately biased towards devices with which the author has been associated during the development stages. However, they typify the level of capital intensity, simplicity of construction and operation, and level of labour productivity which fit the description 'intermediate technology'. This category of technology is likely to best satisfy the requirements of the self-builders who wish to use their own labour productively, to make building elements in substitution for factory-manufactured products which they cannot afford.

Postscript

Geoffrey Payne

What lessons can this book offer for the development and implementation of housing policies and projects serving the majority of urban populations? Clearly, sites and services and settlement upgrading have benefited many thousands of low-income families and represent a considerable improvement over previous approaches. They have also pioneered new ways of working with local communities to produce more affordable housing and services as a basis for long-term development. They have, however, clearly failed to keep pace with the ever-increasing demand for housing and it is unlikely that merely expanding the same approach will increase this trend.

Whilst projects will therefore continue to represent a valuable means of gaining political support, developing professional capability and testing new ideas, a qualitative change of focus would appear necessary if governments and their professional servants or advisors seriously wish to influence urban development and housing provision systems.

Essentially, such a change requires governments to intervene more positively in land and property markets and use their considerable legislative and fiscal powers to greater effect. This may take many forms, such as:

— Formulating appropriate building and planning codes or regulations applicable in low-income areas and distinguishing between initial and long term standards.
— Strengthening those informal housing systems already serving low-income needs.
— Recognizing the need for local communities to exercise more influence over the development of their neighbourhoods.
— Regulating the activities of informal land developers and building materials suppliers, etc.
— Achieving a more equitable distribution of resources and services *between* income groups.

These and other related forms of intervention offer the only realistic prospect for regulating urban growth and assisting low-income groups as a whole. They imply an active and innovative role for government agencies which runs counter to normal practice. They also presuppose an understanding of how such markets operate and the likely effects of specific actions which may not yet exist. Whilst the priority at project level may

265

therefore be to disseminate the considerable experience already obtained, at the policy level it is necessary to develop, implement *and* disseminate new initiatives.

This book is intended as a contribution to that process. Hopefully, the proposed United Nations Year of Shelter for the Homeless in 1987 will stimulate progress and provide a forum for exchanging such experience. Meanwhile, no other opportunities should be lost of translating such ideas into practice.

Index

267